Ginny's Story
of the
Lluest Horse and Pony Trust

by

Ginny Hajdukiewicz

*Collected and edited
and with an introduction and
additional material by*

Barbara Metcalfe & Stella Gratrix

Published in 2023 by FeedARead.com Publishing

The stories contained in this book are entirely the writings and opinions
of Ginny Hajdukiewicz and have been published to celebrate her writing
skills, promote greater awareness of the work she did and to encourage
further support for the Lluest Horse and Pony Trust. No responsibility
is taken by those of us involved in the publication of this book for any
controversial content included. On a few occasions we have changed a
name or two.
No costs, including the printing and publication of this book, have
been taken from charity funds. All proceeds will be donated to the
Lluest Horse and Pony Trust.

A CIP catalogue record for this title is available from the British Library.

Cover photograph: Charity ride on the mountain, 1985 - one of the
first sponsored rides raising money for the Lluest Horse and Pony Trust

Contents

Introduction .... *v*

About Ginny: a short biography .... *vii*

About this book .... *xi*

Acknowledgements .... *xii*

Part One: Beginnings in Gloucestershire 1

Chapter 1 Prince and Jim 3

Chapter 2 Comet 15

Chapter 3 Pepper, Sarah and Queenie 24

Chapter 4 Jerry 31

Chapter 5 Screwy Bluey 41

Chapter 6 Departures and arrivals 50

Part Two: Lluest 57

Chapter 7 October 1981 and the start of life at Lluest 59

Chapter 8 Testing times for Trefor 68

Chapter 9 I've always known that I've been slightly eccentric 76

Chapter 10 Can you take a party this evening? 84

Chapter 11 P Brain and other related problems 92

Chapter 12 Tribute to Jim 99

Jim: A short story by Ginny 99

Barbara remembers 101

Stella remembers 102

Ginny remembers 103

Stella's songs 105

Chapter 13 Mick 107

Chapter 14 Birth of The Lluest Horse and Pony Trust 114

Chapter 15 Rehabilitation of Dancer and Phoenix 121

Chapter 16 Rhona 130

Chapter 17 Copper, Barley and Ben 139

Chapter 18 She is an emotional bitch 145

Chapter 19 I've been here three years now.................................. 151

Chapter 20 The power of the press 158

Chapter 21 Back injury at Lluest... 168

Chapter 22 Ceri 175

Part Three: Beili Bedw.. 185

Chapter 23 November 1986 and new beginnings at Beili Bedw ... 187

Chapter 24 A nose on my arm.. 196

Chapter 25 A happy herd 203

Chapter 26 Mick's injury.. 210

Chapter 27 Gwilym.. 217

Chapter 28 Jake 221

Part Four: Memories and moving forward 231

Memories and personal tributes 233

From Peter Hajdukiewicz.. 234

From Barbara Metcalfe 234

From Stella Gratrix... 237

Life at Lluest in 2023 241

Find out more.. 243

Photographs

Ginny with Prince 1

Ginny with Jim and Pepper 2

Ginny on Jim with her Grandfather and Prince 2

Comet 23

Sarah 30

Bluey 49

Ginny with Dancer 57

Lluest house, with 'Pygsy' the three-wheeler 58

Ben 58

Joker and Jester 75

Chickens 83

Mick 113

Ginny with Cariad and Davy 167

Ceri with Shelley 184

Peter and Ginny with Jester, Gypsy and Joker 185

The foal Rhiannon, with Ginny and Morfydd 186

Joker tolerating Gypsy 186

Dinah the donkey 209

Gwylim and Ginny 220

Checking Jake on the mountain 230

Ginny on some time out with Jester near Cader Idris 231

Ginny at her happiest, as we hope she will always be remembered ... 232

Champ with Shelley, helping to promote the Trust's work
    at a show in Gloucestershire 244

Ginny Hajdukiewicz's Story of the Lluest Horse and Pony Trust

Introduction

G inny Hajdukiewicz was a remarkable woman with an abiding love of animals and a concern for their welfare. She wrote about her animals and her experiences as she managed her riding centre, her trekking centre, and set up the Lluest Horse and Pony Trust to care for neglected and abused horses, ponies and donkeys. Her vibrant personality shines through in her engaging accounts.

In this introduction, we present a brief biography of Ginny and explain how this book came to be.

About Ginny: a short biography

Ginny Hajdukiewicz was born Virginia Jane Rust on 18 May 1956. She spent her childhood at Ivy Cottage, Foxmoor Lane, Stroud, with her parents Mike and Margaret, and attended Stroud High School. Ginny's grandfather, who was once a miner in the Forest of Dean, influenced her greatly by his own love of horses. He was no doubt influenced himself by the ponies he would have encountered whilst working in the coal mines. Ginny was also an avid reader and admired the amazing riding skills of the American Indians that she read about. By 1968 Ginny was working as a groom at stables near the Gloucestershire town of Stroud, and had a favourite pony, named Ballerina. It was there that unfortunately she had a riding accident and badly damaged her neck and right leg. The accident impacted her health a little later in life, but in no way affected her love of horses and determination to pursue her ambition to set up her own riding centre.

After leaving school in 1974 she started work as a clerk for a solicitor in Gloucester. By saving her small earnings she was eventually able to buy Prince, her first pony, from Backwell near Bristol, stabling him at Charley's farm near Ruscombe. He was unbroken and not used to being handled. As Ginny could not yet afford a proper bridle or saddle, she sewed up a headcollar from old sheets, much to the amusement of her mother. This gave Prince a gentle introduction to being handled, and he gradually became used to her. For years afterwards Prince would only allow Ginny to ride him.

Ginny was commuting to work daily with her father, while also having to walk to the rented stables each day to look after and feed Prince. She was determined to somehow earn a living working with horses, and with more savings she bought Jiminy Cricket ('Jim') from Corse Lane, who she also stabled at Charley's farm. It was from there that she started giving rides to local children, using Jim as he was the older and very used to people and traffic. It was the first experience for many of the children of riding, with Ginny taking them on a leading rein along the quiet lanes near the stables. Soon the rides became quite popular, and she was able to collect a small fee for each ride. In a few months she had enough money to buy two more ponies: Pepper and Comet. That was the start of a herd that grew to nineteen over the next six years or so. Ginny was becoming well known and her rides became ever more popular.

By then Ginny had moved her ponies to the Vine Tree in Randwick. Most were 'misfits', as Ginny called them. Some she purchased from sales, and some she took in because they simply needed the tender loving care that she was prepared to give them.

During this time Ginny met Peter Hajdukiewicz and taught him to ride on Pepper. Peter worked in Bristol, and so they decided to look for somewhere to live and keep the ponies that was midway between Stroud and Bristol. Eventually they moved to a flat in the small town of Wotton under Edge. The ponies were hacked over from Stroud to a farm on the outskirts of Wotton, and from there Ginny continued her rides on a local bridleway, while all the time gathering new friends and helpers. Peter left his job in Bristol and started to work for a company in Wotton. For a while Ginny studied shorthand and typing at Stroud college, but she knew that kind of work was not for her, so she ended up buying two more ponies – Gerry and Sarah – instead, and looking after them full time. Ginny and Peter also had a border collie puppy called Jester, who became very much part of the menagerie and who was trained by Ginny to round up the ponies when it was time for work.

In December 1978 Ginny and Pete bought and moved to 22 Walk Mill Lane, in the village of Kingswood on the outskirts of Wotton. They were married on 19 May 1979.

After a year or so, an old stable with an adjoining field became available for rent in Kingswood, thus giving the opportunity to form a proper riding school as a business. A car park was created, and the ponies were moved into the stables after some renovation. There was much more space, so an outdoor school was constructed to give riding lessons. After a battle with authorities, a formal licence to operate a school was obtained, with Ginny becoming one of the youngest proprietors in the country (at the age of twenty-three) to hold such a licence. They called it the Kingswood Riding Centre. The school was very successful, with lots of local demand for lessons, but the immediate riding area was plagued with traffic which was a constant safety concern when the ponies were taken out. This prompted Ginny and Pete to move to West Wales in 1981, giving a complete contrast to Gloucestershire.

Life in Wales was peaceful, but hard work for Ginny as Pete had to stay in Gloucestershire to work and could only visit at weekends and holidays for the next fourteen years. Their first smallholding was called Lluest, and this name stuck, to become the name of the charity that exists today. Lluest in English means 'haven' or 'resting place for a shepherd and his flock'.

At Lluest, Ginny's only income was from a very few local children and visitors during the holidays who mainly wanted to go trekking in the beautiful mountain scenery nearby. However, Lluest was near the coast, and holidaymakers from local caravan sites eventually brought an important source of income. Luckily, their neighbour was a friendly dairy farmer by the name of Trefor who rented them extra grazing in return for help with his milking and other jobs.

Ginny found that she still needed to add to her collection of ponies to accommodate the occasional large group of riders. It was during a visit to a local horse market that she witnessed and became appalled at the conditions, and one incident in particular made her determined to do something about it (as described in Chapter 14). There was no other horse charity in Wales at that time so, with the help of some friends to act as Trustees, she set up the Lluest Horse and Pony Trust.

Five years later, Ginny had rescued a number of ponies for the Trust, for reasons ranging from cases of sheer neglect where owners could not, or would not, look after them properly, to just rescuing a perfectly good riding pony at a market, where it would otherwise have been sold for slaughter. Ginny's determination to promote the charity was such that one weekend, while Radio 1 Roadshow was visiting Aberystwyth fifteen miles away, she took advantage and rode one of her trusty trekking ponies on an exhausting trip there and back to barge her way into the Roadshow and actually get a live interview on stage.

Ginny eventually needed larger premises, and in 1986, with Pete's help, she bought a former sheep farm in the Brecon Beacons National Park[1] called Beili Bedw. The charity also managed to buy its own piece of grazing at the farm, thanks to a campaign about cruelty at markets which was published in *Horse & Pony* magazine and which had attracted many supporters and donations, totalling over £7,000. Ginny struggled again, this time with the National Park authorities to obtain permission to run a trekking business from the new farm, but as with most things she set her mind to, she eventually succeeded. The combination of the charity with visitor open days to see the ponies, together with Ginny's trekking business, brought a significant visitor attraction to that area of the National Park.

Ginny continued to promote equine welfare with a growing passion. She had articles about her and the charity published in a number of newspapers, appeared on radio and television, and also regularly joined the National Equine Welfare Council at meetings in London.

Six years later, and when the Lluest Horse and Pony Trust seemed to be gaining an ever-greater importance in South Wales, Ginny was diagnosed with breast cancer. After an operation she was in remission for nearly two years and all seemed well, but it sadly returned and she battled on bravely for another six months before her tragic death on 13 September 1994 at the age of thirty-eight.

Ginny was a formidable personality; who changed the lives of many she met along the way. There was no stopping her when it came to horse welfare, as she was absolutely committed to believing that indeed all animals should be treated humanely. As a result of her efforts, the markets in the area improved, together with the standard of treatment for the mountain ponies. The charity she founded became a vital rescue centre for animals in distress in the area, and continues its work to this day.

---

[1] Bannau Brycheiniog

About this book

Throughout the time of running her riding and trekking business, Ginny would often laugh about her various amusing experiences with the ponies and riders. Her husband, Peter Hajdukiewicz, would encourage her to scribble her experiences down. She was always jotting things down in old notepads and even on large envelopes, so he bought her an electric typewriter and then there was no stopping her!

This book collects the stories written by Ginny. Some are amusing and some are sad, but together they give an insight into the life and hopes of this remarkable lady. With the help and approval of Pete, they have been collected, collated and typed up by Barbara Metcalfe, and edited by both Barbara Metcalfe and Stella Gratrix, old friends and two of the original three trustees of the Lluest Horse and Pony Trust (the third being Barbara's husband Brian).

The story of Ben was published in The Lady magazine in 1987 with the title 'He was just an ordinary dun colt'. In July 2019 Barbara began work on the rest, some of which had been typed by Ginny and others written in her scrawly handwriting on various bits of paper and old envelopes. Some needed piecing together to form chapters. We have attempted to put them into roughly chronological order, although some recount events in the life of a particular pony over a number of years. We have changed as little as possible of Ginny's original words, although we have changed some passages into the past tense as they were written in Ginny's present in different years. We have included some explanations, and definitions of terms that may be unfamiliar to readers, in footnotes. Part Four of the book presents our memories and personal tributes to Ginny, together with information from the present-day manager of life as it is today at the Trust.

Ginny came across a great many people during her life and work, both as proprietor of the riding stables and trekking centre, and as manager of the Lluest Horse and Pony Trust. Generally she made no secret of the fact that she preferred the company of animals to people, but there are instances during her writing where she drops guard and words of fondness creep in. At times she refers to names with no indication as to whom that name refers. If you were involved in the charity during its early days as we were, you will probably have experienced some of the characteristics we describe. Ginny was dedicated to her animals, but she cared very much about the safety of anyone who rode, worked and accompanied her whilst visiting the 'wild' mountain ponies and the markets.

We hope you enjoy reading this book and that it will also give you some idea of the reasons for the passion Ginny developed for equine welfare.

Acknowledgements

This book has been published with the blessing and support of Ginny's husband, Peter Hajdukiewicz. Barbara, Stella and Peter are grateful to the several friends, all of whom request no recognition, for the time they gave in reading and offering encouraging words in embarking on this project. Thank you all.

We would also like to thank: Dionne Schuurman, the current manager of the Lluest Horse and Pony Trust, for providing the information about the Trust as it is today; Jane Dards (a horse-loving retired technical author and publications consultant) for proofreading the manuscript and preparing it for publication; and Scott Cumberlin, Tony Branson and Dave Collington for their work on the photographs.

We are sorry for the fact that the project has taken longer than we originally thought and hoped it would.

Barbara Metcalfe and Stella Gratrix
October 2023

Part One:

Beginnings in Gloucestershire

Ginny with Prince

Ginny with Jim and Pepper

Ginny on Jim with her Grandfather and Prince

Chapter 1

Prince and Jim

There I was, trudging around a muddy field not far from my home near Stroud, in Gloucestershire, trying to catch a scruffy, wild, skewbald gelding, who rejoiced in the name of Mystic Prince. I was eighteen, and I'd just bought him but couldn't get anywhere near him. Everyone hated the pony, sometimes even me, because, as well as picking fights with his companions, he charged anyone rash enough to enter the field and spent the rest of his time trying to break out onto the road, presumably to kill any remaining person he could find. Sometimes I thought that it might be a good idea to sell him, but who to? Anyway, I wanted a pony, and he was all I could afford. So we were stuck with each other.

'Come on, good boy,' I called, shaking his feed bucket. Prince hesitated, then walked towards me. At last, I thought, I'm winning. I should have known better really, as I only just avoided the front hooves which flew at my head. Prince smirked as he grabbed a mouthful of feed. That was finally too much.

'Right, you horrible pony,' I roared.

I retrieved the now empty feed bucket and, to my own amazement, a surprised Prince retreated. He regained his composure and laid his ears back in preparation to charge. I wondered if anyone had ever stood their ground when he charged, or even if they had tried charging him back. I had good reason to suspect his reasons for hating the human race as I had little doubt that he would have been separated from his mother at market. An electric goad would probably have been used, and that would have hurt him. Prince, unlike most, had the courage to fight back, and he would do so, until the day he had strength enough to finally get his own way and be left alone. Now this hatred was a habit, reinforced when his only contact with people had been when his previous owners had him castrated. He was proud and would be a beauty when properly nourished, but he was a very dangerous pony, almost ready to kill.

We stared at each other while I wondered what to do. I knew that it would be very unwise to fall under those hooves, but I was torn between the gentle approach and teaching the little swine some manners, so that I could eventually ride him. I had spent nearly a month trying to gain his confidence, and I was getting nowhere. I had to admit, I was running out of ideas, until the field itself made up my mind for me. It was a steep field and I was a long way from the gate; running up a muddy field with a mad pony in pursuit and clad in wellies that were borrowed, and a size too big, didn't seem half as attractive as running down it. Prince was now a little way off, circling me, but as he turned, snorting, and started to charge I ran straight at him shouting abuse. He slithered to a confused halt, wide eyed. This was not what he expected when he charged! People were definitely supposed to run away from him, not run towards him yelling rude words. It was all too much for Prince, who had no time to think how to cope with this new phenomenon. He wheeled away, instinctively running away from something that was now behaving as a predator. He raced down to the far corner of the field, turning his back end on me. By this time, I was far too cross to be cautious.

'I've had it with you,' I screamed. Prince tried to back into me,

'You dare,' I roared, and gave him a swift kick up the behind. Somehow, I got hold of his mane and held on tight as he shot round.

'Right, you horrible little runt, no more – I'm cross. One more bite or kick and you're dog food,' I yelled.

I realised that I was in an excellent position to get kicked or trampled again, but had a feeling Prince was much too surprised to attempt it. I let go of his mane and pushed him away from me.

'Get lost – go on, hop it,' I shouted. I then turned on my heel and marched back up to the gate as determinedly as my wellies and the mud allowed. By the time I got there I had company: a muddy scruffy little skewbald who followed dejectedly behind me in meek expectation of his feed. A nose snuffed into my face very gently, assuring me of its owner's good intentions, but I was not impressed and pushed him away again, as it was late and I still had to mix his feed. When I returned with his bucket, Prince didn't knock me over as he usually did, but waited politely for me to put his bucket on the ground. I stood by him as I always did, not that there was any need because Prince was quite capable of defending his own feed; it was the safety of his companions that I was worried about. When he finished, he tried to make friends again, and this time I forgave him and cuddled my new pony for the very first time.

U

I wasn't the only one who was fed up with Prince's behaviour that evening, because the next morning he limped up the field with a nasty cut on his near hind leg. I groaned to myself. It was all I needed, treating a cut leg by torchlight at six thirty in the morning when I was already late. All I needed now was to miss my lift to work.

'Right, my lad,' I said, as I squelched into the field with my bucket of salty water, cotton wool, and wound powder.

'Stand,' I ordered as firmly as I could, hoping Prince would stand still, too nonplussed by my antics of the previous day to realise that I was very nervous.

I knelt down by his back legs expecting a swift lethal kick, but Prince stood quietly while I cleaned the wound and filled it with powder. Luckily, it did not need stitching but it did need to be kept clean. If only I had a stable, I thought, wondering if Prince would stay in one, even if the opportunity to have one arose. Occasionally he turned his head to see what I was up to, but by now I had forgotten that I was dealing with a lethal pony, and I think that Prince had too. He had realised that I was trying to help him.

'Well, pest, you'll need an anti-tetanus tonight when I come home,' I said, giving him a rushed goodbye pat. 'Now behave,' I warned.

I ran the mile and a half back home, which was luckily downhill, changed my clothes and leapt into Dad's car, ignoring the fixed expression Dad always wore when I was late again. I just managed to slide into the reception area before the boss. Unfortunately, I hadn't had time to wash, and the brief towelling I'd given my muddy knees and legs had left a brown stain clearly visible through my tights. Then I noticed a distinctly horsey smell creeping through the office, as my top, which I had forgotten to change, warmed to the central heating and announced its recent close contact with an equine. The senior receptionist huffed to herself and used the air freshener liberally – rather a mistake, as I spent the rest of the day sneezing and she had to man the switchboard.

I managed to phone the vet between sneezes in my lunch break, and arranged for him to meet me at the field at six that evening – of course my boss, now thoroughly fed up with her horsey subordinate, had decided that I should stay late to catch up on the filing. I finally escaped, leaving more than a handful of files hastily shoved into a handy drawer, and just managed to catch up with my Dad, who was waiting around the corner from the office.

I rushed through the yard gate at the same time as the vet drove in, borrowed a pair of wellies and floundered off to catch Prince, who did not recognise the thing in a dress and almost charged me. A roar stopped him in his tracks and I dragged him up to the yard without further incident. His recent good behaviour had lulled me into thinking that he would behave with anyone. His attitude in the field to a stranger should have alerted me, but it didn't. The vet looked doubtful.

'Is he quiet?' he asked,

'Yes, fine,' I replied impatiently. 'I bathed that cut myself this morning with no problems at all.'

The vet grunted. He had already treated one of Prince's horsey victims and had heard tales from various other humans about my pony's behaviour. He advanced cautiously. Prince exploded, and a well-timed cow kick sent the vet flying backwards into a wall. I was determined not to let go of Prince and expected him to carry on fighting, but once the vet was clear he calmed down. The vet wasn't at all calm!

'That pony is a menace,' he grumbled. Then there were some less polite comments, like 'Sell it!'

'Who to?' I muttered.

The vet, never one to mince words, glowered at me.

'The knacker-man of course, that's all he's good for,' he grumbled,

'No, he isn't!' I yelled. 'Just because you can't handle him – he's got loads of potential.'

'Yes dear, but what as?' was the irritable reply.

'My pony,' I snapped, realising now that I could never do as I'd planned and sell him on to get a better pony. Prince nuzzled me and showed no remorse in respect of the injured vet.

'Are you going to try again?' I asked tentatively.

The vet's reply wasn't repeatable!

'But he needs an anti-tetanus jab and you are a vet,' I reminded him.

He gave me a filthy look and then said, 'Here you are then, you give it to him.'

'I've never given an injection,' I complained.

'Well you'll have to learn, because I'm not going near that thing,' he snapped.

So there I was, clutching a needle in one hand and a cross pony in the other, and I hate needles. I wasn't worried about Prince's reaction to the needle, but the thought of driving it into his neck made me cringe. So I closed my eyes and stabbed it in. My hands were trembling but nothing happened, Prince had not moved. For a moment I thought I might have injected myself, or missed completely, but I withdrew the needle and turned to give the vet a triumphant look. However, by this time he had retreated to the other side of the yard, so without thinking I began to walk over to him to return the needle, leading my now innocent pony... Prince beat me to the vet and almost came down on his head! Needless to say, I had to change vets, as I did fairly frequently until ten years later when I finally found a vet who was not afraid of him. Perhaps it was also time to start searching for new stable premises to rent.

However, things were beginning to go well. Prince was tame – well, sort of – and by some miracle I was still employed as a junior receptionist. The work was boring and I hated the ordered life of a solicitor's office, but I had an ambition and I needed money, and lots of it. So I worked as hard as I could, resisted the temptation to tell the solicitors what I thought of their world of squash and golf clubs, and remembered that I was the lowest thing on earth: a junior receptionist. One day I would be free of their world and boss of my own stable, but I thought that dream was a long way off until an advertisement in a newspaper caught my eye and brought the dream a little closer.

The advert was for a 12.2hh[2] iron grey gelding, twelve years old, sadly outgrown. Probably nothing special – or was he? I felt drawn towards the pony almost as if he needed me, and I knew long before I saw him that he was the pony for me. I had enough money now to buy and feed another pony, so when my boyfriend Pete came home from University I suggested an expedition to the little village nearby to meet this potential

---

[2] Horses are measured in hands high (hh) to the withers, which are the top of the shoulders at the base of the neck. One hand is four inches, so a 12.2hh pony is four feet two inches at the shoulder. Ponies are under 14.2hh. Horses are taller.

new four-legged friend. Pete already wasn't too keen on Prince, and of course Prince took full advantage of this by pulling faces and doing his best to terrorise his latest enemy – all five feet ten of him.

Luckily, Pete was finally persuaded to take me on this trip, and we set off one Saturday afternoon in March. As we walked in through the garden, I saw a nice dun 13hh gelding and then I saw the daughter of the house; her arm was in a sling and a quick conversation with the owner, her mother, revealed that yes, she had fallen off the pony they were selling. It seemed that Jiminy Cricket was a bit of a lad. Pete looked concerned, but I laughed and headed off to find the delinquent. I'll never forget my first sight of our Jim because in that instant he truly was ours. His grey-black face was dominated by a pair of wicked, clever eyes that summed us up instantly. He pulled a face at us and turned his back on the door.

'I'll just go and get his saddle and bridle,' the girl's mother said hastily, leaving me to walk in to try and get the little rogue.

'Shift,' I said as I walked in.

Dealing with Prince and his temper tantrums had made me blasé about every other pony I met, as none could be as bad as him. Jim moved over, surprised by my attitude, and I patted him. His owner held out a bridle. I looked at it in amazement.

'That bridle's not for him, is it?' I queried.

I'd never seen anything like it – well not on a 12.2hh anyway. The bridle in question had a 'Pelham and curb' with the addition of a dropped noseband *and* with a standing martingale attached.[3]

'I'm not riding in that. Haven't you got a simple bridle with a simple snaffle bit?' I asked.

'Only a snaffle?' his soon to be ex-owner replied. 'Bbbbut he is *very* strong,' she stammered.

'I'm not surprised,' I muttered to myself, as the owner went in search of a more appropriate bit. 'She's given you enough to fight against, hasn't she? I don't know how you ever moved with all that lot on,' I sympathised to Jim, who was now the picture of equine docility.

---

[3] A Pelham bit with a curb chain is considered a relatively severe bit. A dropped noseband is fastened around the horse's nose below the bit rather than above it, and prevents the horse opening its mouth wide. A standing martingale is a strap that fastens the bottom of the noseband to the girth to prevent a horse throwing its head up.

His owner returned with a snaffle and Jim was duly saddled and mounted.

'I'll stand in the middle and you ride around me,' the mother offered.

'He might think that he is at Pony Club and behave,' she continued. 'He likes Pony Club.'

Yes, I bet he does, I thought. It was maybe the one place the girl was made to ride properly with a sensible bridle. The mother rattled on while Jim and I trotted around her. He was a lovely ride, although I did feel he was a little difficult to stop at times.

'Yes, he is a bit too much for my daughter, but he is so ideal for you as a lightweight adult, and you can obviously ride,' she said coyly.

Yes, I know I can, I thought smugly, forgetting that in my case pride always goes before a fall. Jim was beautiful, lightly responding to my every whim, and I was really enjoying showing my horsemanship off to Pete. But what I didn't realise was that I was also being set up by one of the cleverest ponies that I have ever met!

Continuing, we haggled over the price a little bit, but settled on £120 which worried me a little because it was just too low. Was he really only twelve? Just how dangerous was he? This was hopefully the founder member of my herd of ponies, that would make my dream of owning a riding school come true. The offer of free transport to my home and a week on loan didn't reassure me, but he was only £120 and he couldn't possibly be worse than Prince.

Now all I had to do was to face my parents. I knew that they wouldn't be at all keen on the idea of me owning *another* pony, and I knew they thought my dream of owning a riding stable was just me being silly. How could I ever afford one of those, and even if I could, why should I want one? They had pointed out it would be a waste of my education, but then *I* always pointed out the 'education' had been one thing that I didn't want; I preferred the daily grind of mucking out and feeding at a local stable to the joys of Political and Economic History of the 19th Century at the local Grammar School. There was one person who I knew would be pleased with the progression of my plan though, and that was my grandfather, 'Pamp', who encouraged me to pursue my dreams.

Mum and Dad had got used to making trips up to the field to see Prince but, as I'd feared, they greeted my news of the new pony with some annoyance.

9

'Well, when is the pony arriving?' they asked.

'He arrived today, I've just moved him to his new home,' I announced.

My parents looked at me, taking in the torn jeans and the fact that I was slightly more dishevelled than normal. I retreated to the bathroom before World War Three broke out in the living room and collapsed onto the loo to survey my battered body. What a day, I thought, and what a move...

Jim had arrived in a trailer and was unloaded in record time. His ex-owners thrust the leading rein into my hands and drove away as rapidly as possible. No goodbye pats for Jim and still no request for a deposit. I had a feeling the family didn't care what happened to the little rogue as long as they never saw him again.

Now I needed to take him to the new stables that I'd arranged to rent from my friend Susie.

'Come on Jim,' I said.

I scrabbled up onto him and headed him up the road, hatless as usual and with no saddle or bridle. Jim trotted on willingly. It was so good to be riding a pony again, even a bone shaker like Jim, whose prominent backbone didn't exactly make a comfortable ride!

I continued to wonder why he had been such a problem. He was a lively little chap, full of go and eager to trot as fast as possible. A tractor passed us without incident, and he ignored several dogs that ran out and tried to bite his heels. Life was definitely good; a bright spring day, a new pony and the start of a new life for both of us. As I sat on him, I forgot the real world for a moment and dreamed of the future, which was definitely looking rosier by the minute... That was, until I remembered that the bus must be due about now, and the lane was very narrow. What should I do? Perhaps we should pull into the next lay-by and wait for it, but of course Jim and I met the bus on the next bend.

'Steady,' I pleaded, pulling frantically on the lead rope... Nothing happened. We trotted briskly onwards towards the bus, then past the bus with just inches to spare. I had a quick but vivid impression of a bus full of surprised passengers, most of whom probably knew my parents, so tongues would definitely be wagging. Once well clear of the bus, I tried to steady Jim again. Nothing happened as he still refused to slow down, but I did manage to pull him into the short cut to his field, which was a steep lane. I was sure that he would soon be puffed out and have to stop, but he wasn't. We had probably trotted about a mile by now, and he showed no sign of slackening his pace. It wasn't that he threw himself around if I asked him to stop, he just kept on going at a very brisk trot.

'Walk,' I said firmly.

Jim responded with a few steps of canter.

'If only we were on grass, you little rat,' I thought out loud, 'I'd give you a good gallop and then see how long it took you to listen to the stop command.' My teeth rattled. Jim had obviously learnt that the best way to terrorise any rider was for him to take them for a ride, preferably with *him* taking complete control. It wasn't that he bolted, he just moved on at a good pace and wickedly forgot how to stop. It was just a 'try out', to see how good or brave the rider was, and I had a strong feeling that if you called his bluff and gave him a jolly good gallop he would then behave himself. Strapping him down, like his previous owners had done, was not the answer. A pony like Jim fought impersonal controls, just as he would fight a rider he disliked; but win his respect and you would win his co-operation, too. However, hatless and on the road was not the place to have an argument with my new pony, and as my legs now felt like jelly I had a horrible feeling that I would lose anyway. It was my own fault anyway for underestimating the little toad. It was no good, I just couldn't stop him, so I was going to have to try and throw myself off and pull him up from the ground. I spotted a soft bit of grass verge and tried to leap off as athletically as possible! The problem was that I'm not a natural athlete, so it was no surprise to me when I landed off balance and promptly fell into the ditch that I hadn't noticed, and of course it had to be full of very mucky water. This scenario had of course made me let go of the lead rope, so I fully expected to spend the rest of the afternoon trying to find and catch Jim. I looked along the lane. He had stopped about ten yards further on and was searching the hedgerow for any tasty spring titbits.

'Good boy, Jim,' I said, quietly sidling up to him.

He turned his head towards me, eyeing up the muddy jeans and muddy hair. He then definitely smirked, before graciously allowing me to catch him, no doubt hoping that I would be silly enough to remount so that he could give me an encore. *No* chance, I thought as I staggered on my way; not until I can afford a saddle and bridle and am wearing a hat.

Jim nuzzled me. 'Just my little joke,' he seemed to say, and looked in my pockets for titbits.

'You are supposed to be a civilising influence on Prince, my other pony, you know,' I remonstrated.

Somehow, I thought Jim would be incapable of being a civilising influence on any pony, least of all Prince. In fact, though, it didn't take very long for me to realise that Jim's influence was to become something I could never have imagined. By the time Jim and I trudged into his new home, I was tired and very sore, mostly in unmentionable places. Jim wasn't tired, sore or repentant and danced in on his tiptoes, announcing his arrival with confident whinnies.

My friend Susie showed us to our new stables where I left Jim, and she went off to collect her mare Copper to ride over with me to collect Prince. Trying to lead him a mile and a half through the centre of the village, past cars, lorries and possibly yet another bus, just didn't appeal to me at that moment, but I hoped that Prince would be too busy trying to catch up with the mare to notice anything that was happening around him. I knew him pretty well by then and had noticed his interest in mares wasn't at all like the interest of a normal gelding. He cantered over to the gate to meet me and stood quietly while I put his headcollar on. He trotted out of the field and up the yard to meet Copper. His eyes were bright, his tail held high – it was definitely love; well, sex, to be more exact! Luckily, Susie moved Copper off at a brisk walk along the lane, and I did my best to restrain my scruffy little 'Romeo'. He had never led so easily, walking past all the hazards that normally gave him hysterics, his eyes glued on Copper's provocative rump. She really was a flirt and every so often slowed down to give him a coy glance. As for me, well I was being dragged along as if I was a rag doll, and any minute I expected Prince to decide to brush me aside to get closer to his new love. As we turned down the lane that led to his new home, he sensed the other horses and accelerated to a canter. I had often wondered what water skiing felt like but wasn't at all keen on trying the land variety on a gravelly drive. I would have kept hold of him if it hadn't been for the 'stone thingies' that looked like oversized mushrooms. As I collided with one of them, I cursed the idiot who had put them there and let go of Prince. He galloped around the yard and headed for the field gate, where several of the ponies were gathered to watch the fun. Prince never let gates bother him and charged, but luckily the gates were properly hung metal ones, not ancient wooden ones that shattered on impact. Prince retreated, huffing and eyeing the gate, but decided against trying to jump it; it wasn't his style as it required far too much effort. I grabbed a handy feed bucket and rattled it, and Prince hesitated, torn between the two very basic desires that filled his life. Then he turned towards me. Love could wait. After all, what could any male do on an empty stomach?

He hurtled past me into the empty stable in search of his tea. So that was when he met Jim, who rather resented the rapid arrival of his next-door neighbour and lashed out, rattling the wooden partition. Prince reciprocated.

Oh God, I thought. Perhaps my parents were right. I must be mad.

'Stand still and be quiet,' I roared.

Peace reigned. Prince knew that voice and wasn't going to annoy it any further, and crafty old Jim called a truce. He'd never had any intention of annoying his new owner; well, not when it smelled like feeding time, anyway. He accepted his bucket graciously, and as for me, I slithered onto a bale of hay and examined my bruised middle from the collision with the mushroom, my blistered hands, and a new hole in my trainers. Then I noticed a bruise on my foot that I hadn't seen before. The joys of owning ponies. Examining the rest of my aching anatomy would be best left to the privacy of a bathroom!

As I sat on the bale of hay, I looked out on the afternoon stables and at a gaggle of smart, 'jodhpured' girls going about the task of feeding their smart, well-bred horses and ponies. Why were their ponies so well behaved and tidy, I wondered? Why didn't they get bruised and battered? I realised fairly ruefully that their ponies were all tailor-made for them when they were purchased. In fact, all of them were purchased for a tailor-made reason. My two were also purchased for a reason: they were all I could afford, and no one else wanted them. What did I expect? Anyway, did I want a pony that had a character, or some overgrown status symbol to be paraded around the local shows? I looked back towards my two, who by now had finished their supper and were busily engaged in leaning out over their stable doors to see if they could reach to bite each other.

'Oi, you two,' I yelled.

Two heads retreated to their hay nets. I couldn't help smiling. Yes, I decided, my two were definitely what I wanted, but after an hour in their company did I have enough energy left for the three-mile walk home? I was hungry, and it was getting cold, so after a final check on my boys I limped home to face outraged parents, my bedraggled appearance just begging for a chorus of... 'I told you so'.

Well, what can I say? By the autumn Prince and Jim were both regular visitors to local shows and gymkhanas. Jim won regularly, but Prince, well, perhaps not... He reared, kicked and barged his way through showgrounds, having hysterics at brass bands, funfairs or whatever else was on hand. Prince wasn't a show pony, he was a pony born on isolated moorland who longed for a life unrestricted by fences and roads. Roads were populated by monsters. Given the chance of a twenty-mile ride, or a gallop across a common, he was a saint, and no hill was too steep or gallop too long. Also, he was a one-person pony, whether from fear or choice I wasn't sure. All I knew was that the two of us already held a very special bond. As for Jim, a gymkhana winner, yes, but also he was a total delinquent in other ways. Instead of persuading Prince to stay in his field, he taught him all he knew about escaping from it. Between them they were enough to put anyone off owning a pony for good. But if they were trying to employ their plot towards me, well, it was never going to work!

Chapter 2

Comet

C omet's teeth just missed my hand as I hung his hay net.

'You pig,' I yelled. Comet just laid his ears back and ignored me. Human disapproval had never worried him, and unless the human involved was going to make life difficult for him, he just got on with his life with a sullen look in his eyes.

Comet's problem was that he was too small, because at 12.1hh he was only really suitable for children, and he hated children. It was sad, as he missed out on cuddles. He was a bright bay with a blaze, and he was an excellent jumper who was also capable of doing a fifteen-mile day-ride. Unfortunately, because of his size most of his potential customers were under twelve, so he spent much of his time firmly anchored to a leading rein with a tot on board. Luckily, the tot and her mother were unaware of his evil intentions, as he knew better than to annoy his adult handler. The problem came if you let the child ride him off the leading rein.

I vaguely knew the family that had once owned him. They had sent their children for six lessons at the riding school where I worked, and then considered themselves competent to own a pony. Unfortunately for them and the pony, they decided to buy a yearling, and as *experts* they also decided to ignore the advice they were given and to let the pony grow up before they broke it in. Worse was to come. The family also decided it would be cheaper to break the pony in themselves.

I had seen Comet quite regularly, staggering up a steep hill near where I kept Prince and Jim, hampered by a rider who was too big for him and a saddle and bridle that didn't fit. He was just two years old; too weak physically to object, but the anger was there – anger that would surface as soon as he had the strength to throw his rider. By the time he

15

was three he was evil, biting and kicking the children if they went into the field with him and bolting if the opportunity presented itself when he was ridden. I felt so sorry for Comet. I needed another pony, but did I need Comet? I decided that I did and parted with £50 and a certain amount of blood when he sank his teeth into the hand that was trying to help him.

He was an independent little soul used to living alone, so he didn't try to make friends with my ponies and continued to bite any human silly enough to touch him. Luckily, he was a pretty pony, and after a few months rest we took him to his first show. I was amazed when he came home with a sixth-place rosette for musical sacks. It was then I found out what I had suspected: Comet was a clever pony who would do anything from gymkhana games to jumping, and if you could restrain him from biting the judge or his tiny rider, he went well in the leading rein classes. I could see that Comet enjoyed the variety of his new life and began to respond to my voice, but he still hated any fuss. You did what you had to as quickly as possible and left him in peace.

By the time we had our first riding centre[4], he had a certain reputation. He was fine if you could ride, and won rosettes galore, but put a beginner on him and he would bide his time, then dump them with as much violence as he could manage.

His evil stubborn nature did help to keep him alive some time later, when the vet had to operate on him twice in three days. Comet had a fibroma (a fatty benign cyst) at the base of his ear, and the vet decided to freeze it off using a technique called cryosurgery. This involved putting a needle into the fibroma and using freezing gas to kill it off. Unfortunately, the first operation missed some of the fibroma which was red and angry two days later. The vet had no choice but to operate again the following day. Comet struggled groggily to his feet after the second operation and sullenly survived three months of convalescence afterwards, even more convinced that humans only existed to torture ponies. His showing career was over, though we all cheered when he won a consolation rosette despite an ugly scar. At least he was alive. If the insurance company had had their way he would have been slaughtered, as they refused to pay for treatment, which cost more than the pony was worth. I decided that Comet was probably right about the human race.

---

[4] At Kingswood near Wotton under Edge in Gloucestershire.

Comet stayed with us, moving to Wales and, later again, within Wales[5]. He even enjoyed his life, I think, only he would never have admitted that to anyone! But just think how much more he would have enjoyed his life if he had had a gentler start. A worse thought would be that if I hadn't committed to him, he probably would have been lost to the meat man's wagon.

Comet eventually became a middle-aged trekker and even developed some middle-aged spread! But we were still very careful to only give him competent young riders. Comet should have liked Tanya, a regular young rider who had light hands, sensitivity to her pony and loved jumping. So did Comet, but although he loved to jump – a fact he demonstrated when on the lunge[6], going out of his way to widen the circle to include a jump – he also enjoyed annoying and throwing humans. In fact, felling humans was definitely his favourite hobby. Tanya only weighed about five stone, so Comet realised he could erupt into a series of vicious bucks and send her flying into the sand. Poor Tanya kept coming back for more, repaying bites and bucks with pats until she won his grudging respect.

Tanya understood Comet and said that she loved him even though he was a pig. As for me, I liked him too, but my patience was wearing thin, so Comet's lunge lessons became more frequent as I dared him to challenge my authority. If he had challenged me, I could have fought him and won. But Comet knew better than to challenge strength and reserved his evil tricks for children, the smaller the better. So he spent more time on the leading rein and became more bored and worse tempered, until eventually Tanya was able enough to take him out on the mountain. Of course, he couldn't resist trying to dump her, but didn't succeed and settled down to enjoy his ride. I doubted if he would ever repay her devotion with a whinny, as he never joined in the dawn chorus that welcomed me to the stables every winter morning, but then Comet's attitude was no surprise when you considered his background. He also still had no special friends and, unlike all the others, he had a huge stable to himself as he would kick any other pony that shared with

---

[5] To Lluest in 1981 and then to Beili Bedw in 1986, as described in Part Two and part Three.

[6] Lunging is a very basic technique for training horses and ponies. It is done on a long rein in a circular movement with the aid of a long whip used to keep the horse away from you.

him. He grazed with the herd and followed them up to drink, but I doubted if he would have missed them if they weren't there.

And yet he was so capable of giving confidence to little girls who loved him. One in particular was Rosemary:

I was never very good at keeping rides to time and tended to rely on extra gallops on experienced rides to regain time lost gossiping to Mums and Dads and assorted neighbours.

If you've never galloped a fit horse on a windy day then you haven't lived. Riding Prince towards the gallops I felt as if I was sitting on a nervy coiled spring. He would prance sideways and then trot on the spot, head tossing, snorting his desire to gallop for all his worth. Then I would let him go and have over two miles of pounding feet skidding around corners, kicking up the gravel or turf. Best of all, I had other ponies to pit my wits against.

Although fast, Prince was easily beaten by Peter's horse, Jadine, who was over two hands bigger. At the end of the two miles Jadine was worn out but Prince was just waiting, hoping someone would give him the order to gallop back again. I hope that the love of a good gallop is a thing that will never fade, but as we grew older together we both enjoyed the odd slow ride. Unfortunately, we never seemed to enjoy them at the same time.

I had a feeling when I caught Prince that morning that I was in for a rough ride. It was a grotty November day, drizzly and wet but not wet enough to deter the lone trekker who stood in our untidy yard. Today was supposed to be a day of rest for most people, but I've never liked to follow a crowd so I was going to spend two hours taking one trekker – a ten-year-old child – across slippery mountains. Rosemary (of course it had to be a girl) had an earnest dedication to her riding that only a young female possesses.

'Can I saddle Comet?' she asked hopefully. I chuckled and handed over Comet's tack. I suppose I did bang the stable door – I didn't really want to go out and the sensitive Prince realised it.

'Right then, Prince,' I said. Prince laid his ears back and lifted his hind leg. 'You dare,' I roared, and he turned back towards me. Rosemary leant over the door.

'He's such a lovely pony,' she enthused.

'Yes, beautiful,' I agreed, giving Prince, who was about to bite his admirer, a sly poke in the ribs. 'Right, let's get you mounted, Rosy,' I said cheerfully. 'Come on then, Prince, walk on.' He obeyed reluctantly and dragged his feet all the way up to the mountains.

Swine, I thought. I was already soaked to the skin, my knees had locked, and my hands were rigid on his reins as I hunched my back and leant into the drizzle which was rapidly developing into rain. 'Oh, trot on,' I snapped at Prince, giving him a large boot in the side. Prince approached the canter at a lazy trot. I had my reins in a loop and wasn't concentrating on the ride.

Suddenly Prince pricked his ears and stopped dead. I shot up his neck and swore under my breath. Then we were off at a full gallop on completely the wrong track. Rosemary and Comet followed under complete control while I fumed at Prince and fought to stop him. He bucked and heaved his way across the soggy mountain kicking up peat and murky water, hoping to at least drown me if he couldn't unload me. Gradually I slowed him down and steered him back towards the track.

'You OK, Rosemary?' I shouted.

'Yes, it was great,' she replied. 'We've never been that way before, have we? Isn't Prince fast?'

'Yes,' I replied, wishing that Prince would do as he was told. Yet at times his refusal to obey was based on a healthy desire on his part to stay alive. He was clever, I knew that, and more than once I had been grateful that he could ignore an aid which would have sent both of us into a treacherous bog. He was a pony who reacted extremely quickly, and his reactions were never predictable. He hated pigs, dogs, motor bikes, heavy lorries – in fact anything that it occurred to him might be a danger.

Here on the wet, windy mountain he was in his element, and he was determined to have an interesting ride even if his frozen, soaked rider had different ideas. The track off the Mynydd Bach is steep and stony in places, and slippery in others where the closely grazed grass soon turns to mud.

Comet slithered after Prince, relying on his rider to make all the decisions. Years of experience have taught me that I haven't the ability to make such crucial decisions. So, as usual, I let Prince have his head, sat tight, and tried not to show my evil unpredictable mount that I loved and respected him.

He was not really that good looking, with his heavy Roman nose and his spavin-laden hocks[7], but he had the magical mark of a cat's paws which ran along his neck and his back. He was special. I had always loved coloured ponies for their independence, strength and gentleness, but I soon realised that Prince, although he had the former in abundance, had only a tiny piece of the latter. He eventually learnt to tolerate me, because as long as I allowed him to lead me along mountain tracks to the call of the buzzard he would be a sensible ride. But the moment his feet felt the straight boring roads he declared war and huffed his way past machines that he, like his owner, detested.

The road was boring, just as he had found my attitude boring on our ride with Rosemary. He was cold and wet too, and if he had to put up with me then I was going to have to enjoy it too. I saw his point and patted him. His ears flicked, his head came up, and once safely off the mountain we trotted for home, the perfect partnership. Until, just outside our gate, he noticed a branch blown out of our tree and leapt aside in mock terror.

'You...,' I chastised, but he seemed to laugh, knowing he'd caught me unawares – again. Then, together with Comet, he jogged down our drive to warm stables, waiting hay nets and just the possibility of buckets of feed.

Sadly, however, there are thousands of ponies like Comet in this world who end up in the sales rings; ponies ridden too young, ridden by idiots who buy them as casually as they buy a magazine. When a family decides to buy a pony for their child, it is tempting for them to see it as a cheaper option than riding lessons. It isn't, of course, and, unlike the animal their darling child rides at the local stable, it can't just be left for someone else to feed. If the family are really looking for a bargain, they may like the look of a quiet little pony that is a bit cheaper than the rest. As many parents do not know one end of an equine from the other, they are likely to go for a one on appearance alone, a 'pretty colour' being the best selling point.

At one sale, I spotted a skewbald colt standing tied up next to a piebald and a roan. He could have been a pretty pony. He was about eighteen months old, very stunted and thin but he had a kind eye. I knew his owner, who was often at the market; he was a fat, greedy man

---

[7] A spavin is either a puffy swelling or a bony arthritic growth on a horse's hock (the joint half-way up the hind leg).

who kept his ponies who knows where, perhaps on the marshes, or maybe on a scrap of overgrazed 'horse sick' field[8]. His ponies suffered not only from his neglect, but from his cruelty too. Eventually the skewbald was led into the ring; the auctioneer had just cautioned the handlers to 'treat him gently', but his empty words held no comfort for the colt. As usual at this market they were just words designed to placate anyone who complained about the treatment of the ponies there. The auctioneer didn't really expect anyone to take any notice of them, but he felt that he had done his duty by uttering them. Honour was satisfied on all sides and there was no danger of offending the vendors. The skewbald walked quietly up the ring, dejectedly awaiting his fate. I don't know what the colt was doing wrong, except perhaps showing a lack of spirit. He was in poor condition, no doubt like many others suffering from malnutrition. Of course, they could have fed him properly, but that would have cost them money and they would probably have been afraid of a pony with real spirit. So the owner's friend used a quicker method of injecting some 'instant' spirit, lashing him with a lunging whip. It was not a gentle flick but a vicious crack that finally stung the colt into action. The colt bolted down the ring dragging the owner's son along at the end of the halter rope. For a second I thought that he would bolt through the crowd, injuring the onlookers, but he allowed himself to be slowed down, whether out of gentleness or lack of energy I'm not sure. The lad dragged the colt back towards the auctioneer as my friend Barbara[9] shouted at the man with the whip. The auctioneer said nothing, though I had a feeling I knew who he would have liked to evict, as he glared at Barbara. The colt trotted up this time without any help from his owner's friend, but he was unsold; his colour meant that the owner expected a bit more for him. How I wished I could wave £100 under his owner's nose. But I didn't have £100, and anyway, although that £100 would give this colt a decent life, it would then give his owner enough money to buy two more colts to take his place.

The colt was tied to a rail and left to stand and shiver until the end of the sale. By this time the auctioneer was selling the wild ponies in Ring

---

[8] A 'horse sick' field is an over-grazed field with bare patches and evidence of rampant weed growth. Poo picking regularly can help reduce the condition as it is usually areas of droppings where the weed growth appears, making these areas unpalatable.

[9] Barbara Metcalfe, collator and editor of Ginny's writing and one of the original trustees of the Lluest Horse and Pony Trust.

Two which in winter is approached through a rattling cattle crush, a terrifying experience for a wild pony or foal that has never been confined until the day of the sale. The skewbald, remembering his earlier experience, just stood and shook. He made no attempt to kick or bite as he was pushed into the crush, but his eyes were wild and his breathing rapid. He shot into the ring as the crush gate banged open, narrowly escaping the final bid of a meat man. I saw Barb looking relieved, but I groaned because I knew his new owner. He was a young man, always well groomed, who dealt in 'quiet to ride' youngsters, usually in poor condition. I watched him collect the colt and lead him to the car park, so I followed. The colt was tired, cold and hungry so he stumbled along by his new owner. A child ran up behind him, and the colt barely noticed. Then the young man picked the child up, one hand dragging the colt's head even lower, while the other swung the child onto the colt's back, thumping him down as if he were a sack of coal into the boot of his car. The skewbald staggered and almost collapsed, but somehow kept moving towards the lorry. His owner swaggered – he'd sell the colt soon to some unsuspecting buyer as 'quiet to ride'. I wondered if the colt's confusion would turn into viciousness like Comet – or would he struggle on, only eighteen months old but already described as 'quiet to ride'. He would probably be schooled in a boggy field with a heavy rider on him just to make sure no spirit had survived. Any that did remain would be beaten out of him. It wouldn't take long to school him; the colt knew that resistance was useless so it would be back to market or sold privately to some idiot who wanted a pony for their child and wouldn't know what they were buying. They would be better off if they bought the child a toy pony; at least they could not hurt that pony with their ignorance, and neither could it have hurt their child. Would the skewbald colt be condemned to a miserable life? I had no way of knowing. The dealer was breaking no law; his ponies were poor, ridden too young and worm infested, but that is not illegal. But I do know one thing for sure: those colts' lives will end in the meat man's pen, worn out by too many demands on an immature body and the damage of malnutrition and worms. All that is in question is how long the colt will take to get there.

So, the next time you come across one of these ponies like Comet, stop and **think**. It's quite natural to be annoyed, as I often am, but don't offer a pat that will definitely be rejected; you don't have to make his life interesting. It is easier to keep him to boring work on a leading rein where he can do no damage but think and pass time. One day he may respond, but even if he doesn't at least your conscience will be clear. We created Comet and his type through our ignorance, through our cowardice when we put off talking to the owner of a pony who is obviously too young for the work asked of him. Most owners do not want to be told that their animal is too young, but sometimes one will listen and one pony will have a better life. These youngsters do have potential even if we can't see it immediately, but the most important thing is to remember to love the ponies for themselves. We must fight until the ownership of horses and ponies is restricted to those who are prepared to look after them properly. We must educate parents who think about buying a pony, explaining about the pitfalls, and stressing that their purchase is an expensive addition to any family. In an ideal world, both the owners of that skewbald pony would never keep ponies long term, but I saw them at the sales most months with several for sale – all destined for the same miserable lives. All deserved better.

Comet

Chapter 3

Pepper, Sarah and Queenie

Pepper, Sarah and Queenie all came into my life whilst I was living in Gloucestershire but later moved with us to Wales. They were all very different in character!

Pepper was not a remarkable pony. An aged somewhat tatty dun with a large appetite and a very uneven gait, he was definitely no one's first choice as a riding pony. We met in about 1977 – I can't remember the exact date that I cantered him around an orchard outside Gloucester. He had a kind eye and an easy-going if lazy nature, he could jump 'a bit' and was guaranteed quiet in traffic. He nudged me to see if I had any food, but as soon as I had untacked him, he settled down to eating the grass and looking in vain for any fallen apples. Unlike many of my ponies, he expressed no desire to be part of our herd or my life. As long as he was fed, I suspected he cared very little who carried the bucket.

It was not 'love at first sight'. He was a useful pony: a good size at 13.3hh, and light enough for riders not to think they were riding a miniature carthorse. Unfortunately, in spite of his body, Pepper had the spirit of a very heavy carthorse and often tripped over his feet or any handy tuft of grass. Of course, he settled in to his new home as easily as he had no doubt settled in to his previous one. I suspected that he had come originally from an early life on the Black Mountains. He was clumsy and hadn't had much, if any, schooling. It wasn't until several years later that I realised that Pepper had probably been broken in by being sat on in a handy bog by a heavy man. He was, if he was lucky, two years old at the time. Yet he bore no malice, ambling through life with his eyes half closed, only opening them fully when he noticed a tasty blade of grass.

Pepper could and did jump well, clearing three-foot jumps with ease and rarely knocking one down. Unfortunately, he jumped as he did everything else in life – at his own speed. He would never win a show-jumping class, though he was excellent at 'Chase me Charlie' where his careful steady jumping won him many rosettes, often against far better ponies than himself. He also did well at 'Clear Round Jumping', giving even the most nervous rider a steady guaranteed pop over the obstacles.

When I opened my first riding school in Gloucestershire, he was still young enough to have regular riders who liked him, but for every child who adored Pepper there were twenty-five who would go to any lengths to avoid riding him. He idled his way through numerous lessons, moving only if I joined him in trotting around the school. Luckily, he enjoyed hacking, so when we moved with all our ponies to Wales he cheered up no end. However, the kind of riding we did was pony trekking, encouraging a variety of children and lightweight ladies to take a ride around the hills and mountains.

Pepper settled down, happily dealing with everything from screaming children to a lady who was so terrified, as soon as she sat in his saddle, that she refused to allow him to move or to move herself, even to dismount. Luckily, I knew Pepper wouldn't go anywhere, and I managed to stand for ten minutes holding the lady's hand until her husband eventually decided to lift her out of the saddle. The only casualty of that incident was my hand which was limp and bruised after being gripped so tightly. We reassured the lady, offering her a cup of tea, sitting in our front room. As I gave her the tea, I glanced out of the window. Good old Pepper was still standing by the mounting block fast asleep. I rescued him, still chuckling and wondering, as I often did, whether his quiet acceptance of everything the human race did to him was because he was too lazy to wake up, or because he had a genuine feeling for us.

As my business prospered, Pepper worked hard. Not that I noticed, as I spent most of my time trying to dissuade him from working for our local council, which didn't seem to get round to trimming overgrown hedges. Just as well really, as Pepper munched his way through tons of hedgerow, an assortment of trekkers lunches, passing holiday-makers' ice-creams, and even a mouthful of chips. Naturally, some of the peculiar things he ate, which included his bedding, gave him tummy ache.

Colic can be very serious, so the slightest pain is always a signal to panic and call the vet, especially in Pepper's case as he was always convinced he was about to die. Luckily, an injection restored him to his usual greedy self, often within minutes. The problem then was to stop him eating for a few hours, so that whatever he'd eaten this time could pass through his system.

He was probably the most cursed pony we owned, as he plodded along lanes, ignoring his rider's commands, with a selection of hedgerow goodies dangling from his mouth. Looking back on his career I never remember him throwing a rider or biting or kicking any human even if he was ill or in pain. The only thing he wouldn't tolerate was having his teeth rasped – every attempt to look in his mouth provoked a very impressive display of rearing. He was always sensitive about his mouth, perhaps as a result of early mistreatment, and had worn a rubber bit for years.

By the time we moved again to our next and forever home[10], Pepper was an old pony, probably at least twenty-five years old. He didn't have a special rider, he was just a 'plod' for the nervous or beginners, considered useless for an experienced rider. I had begun to look for a replacement, but I never found one; boring, predictable Pepper was impossible to replace. I'd fed him, mucked out after him and cared for him, but I hadn't noticed how special he was. I owed my business in large part to the special years of his life he had given, if sometimes grudgingly. He saved me endless worry – there was always one in every party, one terrified child or mother who I could give Pepper to, knowing the worst he would do was to stop for a munch. Pepper was never affectionate, regarding cuddles as a waste of time and just a prelude to a hidden packet of polos. His less than endearing habit of headbutting if the polos were not forthcoming lost him a few friends, and one unfortunate gentleman was badly winded when Pepper caught him off balance.

I probably wouldn't have realised how much Pepper really cared for us humans if Ellryn hadn't come to Beili Bedw. Although confined to a wheelchair she was an active young lady who wanted to ride. She was nervous of Pepper's size at first, but was soon riding him in the school off lead rein. He plodded around taking no more notice of her aids than he did of any of his able-bodied riders. Later that week we met Ellryn

---

[10] Beili Bedw, a beautiful farm in the Black Mountains

and her sister on the mountain for a one-and-a-half-hour ride. It should have been an easy ride for Pepper, who enjoyed spending time in the mountains. But he was twenty-seven years old and he hated cold rainy days. It was raining heavily by the time Ellryn, clad in waterproofs, was lifted on. As soon as we asked him, Pepper walked forward, ears pricked, resisting the temptation to turn rump to the bad weather. He plodded on for an hour and a half to give Ellryn the ride of her life and returned to his stable wet, cold and for once in his life the centre of our grateful attention. A swift head butt and a very determined attempt to kick his stable to pieces discouraged us from wasting time with praise – he couldn't eat praise; a bucket of feed made much more sense to him.

A few days later another girl rode Pepper. The young lady could not ride very well but had no intention of learning to do any better. She chatted to her friend, left her reins dangling and ignored Pepper completely. He galloped and even jumped a ditch perfectly happily, completely oblivious to the young lady's scorn. Or was he oblivious? I suspect that he just didn't care and rather enjoyed his one gallop, done when he felt like it. He didn't notice the lack of a pat either, though my cuddle may have been noticed before he dived for his bucket.

Pepper trotted off down the field with his friends that evening as jauntily as he always did, leaving me to reflect sadly on a boring little pony who quietly gave so much to the human race and was always taken for granted. Now that he was about to retire, I realised what a gap he would leave. Somewhere there might be another Pepper if he had survived the rapacious meat trade as a foal. Pepper, who wasn't a pretty pony, had survived all those years ago. How or why we don't know. As for me, I just wished he was thirteen years younger. Pepper? Well, I thought, he'll love his retirement, when his only duty will be to take Ellryn riding – and eat his head off.

Sarah lived for herself and wasn't going to change for anyone. She was Sarah and you could take her or leave her. I took her, and kept her, despite threatening countless times to sell her to the knacker-man. Most ponies seem to have a tipping point, a point when despite a poor start in life or a basically idle nature they suddenly put their heart and soul into their work. All my ponies were willing except Sarah; all were rejects come good except Sarah. She was a reject all right, but good she certainly wasn't. She was guaranteed to make the legs drop off an experienced rider and reduce a perfectly good trek to a funeral procession. She never moved rapidly unless being chased, returning to her field or approaching a meal time.

She was stunning to look at, black with three white socks and a star, but I am sure she would hate the human race – that's if she had the energy to do so. As it was, she contented herself with merely annoying us. I often wondered if some swine taught her reverse commands but that is unlikely as I found it more or less impossible to teach her anything, apart from how to stand still. When a ride left the yard, the pony's names were called in the order I wanted them to leave in. Except that we seemed to have about five 'Sarah's before the pony in question raised herself enough to put any foot forward, let alone her best one.

Sarah moved with us to Wales and became part of our trekking centre. As she sleep-walked across the mountain, there were frequent pauses while she admired the scenery and sampled a variety of vegetation. Yet even this example of horseflesh had her admirers.

'Are your ponies quiet?' asked the woman, somewhat nervously. Her two young children had already mounted Bluey and Mick[11] and were laughing at Mum who was obviously coming apart at the seams.

'Don't worry,' I replied, 'this one is guaranteed not to move unless you drop a bomb, and even then she'd stop to see if it was going to explode.' The woman laughed nervously and advanced on Sarah, who heaved a deep sigh as the woman collapsed into the saddle.

'What's your name?' I asked.

'Margaret,' she replied. 'Don't leave me. Can't you put me on a leading rein?' The children laughed and looked as if they regretted bringing their mum.

'Come on, then,' I said, leading Sarah out of the yard. Sarah dawdled all the way around the two-and-a-half-hour trek, much to Margaret's relief and gradually she gained confidence. By the time we reached the top of the mountains she was chatting away, enthusing over a buzzard and enjoying the view. Sarah had one, or was it both eyes closed as she plodded along. No, she isn't particularly kind. In fact, she can be very cunning, but it is easier to carry your load at a steady pace than to try and remove it.

Of course, trotting or leading a ride is a completely different matter. Sue had only just started working for me when I broke my ribs and

---

[11] Bluey and Mick's stories are told in Chapter 5 and Chapter 13.

hadn't had time to warn her about Sarah. At the end of a two-and-a-half-hour trek she was sore, breathless and hot, and Sarah hadn't a hair out of place or even a tiny sweat mark.

'She's a cow,' muttered Sue in disgust.

'Quite possibly,' I agreed. 'But unfortunately, we're stuck with her.'

Sue was never a person to give in. 'I know,' she said, 'I'll take her out on my own. That should wake her up.'

It didn't – although it almost resulted in Sue falling off.

'Right,' said Sue, or words to that effect anyway. 'I'll take her out with little Sue on Jadine[12] to the gallops. She'll go, to keep up with Jadine.' She didn't, and Sue gave up in disgust. People usually did, because Sarah was stubborn and so uncomfortable that it didn't seem worth any effort to improve her.

So she spent her life plodding the hills with a succession of nervy mums who mistook the vacant stare for kindness, and who luckily were unable to interpret the looks she gave them as they mounted.

Some ponies are completely unchangeable. Sarah was one. Queenie was another, but her problem was completely the opposite. She was so willing that she anticipated aids and leapt off in all directions before she or her rider had made up their minds where to go. Lots of people fell off Queenie, but she loved people and always slithered to a halt when yet another jockey decided to try flying lessons. She jumped anything, with or more frequently without her rider, but she was superb as a leading file. She was barely 12hh, but with her long stride she set a pace that Jadine at 15.2hh could feel proud of. She was mostly used as an escort pony, although occasionally carried children on a leading rein.

We met at a sale in Thornbury, near Bristol. I went there to buy hay nets, but as the tiny pony was ridden into the ring by a twelve-and-a-half-stone man, hay nets were forgotten.

'Quiet to ride,' said the auctioneer.

'Yes, if she's weighted down,' I muttered to Barb.

The meat man nodded his bid. I looked at Barb who delved into her bag. We grinned at each other, and minutes later I was the proud owner of Queenie, in debt to a friend and still in need of hay nets!

---

[12] Jadine was officially Peter's horse, but was used in the trekking business when appropriate.

At the time, we were waiting to see if planning permission had been granted for our first riding school in Kingswood, near Wotton under Edge, and this was definitely not the time to buy another pony. Pete was furious when he found out about Queenie. Despite planning permission coming through, as I was confident it would, he decided against letting me attend any more auctions without him.

'She's mad,' he said, after watching an experienced girl sail over the school fence while Queenie danced on the other side.

'Quite,' I agreed, but had no chance of further comment. The rider who had just fallen off leapt to Queenie's defence.

'She's lovely. If you sell her, I'll leave.'

That summed up everyone's reaction to her. No matter how many times a rider fell off, it was never Queenie's fault. She was incapable of throwing anyone, or hurting anyone, but her bounding energy and joy in life was impossible to control. No doubt a psychiatrist could have made a few comments about the reaction of the horsey type to a mad pony like Queenie. I think it stems from a basic respect for what is still, in many ways, a wild animal. Yes, riding Queenie was a challenge, a proof of courage, and somewhere in the back of her riders' minds must have been the thought that one of them might be the one who finally got the better of the fastest, craziest pony in the stable.

Sarah

Chapter 4

Jerry

I can't remember seeing Jerry amongst pens where horses and ponies wait for their fate to be decided. In fact, the first time I saw him was when he was ridden into the auction ring at Stow Fayre. He was a thin 13.3hh gelding of unknown age, but I suspected that he was quite old. He was advertised as genuine in every way, although I hardly heard the description when he looked at me. His kind vague eyes looked trustingly around the ring. His child rider was trying not to cry. Then one of the meat men started bidding. Jerry trotted trustingly towards him. He was going for a song, and fattened up... I didn't hesitate and bought a fifteen-year-old pony that I didn't know anything about. Even after I rushed up and patted him and looked at his teeth, I wasn't sure if I had guessed his age correctly. I never was sure.

'What's he like?' I asked his owner.

'Oh, I'm glad he didn't go for meat,' the mother replied.

I wondered why they had found it necessary to sell such a nice pony through an auction where they couldn't check out his new home.

'Oh, he's lovely' the father replied. 'He's a great ride but he's too strong for my daughter.'

Oh, great, I thought. He bolts.

'What has he done?' I asked politely.

'Well, he's Pony Clubbed and hunted, but a bit strong,' he said.

'I don't hunt,' I said firmly, 'I don't approve.'

For some reason the father looked relieved.

We said our goodbyes, and I took Jerry, who was apparently a New Forest cross thoroughbred, home to my then-illegal business, which was flourishing in a quiet corner of the Cotswolds.

31

The next day we went riding. I left Prince, my usual crazy mount, in the stable and took another in the shape of Jerry. He was thin so I decided to take it steady. We did until we opened the gate which led us on to a green valley sloping invitingly upwards.

'You go on,' I told my ride, who were old customers and excellent riders. So they set off on Comet, Jim and Pepper, with Jim as usual in the lead.

'Walk on, Jerry,' I said quietly. Jerry flicked his ears, threw his head in the air and followed his new friends. I didn't mind that, but when we quickly caught up and then overtook, I did start to wonder. If I tried to stop, he simply threw his head and then bolted with his head almost between his knees. Luckily it was a long valley. I remembered a boggy patch near the top that should steady him up, I thought. It didn't, although it did dirty his tack. The boundary fence of barbed wire was getting closer and I was starting to wonder if I had bought another crazy pony. It was a possibility! Jerry wasn't going to stop and every time I took a pull at his reins he just pulled back harder. I tried to turn him in a circle, but after nearly brushing the ground with my foot as he tried to gallop on a tiny circle, I decided against it. We were about twenty yards from the fence, and it was an impossible jump.

Oh hell, I thought, I haven't fallen off for a while. Shame about the stones.

Jerry felt me go loose in the saddle and slithered to a halt. I dismounted hastily, my legs were weak and my pulse rate would probably have given a doctor heart failure. Jerry nuzzled me gently.

'Can I ride him?' asked one of my more suicidal companions.

'No, you can't,' I snapped. 'If I can't stop him, you certainly won't.'

Of course, I was wrong as usual.

Jerry spent several weeks taking experienced riders only, but inevitably a beginner fell in love with him. He was a saint with her, plodding along the lanes on a leading rein. I didn't risk letting him go anywhere near grass.

We were soon on the move, and Jerry moved with us to our first legal stable just a few miles away[13]. There, much to my surprise, he kept the title of Ginny's fastest pony, as well as plodding quietly around the grass field with a beginner.

---

[13] At the village of Kingswood near Wotton under Edge.

Until Jerry's arrival, Prince had been King of Ginny's mob, the fastest craziest horse, and he wasn't going to be beaten by the speedy upstart I had introduced. Therefore, I wasn't really surprised when I found Jerry with a badly cut hind leg. I had seen Prince's handiwork before, but this was one of the worst. The harassed vet arrived soon after my panicky phone call. 'Gentle Jerry' soon showed that, although gentle, he was a complete coward. The vet approached him, and seconds later he, together with his assistant, myself and my friend Paula, were all holding various bits of our anatomy.

'I'll tranquillize him,' the vet suggested. He did so with some difficulty and soon had to top him up with more.

We led him into the field. The vet bent down to examine the leg and swore as he got trampled on.

'Right, get some rope, we'll throw him,' he shouted.

'Do we have to?' I asked.

The vet scowled. Paula ran off to get some rope from her Dad who was a road haulier. The vet soon pulled Jerry to the ground and Paula and I were instructed to lean on the rope and keep him there. All was peace as the vet froze the leg. Then we had trouble with wasps! They buzzed around Jerry, the vet, Paula and me. Jerry struggled, dreading a sting, and the vet cursed insects in general and wasps in particular. I've never heard wasps described with such a variety of adjectives – none of them printable! What fun, I thought. Then, as the vet worked on the wound, there was a thud and groan from my left side. Paula was on the ground.

'Get up,' I yelled at Paula, who didn't look too well. 'For God's sake get up, I can't hold Jerry on my own,' I pleaded.

She looked up but stayed where she was.

The vet glanced at her. His glance summed up why vets hate working for undersized emotional females. After a few minutes Paula got up and then he finished his stitching. Untying Jerry was easy and he followed us back to the stable. He was as lively as ever, even attempting a dance. The vet left hastily before I could take him to see the rest of my charges, while his assistant looked as if he felt he may not have chosen the right career.

Customers were waiting, so I mounted them up and ushered them to the school. I had planned a jumping lesson, which was not a pleasant prospect as 'Screwy Bluey'[14] had taken Jerry's place and Bluey didn't jump.

'Ginny!' The yell sounded panicky.

I dropped my lunge whip and raced over to the yard. Paula was in Jerry's stable; he was reeling around crashing into the wall and Paula was taking a risk being in with him.

'It's that damn tranquilliser,' I said, rushing in and grabbing Jerry. 'We must keep him still and stop him plunging around.'

Jerry realized that he was under control and dozed off, leaning his head on Paula's shoulder.

'You're crazy,' I said, to Paula. 'You nearly faint because you see a drop of blood, but you race into a drugged pony's stable. He could have killed you.' I groaned.

She grinned. 'I'm not squeamish usually, but the vet dropped the needle into the wound. He was fishing around for it'.

I laughed, 'Oh, is that all. He did get it out, didn't he?'

'Yes' replied Paula.

Jerry's leg healed quickly and the vet came back to take the stitches out. Jerry nuzzled him and was remarkably forgiving, until the vet looked at his leg. I think it was the sight of the scissors, but whatever it was, Jerry tried to dance a tattoo on the vet's head.

'Oh, bugger it,' the vet cursed. 'Here's the scissors. He's your pony.'

'They're your stitches,' I retorted, but the vet was already escaping.

'You won't have any trouble,' he said as he was climbing into his car.

I went back into Jerry's stable, scissors well-hidden and bent down to look at his leg. I managed to snip a stitch before he realized what I was up to, but I found myself on the floor when I tried to cut the next one. So I decided to ask his favourite people to cut the stitches. Each one managed to cut a stitch, but as soon as they cut it Jerry would rear or kick in panic. The last stitch was cut by a seven-year-old, who wandered into his stable and cut it because she was in a hurry to get on her pony; she'd overheard me saying that the ride would have to wait until I'd dealt with Jerry. Of course, he didn't kick, even when she pulled the stitch out, and no doubt she did it clumsily. I was very cross, not because I thought the child was at risk – I had a suspicion that Jerry would never hurt a child – but because a child had managed to do what I hadn't been able to!

[14] 'Screwy Bluey' was another of Ginny's misfits, whose story is told in Chapter 5.

A few months later I had every pony out on a day ride. Jerry's rider was an old friend of mine, and I've always thought Mary an excellent rider. Jerry agreed, and so when we met the local hunt he decided to test her skill. The hunt careered through the valley after some unfortunate fox while we looked on from the top of the valley. Jerry was dancing around whinnying. Prince, who hates dogs of any description, fidgeted, and soon Jim and Comet were cavorting and joining in the melee. Pepper, who seemed to have no interest in either mad gallops or hunts, munched the hedge.

'I wish I knew where they were going, Mary,' I said. 'You'd better lead that idiot, he's very strong.'

'No problem,' Mary laughed. 'If I can control sixteen-hand hunters I can control this squirt.'

'Come on you lot, follow me,' I said, wondering just how good Mary was.

I turned Prince and headed for the woods, hoping that the hunt would stay in the valley. Jerry didn't want to leave the hunt. I heard a gasp and turned round in time to see Jerry rearing up. He somehow spun in the air and came down facing the hunt.

'Get off, Mary,' I yelled.

She laughed and ignored me. Seconds later Jerry and Mary were galloping down the hill. Luckily both were excellent jumpers and used to jumping unknown hedges on steep banks. I watched them until they reached the bottom of the valley. Surely, she'll stop him there, I thought. She didn't and they hurtled after the hunt. Apparently, they caught up with the back markers quite easily. Mary tried to steady Jerry, but he ignored her and was soon level with the master who was doing a wonderfully sedate canter. Or rather, he was until Jerry caught up and upset what was probably his young horse. Neither Jerry or the apprentice hunter liked to follow another horse. Luckily, the master had plenty of gadgets that many 'knowledgeable' horsemen use to control unruly mounts, and his horse was soon cantering sedately again. Jerry, ridden only in a mild snaffle, was in his element and forged on to catch up with the brown and white things in front. Mary, a keen hunter, winced as she shot through the pack and prayed that she had not been recognized. She says that she was sure she overtook the fox too, but then fear can do strange things to people.

Jerry and Mary re-joined us at our picnic place. She was very quiet during lunch.

'Do you still think he's a squirt?' I asked wickedly.

'Yes, and he's a swine as well – you should put a standing martingale on him,' she muttered.

'Perhaps a double bridle as well?' I asked innocently.

'Alright, alright,' she replied. 'I know how you feel about gadgets, but don't you think that pony needs something to help his unfortunate riders?'

'I did tell you to get off.' I said

'And then get kicked,' she snapped. 'No thanks.'

'He wouldn't,' I said. 'We met the hunt a few weeks ago, and he had Mrs Smith on him,' I added.

The ride laughed. Mrs Smith was one of the most neurotic women I had ever met, and she spent most of her time clinging on to the saddle, screaming.

'Not Mrs Smith from the village?' Mary said.

'Yes, that's the one. And he ignored the hunt. He's a very clever chap. After all, would you take Mrs Smith for a trot, never mind a hunt?'

Mary looked at Jerry who was grazing peacefully next to Blackie.

'You mean he's OK unless you can ride?' she asked.

'Yes. I expect all the experienced riders he's belonged to have bombed him around and relied on gadgets, not schooling, to stop him,' I said. 'He's got a mouth like cast iron, the fault of previous owners,' I added.

'Then I'll stick to sixteen-handers with gadgets, thanks,' she asserted.

She did, too, and Jerry never had the opportunity to take her riding or hunting again.

U

Once we moved to Wales, Jerry had to take even more beginners, and his gentleness won him many friends. Then one day, on a beginner's ride, Sarah tried to bite him. Jerry, cowardly as ever, jumped aside and staggered and slipped. I rushed up and dismounted his rider. Jerry was leaning to one side and obviously in agony. Reluctantly, I carried on with the ride and sent Jerry back with Alison, one of my helpers. Stella[15],

---

[15] Stella Gratrix, a long-term helper of Ginny's and one of the editors of this book.

back in the yard, called the vet who diagnosed that Jerry had trapped a nerve in his neck and would be fine in twenty-four hours.

The next day, while I was away on the day ride, Jerry had the first of many strokes. The vet came again and again. He tried gently to tell me that there was no hope, and Jerry should be put to sleep. But it was my decision and no one could make it for me. I couldn't face holding Jerry for the inevitable. He didn't even recognize my voice and he was rearing and trying to throw himself over the stable wall. Blood was pouring from his face and legs and the attacks were coming every few minutes.

'Stella,' I said, 'call the vet and ask him to bring the humane killer.'

Stella rushed into the house. I stood by Jerry. I couldn't touch him because he was never still. I loved him and I couldn't face losing him, but I couldn't let him continue banging his head against the stable wall.

'The vet's out on a call,' Stella said, leaning through the window. I was crying and Stella was trying not to.

'Stella,' I said, 'go back and ask for a very heavy dose of tranquillizer. The vet won't be able to shoot him like this. Look, the dose might finish him...'

I hardly dared admit that I had an idea.

I remembered James Herriot's lovely books and the story of the poodle with life-threatening diarrhoea. He tranquillized it heavily and the dog's life was saved. Stella and I both agreed that Jerry was a coward. He has never been able to face physical pain, but by throwing himself around and fighting he was making things worse. Unfortunately, Stella couldn't drive at that time, after being mugged and suffering a serious arm injury, so she phoned Trefor the long-suffering farmer from next door, who raced down to Lluest, picked her up and covered the distance to the vets' in record time. Luckily, Jerry was going through a calm period when they returned, so Trefor rammed a full dose into his rump. Five minutes later Jerry collapsed. We threw a lot of straw into the stable and waited for him to die. Although he was still having attacks, they weren't hurting him now. In fact, at one stage I had the strange feeling that he was just chasing hounds as he had probably done for most of his life.

Trefor went home, and our guests Diana and Marion returned with the children. If you've ever had ten fourteen-year-old girls staying in your house you will know that ear plugs are a necessity, but all the girls were quiet. They sat by the open window waiting for news and occasionally weeping. Diana and Marion tried to cheer me and Stella up and force some food down us, but we weren't hungry. Finally, they persuaded me to leave Jerry and come inside. I could do nothing for him but wait calmly, and I couldn't even manage that.

I did go to bed eventually, but didn't sleep as I listened to Jerry thrashing around. Then at about two o'clock in the morning there was silence. I cried and hugged Jester[16] desperately. I was sure that Jerry was dead. The next morning, I thought that I heard the sound of a pony moving around. Ghosts, I thought. Six o'clock was far too early to ring the knacker-man, and anyway I wanted the children to be out of the yard when Jerry was taken away.

Finally, I walked over to the stable. Jerry was standing quietly and looked up as I walked in – at least it was his body, but his eyes were vacant and his tongue hung uselessly from his mouth. I offered him some hay. He wanted to eat it but he couldn't move it from his front teeth to his back teeth.

Well, I thought, I've just delayed the inevitable. Stella appeared. She looked dreadful.

'Did you sleep?' I asked.

'No,' she replied. 'Did you?'

I shook my head. 'He can't control his mouth or his tongue, I'll try pushing a carrot in.' I did, and with my help Jerry ate it.

Alison appeared around the stable door.

'Is he better?' she asked.

'Well, he's still alive,' replied Stella, who is always an optimist.

As she often says, someone needs to be, and no one could describe me as an optimist! Poor Jerry struggled on dutifully eating the odd wisp of hay. He looked dreadful, but Stella was right, he was still alive, and I didn't feel quite as helpless or inadequate now because I knew what to do. I would give him two days, and if he couldn't feed himself by then I would have to have him put to sleep. Mr R the vet phoned to ask how he was, and he accepted my decision. I could sense that he wasn't happy, and I wondered aloud if he was worried about the bill which I wouldn't be able to pay.

'Don't be daft,' said Stella abruptly. 'He's worried about you. Jerry is dangerous. He could land on you, and Mr R doesn't want that on his conscience.' She was right, of course.

---

[16] Ginny's border collie.

So Alison, Stella and I sat with Jerry encouraging him to eat the nicest bits of hay, honeyed carrots and herbal bran mash. After two days he could control his tongue and eat very slowly without our help.

Then the vet phoned again. 'I'd like to come and see him,' he said. 'Make him walk for an hour, briskly,' he added.

I was about to argue when he hung up. I rushed out to Stella.

'What am I going to do?' I asked her. 'It will kill him,' I whispered.

Stella shrugged. 'Do you want him to spend the rest of his life like he is? Do as the vet says. He must have a reason, and you know he wouldn't ask you to do it if he thought it would kill Jerry.'

She was right. Reassured, I clipped a leading rope on to Jerry's halter. I felt sick and shaky as I led him out of the stable. He nearly crashed into the wall, and I realized for the first time that he was blind in one eye. Jerry reeled into the yard but he followed me up the drive. He couldn't walk straight but gradually he did increase his speed. Stella and Alison watched us and for the first time we all had smiles on our faces. When Mr R arrived, he couldn't resist checking Stella's injured arm, then he turned his attention to his real patient.

'Mr R,' I said straight away, 'I can't afford to pay you and I don't know when I'll be able to.'

'Look, all I'm interested in is getting this chap better,' he replied.

Mr R gave Jerry a variety of drugs just in case he had an infection. He listened to his heart and said that Jerry had a defective valve. Jerry didn't object to the injections, which were given into his chest so that he couldn't see what was going on, but he did object to his eye being examined. Mr R spent nearly an hour with us, most of which he seemed to spend patting his patient.

'Well,' he said, 'I had better go. Watch his kidneys and make sure you exercise him, and don't forget to ring if you want anything.'

Mr R never sent me a bill and probably wouldn't have unless he knew I could have paid it without any difficulty. As for Jerry, he improved slowly and ate normally. Unfortunately, he never recovered his sight, and at first he crashed into walls continually. I almost gave in, because every morning I had to clean cuts. Then one morning I noticed a minute cut on his good side.

'Alright, love,' I murmured and leant down to clean it up. Jerry leapt in the air and looked shocked. The school party and Stella had left by this time so I just gritted my teeth and advanced on his bad side. He didn't react; I don't know whether he had lost the feeling on that side or whether he only panicked if he could see you touching a wound. Whatever reason I was very grateful. I soon decided to risk letting Jerry loose in a big field. He turned several circles trying to adjust to the strange lopsided pictures he was receiving. Then he squealed, leapt in the air and came down bucking. He pranced around for a few minutes while I watched half laughing and half crying. He was on the mend and soon he rejoined the herd. Even Prince now treated him gently, and the ponies seemed to take it in turns to guide him around. He couldn't find the water trough, so I carried water to him two or three times a day. I still carried a herbal feed to him twice a day, and one morning he managed to walk to me in a straight line. Other important improvements followed quickly, the hysterical circles lessened, he regained condition and finally he located the water trough. Sometimes he would race after the other ponies. He accepted his retirement and I think that he enjoyed himself. He was spoiled, had lots of visitors and for the first time he had a best friend in Mick[17], who in many ways was a smaller version of Jerry, spending his days shepherding Jerry around the field. When Mick was working, little Folly took his place. She loved to play and dodge around Jerry, flirting and provoking him, but he grazed quietly, and gradually he was teaching Folly how to behave. I did wonder whether I had been right to keep Jerry alive and if I had just avoiding my responsibilities, but now I know that I was right. He became a happy pony again and adjusted well to his new life.

---

[17] Mick's story is told in Chapter 13.

Chapter 5

Screwy Bluey

'Wherever did you get this one from?' asked the farrier. Bluey turned a friendly head to Ty, closed his eyes and reverted to his normal state of semi-coma.

'What's his breeding?' asked Ty, returning to his attack. 'Look, when you buy a pony, please look at its feet, it's important. It doesn't matter how sorrowful they look and what might happen to them, just don't buy rubbish, because they drag you down every time.'

I smiled but ignored his well-meant advice. I had a stable full of rejects, and although I always looked at the misshapen feet and crooked jaw, they didn't make any difference, because if the reject had kind eyes, he had a home for life.

Had I suffered because of this policy? Financially, yes, but I knew, as all my customers did, that they would never meet a finer group of ponies. Certainly, some of them looked a little unusual at first, and many more had serious vices, but gradually they developed into a team – my team.

It was a bleak autumn day when I first noticed that small white pony standing motionless amongst a large herd of ponies. I knew something special was about to happen. The little pony was obviously in pain and the farrier who knew him confirmed that he was badly neglected. Welfare organisations had been involved but no conclusion to the little pony's suffering had been reached, so I bought him for £20. As usual, I commandeered my long-suffering friends, Barbara and Brian[18], into collecting my latest recruit. He was not exactly a sensible purchase. He

---

[18] Barbara (editor) and Brian Metcalfe, two of the original trustees of the Lluest Horse and Pony Trust.

was crippled because of laminitis, an inflammatory condition of the feet. This had been caused by neglect of his feet, which resembled oriental slippers curving upwards so that walking was difficult. As far as I could make out, Bluey had been in this condition for most of his three and a half years. In the summer he became overweight, as he managed to hobble within range of easy pickings of grass which exacerbated the condition, but in the winter he was skin and bone. Gradually, this pony, who was basically intelligent and friendly, lost interest in life and waited for the inevitable. As he stood in his field, in constant pain, the world passed him by, unseeing and uncaring. So why did I care and take the gamble? An instinct told me to. It was as if someone with a great deal more experience than I had was standing at my shoulder giving me whispered instructions. I knew that Blue Boy (as I renamed him) would come good, and even as Barb, Brian and I half carried him to the trailer I was making plans for his future.

I decided to ride in the trailer with him and was impressed by his friendliness. Most ponies with his background are bad tempered and will kick or at least bite you if you hurt them, but he always stood patiently for injections and during the painful trimming of misshapen feet. Severe laminitis is a very painful and potentially crippling condition, where the tissues, (the laminae), inside the hoof become very inflamed, causing extreme pain and subsequent hoof malformations. At first, I had Bluey injected with cortisone which brought an immediate improvement, but unfortunately once the effect wore off his condition deteriorated. So I read the marvellous book written by the herbalist Juliette de Bairacli Levy, and followed her treatment for laminitis. Cooling seemed to be the key, so Bluey's sawdust bed was thoroughly soaked as Bluey, too, was hosed down with water as frequently as possible. Then I decided to try and remove the fever by bandaging ice cubes onto his lower leg. Of course, I didn't have a fridge so various customers were surprised to receive phone calls requesting them to bring ice cubes to their riding lesson. I suppose the fact that no one queried this may have been a reflection on my highly individual way of running a riding establishment. Part of the treatment was supposed to consist of walking on grass in the early morning dew. Now Bluey didn't mind eating grass but wasn't prepared to walk on it. It usually took six of us to drag and shove Bluey for the recommended ten minutes, and gradually my friends began to express their doubts. However, mentally, Bluey was improving. Cautiously at first, in case this promising change in his circumstances dwindled to nothing, he took an interest in his surroundings. He tried to make friends with his neighbour, Jadine, my husband's 15.2hh mare, and he occasionally hobbled over to look over his stable door.

Unfortunately, there was still no improvement in his condition, so my next idea was to stand him in the pond for a couple of hours. As soon as the first ride appeared, I commandeered immaculately dressed mums, scruffy dads, jodhpured girls and the usual regulars who were always clad in tatty jeans. One of the girls led Bluey, and another walked in front with a bucket of food which Bluey probably knew he wouldn't be allowed to eat.

'Well, you could always hope,' he thought, so he staggered forward.

All went well as he lurched across the fields, encouraged at every corner by bemused humans. When we reached the edge of the pond, Bluey had to negotiate a small slope which was slippery with the November rain. It looked an easy job to just shove him down, or so we thought! Then, he showed a totally unexpected side to his character. He dug his heels in and refused to budge.

'Push,' I shouted, and most people did – not that it had any effect.

'Right, you take his lead rope Mrs W, and pull like hell,' I yelled.

She tottered down the slippery slope, her immaculate skirt rapidly resembling the murky depths of the pond.

'OK you lot,' I said encouragingly. 'Now we'll carry him. He isn't heavy and there are quite a lot of you.'

One of the Dads muttered that he had a bad back, but quietened down when I pointed out that exercise is good for bad backs. So we all pushed, pulled, lifted and eased to the best of our ability. We even slapped, but nothing happened.

'Come on Mrs W,' I puffed. 'Pull!'

She did, but unfortunately lost her balance. Just at that moment, Bluey showed the sense of humour we would all come to regret, and half-leapt and half-fell down the slope and into the pond. Several customers joined him there, including the now bedraggled Mrs W. We left him there for several hours up to his knees in the water with various stable girls holding him. Eventually it was time to reverse the process and haul the pony out.

'Oh, just let him go,' I suggested. 'He'll come out when he hears the feed being mixed.'

But Bluey was being stubborn again. Finally, a few wet, muddy girls and an equally wet owner dragged, pushed and coaxed the invalid out of his private swimming pool. Now it should have become easier, but it didn't, and I finally gave up. In came plan B. I filled four buckets with water and popped a leg in each one. Bluey stood quietly with his unusual shoes, quite unaware of the effect this was having on various new customers. One morning, I was giving out saddles at a tacking up lesson and became aware of a prowling father's angry stare. I ambled off on my rounds, starting as usual at Bluey's door. Inside, the disgruntled dad was helping his daughter to tack up.

'Does he actually move?' he asked icily.

'Oh yes, if you make him. I thought buckets made a nice change from shoes. It's cheaper, you know.' I smiled.

Dad didn't seem amused, but soon thawed when I explained Bluey's history, and that his daughter was not riding Bluey at all but was supposed to be in Blackie's stable.

Bluey was soon becoming a favourite with all of the children, but he still didn't improve and I wondered if I had done the right thing. The farrier came every few days, each time trimming down until he drew blood. Bluey, in his pain and discomfort, could easily have bitten me as I held his head, but instead only nuzzled me gently. Not for the first time I noticed the kindness in his eyes. So I went back to my books. But as the months passed Bluey hardly improved at all. Then one day he was being exercised next to the hawthorn hedge. Spring was well on the way and the tangy hawthorn buds were coming to life. Bluey was used to being dragged around the field by this time and didn't usually try to eat, but as soon as he smelt the fresh hawthorn growth he lunged over and started tearing into the hedge, prickles and all. His 'leader', who was only eight and tiny with it, rushed to confess, somewhat nervous of my reaction. I raced out, giving Bluey a large slap on the rump, and then that little voice in my head spoke again. It was a gamble but I left him to it. That night he seemed a little happier as he slobbered over his Epsom salts and bran mash. The following morning he was slightly better, and acting on impulse I equipped all the customers with buckets and showed them the hedge. Bluey ate the hawthorn faster than we could pick it; no doubt helped by the sight of our blood-stained hands. At last he had comrades in his suffering! His recovery, although not complete, was certainly moving along rapidly and, despite setbacks if he overate, he was soon ready to give his first ride.

Of course, in a fairy tale he would have been willing and ever grateful for our care in saving his life, but Bluey was not an ethical spirit; he was a down-to-earth solid little pony with a large appetite and a cautious and basically idle nature. If he could take a short cut he did, and he frequently embarrassed me by coming to a halt in the middle of the road, to the amusement of the villagers. And once he had stopped, nothing and nobody would move him except to head him back home. Gradually, he refined his trickery into a theatrical limp, which was only present on the way out and disappeared miraculously when he was turned for home. The farrier pronounced that he was malingering. I knew that he was, so did most of my customers, but unfortunately the great British public didn't, so rather than face the accusing stares, Bluey got his way and stayed at home. By the time we moved to Wales the mere thought of riding Screwy Bluey was enough to send children scurrying for the exit. Even I couldn't get him going, although we tried a variety of tricks. My Mum had bought a squeaky toy for Jester, my ever-faithful border collie, and I noticed that most of the ponies were afraid of the noise. So, Diane (an experienced girl) rode Bluey out of the yard. As usual he held the 'injured' foot in the air, and as usual he often forgot which foot 'hurt'. This time I walked up behind him, and as soon as he stopped I squeaked the toy loudly. He remained motionless! Katy (the other new pony recruit), who was several yards in front, jumped in the air and did a lap of honour around the field. Bluey got the day off again and he continued to loaf around when we later moved to Wales, only working if threatened and always taking a different route to the other ponies. However, he was still friendly and was obviously fond of me, and even condescended to obey my instructions sometimes!

I chose his riders carefully, giving him the children who were less confident and not so experienced. He seemed to know them, and plodded on as a lazy rogue. Sadly, there were a few he took advantage of – especially if nerves caused his nervous young rider to jab him in the mouth. On one particularly demanding day, when we were out on the ride and I was soaked to the skin by the light rain, I was very alarmed to see the treacherous mist sliding in over the mountain top.

'Hurry up please, everyone,' I shouted.

Everyone hurried except Bluey, who suddenly veered into the bog and to my horror sank into the mire. Somehow, he struggled out, still complete with his rider clinging on, and somehow he made it across the bog, mission accomplished. He had avoided perhaps half a mile of track. He was eating contentedly when I caught up with him. His rider was soaked with evil smelling mud and muck but luckily was unhurt. I had hardly stopped shaking after this incident, when we reached the 'canter'.

'OK, Mair,' I shouted to my leader, 'canter.'

All the ponies struck off as one, except Bluey who, after another jab in the mouth by his rider, veered to the side and shot almost vertically up the steep mountainside. Prince and I followed Bluey and his wailing rider. But try as Prince and I might, I couldn't corner him. Finally, he trotted to the steep edge of the cliff and gazed down to the valley floor which appeared seemingly cushion-like with the gathering fog, but in fact was at least six hundred feet below us. My courage deserted me. To hell with it, I thought. No sense in two dead ponies.

'Try to turn him,' I said quietly, but was only screamed at in temper.

'I hate this pony,' was the reply.

Bluey, his point made, turned gently and walked the few steps back to me. Again, I noticed those kind eyes and realised that, in spite of provocation, he would never actually hurt his rider, just educate by the means he had available to him.

Then a mini miracle happened: Zoe arrived. She was a small girl who would help to change Bluey's life. Perhaps because of her size, she was a stubborn girl, unafraid but kind. I hated having to land her with Bluey, but for her it was love at first sight. He refused to go on the outward journey, refused to stop on the return and made her the butt of a great many jokes, but she stuck at him until her arms and legs were dropping off, and much to our surprise she booked for a return trip the following year. Bluey characteristically idled his way through the rest of the season, and although he was always friendly with the children he preferred it if they didn't try to ride him.

As winter approached and he grew his coat, I thought wryly that he might have won; perhaps I should find him a good home as I couldn't afford passengers. Luck for Bluey arrived in the form of a blizzard, which came unexpectedly. Faced with the prospect of his death, I realised that I didn't want to lose him. It was a real emergency; the weather had already closed in and the ponies were out on the hillside with the conditions worsening by the minute. When I finally reached the terrified ponies, it was Bluey who first came right up close to me. He had the confidence necessary to follow me into drifts of twenty feet and show his timid companions the way home. Then I knew that Bluey had come into my life for a reason, but what I didn't know was that I only knew half of it.

The next summer Bluey started work under protest as usual, and memories of Ty the farrier's comments rubbed salt into my wounds. Everyone laughed at my ewe-necked pony[19] who looked like a demented giraffe without the spots, and to make matters worse the little swine was going bald. Every time you touched him great clouds of white hair flew off, covering everyone and everything within ten feet. One morning, in despair, I gathered up the discarded hair and started laying it on the bare pink skin. Stella, friend and holiday helper, back for another summer, laughed.

'Thatching?' she enquired.

I swore. We heard a car coming down the drive and raced out into the yard to see if it was a prospective customer, leaving Bluey with one hairy side and one bald side. The car contained a family who were interested in riding so we took them on a tour of the stables. Of course, I forgot to miss out Bluey's stable.

'Clippers aren't working properly,' I fibbed, and I might have got away with it if Bluey hadn't shaken himself and snowed all over the unimpressed family.

It was all very well fibbing to customers, but I hadn't a clue what was wrong. It wasn't lice or mange, which are both common causes of baldness. Possibly it was a mineral deficiency, but he had a mineral lick and a good diet and he was the only one like it. Other possibilities included rain scald. This is when excess exposure to the elements results in the coat becoming over-dry, losing its oil so that it falls out. As Bluey was 'white' and therefore had delicate hair and skin, this seemed likely, so again he was well dosed with assorted herbs, had yet another rest from working, and he had the added delight of embarrassing me by standing in the field as close as possible to the road. Eventually his summer coat grew and, apart from his ewe neck and a scraggy mane, he looked almost presentable. Although the soles of his feet had dropped, he was sound as long as he was properly shod. But he was still lazy and none of the children wanted to ride him.

Well, that was the situation until Zoe came again. After the first day her legs must have felt like lead, but she was still determined. On the

---

[19] A horse with a neck that has a longer underline than top line is said to be 'ewe-necked'.

second day, as we headed for the gallops, she huffed and puffed considerably more than Bluey did. Jim was at the back with Bluey, and I, in the hope that old Jim wouldn't overexert himself, held Prince to a steady jog. When we turned into the start of the gallops, Stella, who was leading, stopped to see if I was OK. It was instant chaos, with ponies barging and leaping around ready for the off. Jim took the opportunity to avoid my over-protectiveness and careered onwards, knocking Bluey out of the way as he did so. That really did it, and thirteen would-be athletes were off in a flurry of hooves and tossing heads. There were shrieks from excited riders and a few bucks from the less sober ponies which included the thirty-one-year-old Jim. I tried to stop Prince to retrieve Bluey, as he was sure to have been left behind, but then I noticed him sandwiched between Pepper and Jim and running for all he was worth. I chuckled – you couldn't call whatever action he was using a gallop, but at least he was moving rapidly for once. I drew level and noticed the haunted look in his eyes – he was terrified by the speed and I think frightened of falling.

'Steady up, Zoe,' I yelled.

Jim and Pepper pulled ahead, engaged in their own private race, and quickly overtook the flagging Sarah.

'Collect him, Zoe,' I shouted.

She tried to, but it was useless, and Bluey's legs continued their random movement in various directions.

'I'm going ahead, Jim's overdoing it,' I said, passing at speed.

I looked back, aware of a white shape close behind, and saw Bluey find his legs. He streaked after me, totally in control and enjoying every minute of it. Needless to say, Jim thwarted every attempt to pass him, and Prince, whose disposition usually terrorized horses twice his size, gave way to a 12.2hh old grey pony. At the end of the gallops, ponies were being walked around to cool off, and there were a number of excited voices – one of which was mine. I was proud of Jim and for the first time I was proud of Bluey, and he knew it. Zoe was over the moon as Bluey pranced home. Now I found myself telling her not to keep trotting. Bluey was showing off, no doubt with a little encouragement.

He continued to give a good ride to experienced riders, so much so that at a later date I was a little worried about putting a young rider called Julie on him. I had met her when leafleting on a local campsite and had taken an instant liking to the whole family. They were from the north west of England and full of the directness I had come to expect from people of the mill towns. They were friendly and honest, and because of a bad experience at another trekking centre it was particularly imperative that things went well. So we set off with Julie on Bluey and her sister on Jim. Both were securely on leading reins. All went well until we reached what turned out to be a new slaughterhouse. Unknown to me it had opened, and as soon as the ponies caught the smell of death they tensed and started prancing. Even the steady Jim was nervous, but despite that he was sensible, ever conscious of the precious burden he carried. Bluey was also sensible and proving once more his true worth. Yes, I thought, he could be a good pony, but I still had Jim who took any children I thought needed special help, and those I knew he would like.

Bluey

Chapter 6

Departures and arrivals

That Friday began as many others had done – with a rodeo. Jim, Sarah, Prince and Pepper decided that life was too much hard work and so, as usual, we were late starting.

The riders were a good bunch, and the ride was a happy, carefree one. It was also supposed to be the last ride at Kingswood Riding Centre, and as I looked back down 'Acid Valley' I knew that I would never see or ride up it again. It was reasonably warm, but already the icy tang of winter was in the air. As I turned away from the valley, I remembered other valleys in the Cotswolds that had been special to me: Tyley, red and golden in the autumn and gently green in the spring; Acid; Kilcot. The list was endless. Then I remembered fields which had once run up to the woods in Randwick and Ruscombe, and houses creeping up the valley gradually spoiling the country. I remembered the holiday cottages, the 'townies', the litter, the factories in the Stroud Valleys, the nuclear power stations and the pollution so close to my beloved Tyley Valley. I was sad, but then I remembered a lake nestling in exposed mountains where houses could never climb, and where only buzzards and sheep could live. True, there were problems to be encountered in Wales – a different language, holiday cottages and an extremely large mortgage – but there was hope and space to live.

Later, as I unsaddled Prince and said my goodbyes, I tried to find a quiet corner. However, that wasn't easy, as preparations for my leaving party were in full swing. Then, at four o'clock a ride I had forgotten appeared, and so I took that last ride through the village.

The party went well, but some of the revellers were found sobbing into the ponies' manes. Others had to be dragged off to a Sunday school play. I hoped they were sober enough to do it credit, as I've never had any idea how strong a cider shandy should be! At the end of the party, when they had all gone home, I looked again at the buildings. Soon they would be derelict and quiet again, there would be no more shouts or laughing voices, no one would ever whoop again as Jim had yet another bucking fit, and there would be no more cheers as Bluey got forty-odd faults jumping a six-inch course. And as I looked back, I felt again the laughter and the tears and just for a moment I could hear the laughter again as if it was held in the stone. Perhaps one day another person with more staying power than I had would make the stones laugh again.

Saturday came, and long faces and red eyes greeted me as I staggered (probably something to do with the cider) trying to catch a bleary-eyed troop of nags. The children saddled up for their very last ride, and for an hour bedlam reigned. Then, as we haltered the ponies for the journey to Wales, the horsebox pulled in. Comet went up first, and Sue, sobbing, kissed him on the nose. Then Jim went up nervously, with Carol red-eyed and tense on the leading rein. Vickie put Blackie up, Jacky led Bluey, and Stewart (my landlady's son) led Star; it was difficult for him not to cry. Folly went up next, with Sally leading Queenie. Pippa, as no one was attached to her, went in without tears, but Karen, who realised she may not see Kate again, was crying loudly. Helen took Pepper without any fuss, and I was grateful not to look on another sad face. Jerry was next, led by Russell who put on a brave face. Pete loaded Jadine, then I loaded Prince – or tried to load him; I was near to tears myself when he whipped round and 'legged it'. He was over the gate and back to the stable in a flash. The children were galvanised into action and Pete seized Prince who took him for a walk. Mr Jones (the lorry driver), who failed to see why a 13.2hh should cause so much trouble, hauled him up the ramp, and as Michelle went up with Sarah the lorry was hastily closed.

I hate goodbyes and mine was somewhat gruff, but through the tears there were good wishes and a brave attempt at cheerfulness. Then we pulled away from part of my life, leaving a sea of eager faces that it would be hard to forget. For some time afterwards I could still hear their chatter: sometimes irritating, sometimes sad, but always interesting. I think that it was then that I realised I did enjoy the company of children as well as the company of animals. I also realised that unbeknown to myself I had developed the ability to care about people. It is a wonderful ability, a softening one that comes with age and maturity. I looked forward to meeting the natives at Lluest, our new

51

home, but most of all I looked forward to having the peace and quiet shattered by as many screaming children as possible. I also looked forward to the reunion with the pregnant tabby cat that we had inherited with the farm. Although she was very much a farm cat, and surely well capable of catching the odd small rabbit, we had left food out for her on previous trips.

U

Lluest is a smallholding in Carmarthenshire, nestling into a windswept plateau, sandwiched between the mountains and the sea, which is about four miles away. The cottage, set in three acres, was small and fairly nondescript. It looked out onto a small yard and into two cowsheds. Luckily, whoever had built Lluest had had the good sense to build it into the side of the field so we would be shielded from the worst of the weather. The previous owners said that they had not been snowed in but we were later to experience that this probably wasn't true!

The journey was completely uneventful, and the unloading at Lluest was proceeding remarkably well when Prince decided that the red yard gate was in the wrong place. Then things got back to near normal as I struggled to persuade my fourteen mavericks to return to the yard so that the horsebox could get out. Jester instantly leapt to my aid, but unfortunately she didn't know which way I wanted her to drive the ponies. So they all stampeded over the garden up the drive, into the pond, and eventually into the yard and straight out the other side. We waved the lorry away and set about moving tack into the house, then I heard a noise and looked up to see Prince running loose again having vandalised our one remaining fence. The yard now looked as if it had been hit by a hurricane; there were piles of dung everywhere, a broken gate, and bundles of stable equipment dotted around. Periodically one of the ponies came whizzing through, followed in due course by the rest of the herd.

Then the missing element of chaos – children – arrived, plus two crazy dogs and a cat. Supervising this car-load had been quite a headache for Barb and Brian. And the clutch had been playing up on their car. They were on their way home to Gloucestershire after a holiday in Mid Wales. Together we set the tack shed to rights and cooked a meal – our first at Lluest. To celebrate, we took Barb and Brian's children to the pub and consumed some alcohol, and later took a bottle of forgettable plonk back home. We were still a little too sober and Brian could still stand, so we started on our home-made wine. You have to be a little tipsy to drink it as it doesn't taste too good. Its bouquet resembles a farmyard, but it's got a kick like dear Jim. Finally, the conversation dwindled and three tired dogs, one cat, two children and four weary adults staggered off to bed. I wished I lived in a bungalow, not a crazy farmhouse with a moving staircase.

Breakfast the next morning was omitted, as chasing ponies on a full stomach and a hangover generally meant not catching the said ponies. It was bitterly cold as we walked the two miles up to the grazing rented from neighbours Jeff and Margaret. It proved to be interesting, as the ponies all decided to stay in one small patch of the fifty-acre field. After breakfast and a few more jobs, Barb and Brian and their family returned home to Gloucestershire, and the following day Pete also returned to work in Gloucestershire. He would be away now until Friday.

By now Kitty, the inherited tabby cat, had given birth to two kittens, who I had named Tiger and Bella (later renamed P Brain[20]), but so far neither had shown up – maybe they had been scared off by our arrival. When all was quiet, I did at last spot the two kittens running across the yard with their mother. Tiger was a tabby with a violent disposition, and Bella was a tortoiseshell. They were real wild cats. The slightest movement was answered with a barrage of spits of indignant yowls. Try as I did to befriend them, Tiger was still very wary, so I decided to grab him. He didn't approve of this and sank his teeth into my finger and scratched my hand. Finally, I managed to restrain and stroke him. Then I gently put him down expecting him to run away, but he spun round and attacked me again. I wondered why I bothered with animals at all.

I soon had to think of earning some money, and on the following Saturday afternoon Nigel arrived for a ride on Jim – my first customer at Lluest. When later I went to check the ponies they seemed in a restless mood, and I quickly realised that there was one missing. Jim didn't often wander (unless it was into someone's kitchen), and I was very worried and searched the field for two hours, and then Jeff and Margaret joined me. Our neighbours thought that Jim was probably in a bog somewhere, which cheered me up no end. After another hour or so, we stumbled on a weak, muddy pony struggling – yes, in a bog. Jim was near exhaustion and very cold. He was stuck fast and up to his shoulders in the mire. Jeff hurried to get a rope and I stayed with Jim,

---

[20] P Brain's pea-brained and pee-related problems are recounted in Chapter 11...

who seemed close to death and was lying flat in the muck. I covered him with my coat and jacket. Jeff re-appeared with the rope and we tried to pull Jim out. It was hopeless and as he fell back once again, he trapped Jeff's leg. By now our wellies were full of water and I was trying hard to choke back my tears of frustration and fear. Margaret rang the fire brigade, who were supposed to be on strike, and we waited while Jim grew steadily weaker. As he laid back in the muddy water his head sank lower so I held it with my arms. Jeff finally freed his leg, while I stripped down to a small sweatshirt and piled my lovely new coat and woollies on Jim. Then we heard a siren which seemed to be going the wrong way. It was, we found out later, quite lost and therefore asking the way at various houses. I was imagining how the conversation might be going – once directions were given, no doubt discussions about sheep prices and the weather. However, eventually they arrived. By now I was pretty hysterical and wasn't comforted by them playing tug of war with Jim. Ropes and pulleys were put on the strap around his middle and he was hauled out inch by inch.

Miraculously, as soon as Jim was on firm ground he tried to get up. He staggered across the field, falling many times on the way. The firemen, every inch true professionals, laughed and joked the whole way, trying to lift my spirits. They encouraged Jim and helped me to rub him down. Then the vet arrived to check him over. He was given an injection, but was too sick to complain. The main concern would be pneumonia, which I could readily believe as I'd been in the bog half the time that Jim had and I could hardly move. The firemen and vet left, and we tried to dry Jim further. He was shivering with cold and fear, but kept trying to eat the hay wisps we were rubbing him down with. There was no stabling at the grazing we had rented, so Margaret found a lovely man (who had just been ill himself) to transport Jim back to Lluest. I wondered how long he would take to get to us but he was there in minutes and took charge of the situation. Jim was bundled into the trailer and Jeff, Jester and I raced ahead.

Jeff bedded down the stable after chasing me off to get changed. Minutes seemed to take a long while to tick past, and we worried that Jim had collapsed in the box. Just as we were about to race back to find him, Mr Evans came into sight driving as slowly as any respectable hearse. For the very first time I spoke in praise of what seemed to be the local habit of driving up the middle of the road at ten miles and hour. I would never ever be impatient if I had to wait for one of them again.

Slowly, I was learning that you couldn't dominate this country or its people; they dominated you, in their quiet evasive careless way. No plans would ever come to fruition unhindered; no schedules could be adhered to except the schedule of the seasons, and even they were apt to throw surprises at you! As the ramp dropped, I had my next surprise – Jim was eating the bedding and came down the ramp and into the stable with a much firmer step. We all rubbed him down and talked to him. He was still soaked to the skin and shivering but he kept eating. Our nearest neighbour, Annette, arrived with a present: a best bale of hay. After assuring themselves that Jim and I were OK, our new friends went back to their disrupted work – their evening rest would be a little late, and no one would blame me or begrudge it in any way. No one would think it anything out of the ordinary. Tomorrow it might be a cow in a bog or lost, and in their calm way they would cope with that crisis too.

Jester stayed with Jim while I made a hot water bottle and a cup of Bovril and put my folding bed in the stable next to Jim. The radio played merrily, and I tried not to think what life would be like without Jim. I knew that I wrapped that pony in cotton wool. I had often stopped him from galloping because of his age, often lowered the jumps. I had been selfish really, because he loved all that, and at every opportunity he had managed to avoid restrictions. He had been retired before, but somehow always managed to get back into work. He never complained and was never lazy. His sense of humour was infamous, and more than one expert rider clothed in immaculate riding kit had staggered away from a lesson on a smirking Jim with mud all over their rears. Little horrors all flew off him, but he was gentleness itself with any nervous child or tiny tot, and his patience with the disabled made him many friends.

So, on one particular day, when one of our better riders who annoyed some of the helpers by her pomposity agreed to a dare to ride him bareback, we all waited with bated breath. She vaulted on and, as we all whooped, Jim erupted into a series of bucks. She stayed on until about the third and Jim thundered up the field solo. He was brought back and, after questioning his parentage, she remounted. This time he changed his tactics and galloped up the field properly. The young lady in question, convinced she had won, promptly galloped back, but she got faster and faster, and Jim headed straight at the fence and ditch. We all jumped to safety and Jim skidded to a halt with his nose touching the fence. The young lady slithered to the ground, and we all hoped no mamas were around to hear what she called a most innocent and gentle pony. As he was led back to the stable his step was lighter, and I swear that he laughed at her from that time on.

Then there was the time a knowledgeable father had attempted to give a lecture on stable management. Unfortunately, Jim was subject to passing wind and every learned pronouncement was accompanied by a series of very noisy explosions. The whole thing proved to be too much for most of us and we retired hiccoughing, partly gassed and partly hysterical.

Jim had given me so much. That night, back in his stable, I decided that if he pulled through I would ride him again, which we both enjoyed, and that we would gallop and I would allow him the odd fast ride. Meanwhile, I rubbed him down every half hour and tried to keep myself warm. It was a frosty moonlit night, and faithful Jester, although cold, had curled up at the end of the sleeping bag. There was no complaining as I disturbed her to give Jim his rub down. In fact, she was a lot more charitable than I am when she disturbs me on the odd night for a little walk. The cats, Kitty, Tiger and Bella, were also asleep in the stable, and slowly the heat built up and in spite of the frost we began to warm up. Jim's breathing improved steadily, and he produced the necessary puddle and pile of dung. Then he started to try and knock down the bar to the stable and get out, and I knew he was going to pull through. I fed Jim, Jester and the cats and I wondered whether to go back to bed, but somehow I just lingered, leaning over the wall, looking at a thirty-year-old pony that had fallen in a bog and was now demolishing my new stable. He soon improved, and within a week he was working again and causing chaos as usual. He also made the front page of the *Cambrian News,* and I swear he laughed when I showed it to him. Of course, he suffered no side effects, but I developed a bad cough and cold and was ill for three weeks. The moral being that if you find your pony up to its eyeballs in a bog, don't climb in with it or give it your clothes. Leave it to the fire brigade – they're used to it.

Part Two:

Lluest

Ginny with Dancer

Lluest house, with 'Pygsy' the three-wheeler

Ben

Chapter 7

October 1981 and the start of life at Lluest

The following weeks passed fairly uneventfully, trying to adapt to life in a remote part of Wales. I hate waiting in shops and usually leave any shop that I'm kept waiting in for a long time. That, however, was impossible as there were only two shops, ten miles apart. Most of the visitors to the shops seemed to go primarily for a chat and, as an afterthought, to buy some food. Of course, I always rushed in like a whirlwind, picked up a few goods, and waited impatiently for the piece of bacon to be wrapped. This process was usually held up by a rapid torrent of Welsh which I didn't understand. Various remarks would be addressed to me, which always made me feel uncomfortable as I rarely noticed the change of Welsh back to English, and I was generally unable to give an answer, not having noticed the question. Luckily, the Welsh are a tolerant race and the shopkeepers soon got into the habit of serving me quickly. As the weeks went by and I saw very few people, I began to see why the shops were so important - they were one of the few links with the outside world and one of the few occasions that many women had to talk to anyone outside the family.

Lluest, like most small Welsh farms, was fairly isolated at the end of a track, and unless I happened to be at the end of the track, by the road, I rarely even saw the postman. Milk was delivered by Annette from the neighbouring farm, who sometimes came in for a coffee, and there were shared cups of tea with another neighbour, Margaret. The high spot of the week was 'coffee' on Thursday mornings. These events were well supported by mums in various stages of pregnancy, with or without toddlers at heel. Then there were the older women whose children were at school. And then there was me, the only childless and non-pregnant female around for miles. I smiled sweetly at the babies and hoped that no one would give me one to hold. With that uncanny instinct new mums seemed to possess, I was never offered a baby, and thoroughly enjoyed these mornings. They were held at a different place each week and soon it would be my turn. Lluest was very rugged, cold, draughty and full of cats and a dog. Most of the locals didn't allow animals in the house and I couldn't help wondering what they would think of my house, should they visit, and I also hoped that no one left the garden gate open if they did, because Jim was in the habit of wandering into the garden and from there, if at all possible, into the house.

Autumn 1981 progressed into winter, and the next months were spent preparing for the trekking season that would start the following spring. The story of Jim and his unfortunate experience in the bog at least gained us some publicity and made us some friends. My life until spring would be an endless round of mucking out, feeding and watering, helped by frozen water pipes and power cuts. I also helped out at the neighbouring farm in return for extra grazing from Annette's husband Trefor[21].

By the following spring, on one of our treks we had met a handsome collie dog, and with his owners' blessing we decided to let Jester have her first litter. She gave birth to four puppies. We kept a male who we named Joker. The other three went to homes already known to us, including my Mum and Dad who by this time had moved from Gloucestershire to a nearby cottage.

I also met Stella and Mair, who would become my 'staff'. Stella taught children with special needs, and she joined me for the holidays and returned home to Wolverhampton afterwards exhausted, as I am a slave driver. She could compose songs, cook, clean, add up, and organise. I do not possess these skills, and I relied heavily on Stella who, with her quiet, dry sense of humour, can usually keep things in perspective. Mair, a local girl, was a hard-working, cheerful, noisy, untidy fourteen-year-old. She was an early riser and usually managed to wake everyone up.

That first trekking season in the spring/summer of 1982 was a success, despite concerns about the country's circumstances, such as redundancies that I feared would affect the business, and then all too soon the air became full of winters messages. Life seemed fragile, and

---

[21] More about poor Trefor in the following chapter...

despite a full hay barn I worried that the next trekking season seemed so far away.

Autumn came and with it the time for preparation. All the animals were restless, refusing to stay put in any field, always moving on in search of greener, easier, pastures. We all 'laid up' stores at that time of year, the tack shed turned once again into a granary with bags of oats, bran, pony nuts and maize, all jostling for space with wheat, and mash for the hens. Apples and carrots were safely gathered in and a visit to the cash and carry resulted not in a well-stocked freezer, but a large crate of Guinness for Jim.

The ponies were changing from sleek, well-muscled athletes into chubby, hairy creatures, their mixed origins very visible. Even the hens seemed determined to eat plenty, driven by a hidden clock to prepare for the coming winter. Then, amid the gales and fears of approaching winter, came the traditional end to our season.

Late October 1982 half-term brought Stella, and visiting friends Mick, Carol and Lisa, for the weekend. Suddenly, Lluest was complete and cheerful again, giving the animals and myself strength for whatever was ahead. The ponies were pleased to be ridden again after their short break since the end of the summer holidays, and as we approached the gallops, steps lightened and heads tossed. Somehow, our resolution to start at a collected canter was forgotten, and we set off galloping through the leaves with the sun peeping out of a cloud and the wind in our faces. Prince bucked and I whooped the freedom, joy and excitement that we all felt, which seemed to encourage the sun, beaming on us as we jogged down the lane to the long gallop. The gallop was predictably uncontrolled, so we walked up into the mountains to cool the ponies off. We ate our lunch, sheltered by the wood, and talked about ponies and old times. It was quite warm and, as I lay on the bank looking at the nags, I felt at one with life and began to recall the time earlier in the season, when I felt that we were existing in another world. Stella and I were taking a small trek when the mist rolled in. The complete silence that descended healed all ills and restored tranquillity, but it also had a spooky quality. Stella then tried to dispel (or was it to enhance?) the slight uneasiness, as she joked about a Stone Age man staggering out of the mist brandishing a club, but on my own at the back of the ride I shuddered and urged Prince to keep up with the rider in front. Then Jim snorted and the spell was broken, and I realised that, knowing Jim, he would treat a ghost, however old, with the same lack of respect that he had for any interference.

The next day, I was thankful for the clear skies, and when we rode on after lunch we decided to climb to the summit of what would be the last climb of the season. At the top we let the ponies loose to graze and gazed at the view. All the mountains of Wales are visible from our 'little mountains': Prescelli in the south, Pumlumon, Cader Idris, and Snowdon away in front of us. Then to the sea, which was bright blue, with Bardsey Island and the Llŷn Peninsula rising out of it like green and brown gems. Immediately below us, the wind turned the glass-like Llyn Eiddwen into a choppy slate blue that was imprisoned by the mountain. The air was fresh as the wind quickened and drove the clouds across the sky, as we led five tired ponies down the path. Stella had a surprise for Jim (and Carol); as he ate his feed, she sang her 'Tribute to Jim'[22]. Although the song is quite amusing, we all had lumps in our throats and Carol cried into his mane, because she was leaving first-thing the next morning. We were all up at four, waving goodbyes to Mick, Carol and Lisa. Pete drove them back to Gloucestershire.

I turned my attention to our other new customers staying in Stella's caravan. They were friends of Stella's; June, a head teacher, had ridden, but John, an artist, was a novice. They were great fun and soon fell in love with the ponies, especially Jim. Their first ride was very special – it was another clear day, but this time the air was very still, the lake was like a mirror, reflecting the trees and mountains that surrounded the whole image, which was a fragile one, waiting to be broken by the rough days of winter. Soon the frosts would come and these soft tracks would be frozen and too slippery for equine feet. If we had another bad blizzard, Lluest would be cut off again from the outside, and it would be difficult, if not impossible, to reach the lake. The winter isolation brought a kind of calm, though: often no TV, and definitely no news, so wars and misery passed us by. I thought about all this as we meandered across the mountains and enjoyed the day, so precious because it was one of the last rides of the year. On the way back I took a long look at the countryside, savouring the dying days of October. The clocks had changed and now it was time to consolidate the gains of summer. Tack

---

[22] Stellas's songs are included in Chapter 12.

had to be soaped ready for its winter rest, numnahs[23] washed and mended, girths and brushes washed and stables filled with sawdust.

Our second season was over and had been successful, but, looking ahead, problems still remained. Trekkers would have to be marketed to and encouraged to come, and with many regulars again facing redundancy, the prospects were not good. Advertising was a problem – how much, when, who with; the questions seemed endless. Months of planning and preparation had just two months to produce results, and bad weather or redundancies could spell disaster. Lluest was quiet again: Stella had gone home, Mair was back in school and Pete was in Gloucestershire. The previous months had been hard work, but mostly tremendous fun. Ahead of me again was the inevitable round of feeding, watering and mucking out. There was also the nagging fear that my beloved Jim would not have the strength to make it through the coming winter. The ponies had all been wormed and, hopefully, were all well-prepared for winter, but this land gives no guarantees. Nor did I seek any. Jim had lived a long time and seen many things. He had touched the lives of so many people and given so much to those he had favoured with his friendship. He, I'm sure, would accept the inevitable without fear or grief, and so must I. I was sure his spirit would never leave us, and he would be reborn every spring as I heard the shouts and laughter of the children and remembered.

Gradually the ponies came in for the winter. Jim and Pepper were always first. One afternoon I leant on the gate, Jester and Joker by my side, and watched the rest of the ponies grazing. I was proud of them all, and not a little surprised that those magnificent friends and partners belonged to me. It had been their season and they had risen to it. Novice riders had been handled with kid gloves by ponies who really were only used to experienced ones. They had worked long and hard. Now it was time to rest and prepare for the next season. The sun shone on them as they filled their bellies and grew their coats against winter's icy fingers and chill winds. They were all calm. They had done their bit. They, like me, had prepared well and now trusted in destiny and in this land. A curlew flew overhead, and with his cry ringing in my ears I walked back to Lluest. My step was light and, as I called Jim in, I was thankful for life, for that day. The sun was setting, and like my ponies I trusted in something beyond my understanding; a force, that thankfully

---

[23] Numnah is a pad that is placed beneath the saddle to prevent rubbing.

was beyond my control. Nature was once again our mistress, and I welcomed her.

Christmas came and went, and celebrations for New Year 1983 began with the arrival of Barb and Brian, their two children and two dogs, Sophie and Alice. We were to celebrate as usual with home-made wine. At midnight, we all stood up to sing Auld Lang Syne. I've never been able to sing in key, particularly when I've been drinking. Perhaps that is what upset Joker, who had never seen in the New Year before. At first, he just looked, but by the time we sang 'never brought to mind', swinging our arms exuberantly, it all became too much. He leapt up at us barking, frightening P Brain (our thick, un-house-trainable cat)[24], who did a somersault and fell at Brian's feet. Barb and I collapsed laughing, but Brian sang on, oblivious to the confused heap at his feet. Not to be outdone by Brian's solo performance, young Joker began to howl again and leapt about even more. He landed on Sophie, who growled and fell over Alice, who turned on the cause of the trouble. Jester, who had been carefully ignoring the general mayhem, having witnessed several previous drunken parties, knew that her puppy was being threatened and leapt to his defence. A brawl developed, but Brian sang on as Barb and I tried to separate the dogs. At last, order restored, Brian stopped singing and staggered off into the night. He returned a few minutes later clutching a lump of coal to bring good luck. I hoped that his gesture would work.

The children had fallen asleep, so the party broke up and we all weaved our way up to bed. I didn't wake again until the ponies demanded their breakfast. I staggered out of bed, dressed quickly and ran downstairs. My head was throbbing and my mouth was dry and fuzzy. Outside, the ponies banged their doors and rattled their buckets. I felt too delicate to shout at them as I usually did, and they (realising that I was feeling delicate) took full advantage of the situation, grabbing at each other's food and nearly knocking me over. Pepper and Jim were the most trouble. As usual, Jerry decided that I needed a wash and hurled his half-full bucket of cold water over me. Not for the first time I questioned his parentage as I refilled his bucket. I distracted him with

---

[24] P Brain's story is told in Chapter 11.

his hay net before I put the bucket in, just in case he decided I needed to wash behind my ears.

Barb, Brian and the children were up by this time, and Brian, Shelley and I groomed the ponies while Barb cooked some breakfast and shouted at Pete to get up. Mair needed a lift, so Brian and I zoomed off to collect her. On the way back, we passed the hippy encampment and devilment got the better of us; we blasted the horn, no doubt causing a few of them to lose their cool. The girls (the only ones not suffering a hangover) organised the ponies while Brian and I tried to find a comfortable way of wearing our hard hats. None of us were feeling very lively as we jogged out of the yard. The ponies, however, were full of beans and ready for anything. The children chatted while Brian and I laughed at Pete, who was only semi-conscious as he rode Jadine, his big bay mare, down the lane. Prince shied several times, testing my reaction. Jerry decided that Brian was not quite in control and set off at a respectable pace heading for the gallops. We all followed at a sedate pace, until we caught up and let the excited ponies gallop along the track. It was a bright sharp day and our hangovers disappeared as we raced along. We must have looked a motley crew as we trotted up the lane into the mountains. All my ponies were a shaggy, scruffy lot, bought from a variety of auctions. Their breeding was mostly mistaken and they were all rejects, but despite that they were the nicest bunch of ponies that I had ever met. As we turned into the mountains, I was disturbed to notice old snow lying on the grass waiting for company. These mountains, little as they are, can be dangerous. I have been lost on them in mist and have only found my way home because Prince is never late for a meal and isn't about to let the shortcomings of his rider break the habits of a lifetime. I was cold and uneasy trotting across the mountains and decided to turn back. Once back and the ponies safely bedded down, Brian and family left for home. Pete followed the next day to return to work in Gloucestershire.

So, I was alone again at Lluest, as I am for most of the year. I missed Pete and my friends, but only for a few minutes after they had left. I was too involved in my work, and I enjoyed the solitude and with it the chance to spend the whole day with my animals. Somehow, I resented interruptions; probably because I was clinging to the moment, as a drowning man is supposed to cling to straw. My problem was that Lluest was that straw and it was being blown along by the winter wind always just a little further on, just out of my reach. Every day seemed colder

65

and gloomier than the last. The water pipes in the stables froze solid and were soon joined by the pipes in most of the house. Some mornings I even had to break the ice in the loo.

On one particular morning, at eight o'clock, it was still dark and the wind was howling. I tugged at the door but it was stuck fast. I tried the window and it opened a little, but I was horrified when I discovered that it was covered with snow. Lluest was in the middle of a snow drift. I raced upstairs, where the snow was halfway up the window. I panicked. The electricity was flickering and the telephone was cut off. I struggled into my waterproofs and managed to open the door at last; I was nearly buried by the resulting avalanche of snow. Joker and the cats wisely retreated into the kitchen, but Jester's faithful nature got the better of her and she joined me as I struggled through to the stables. Thankfully, the ponies were all OK, and though I dreaded opening Jim's door he was demanding breakfast as usual. There was about a foot of snow in each stable. Most of the stable doors were buried under deep drifts, so feeding was slow as I had to continue to clear a way in.

I finished about an hour later and then tackled the hens. The hen coop was in the most exposed part of the yard and the full force of the blizzard hit me, stinging my eyes and making me feel sick. When I got the door open, the snow was nearly to the top of the coop and the hen's heads stuck out of the snow like the cherries on an iced cake. There were only five heads and there should have been six. I scraped at the snow and frantically uncovered 'Scrag bag'. She looked dead, so I grabbed two of the living hens and carried them into the kitchen. Roady and Lottie don't usually like being carried, but they were too cold to resist. I deposited them into a box and went back for Beaty and Henrietta. Lastly, I rescued Rosy and as an afterthought I picked up Scraggy too. I set her in the middle of the others, and boiled the kettle for a hot mash before the power failed. She survived, came through the winter as we all did, and longed for the spring that would surely come.

My favourite day of the year is the day when the first smell of spring wafts in on the westerly winds. Our spring was always late, and so much sweeter than any other because we had to wait so long for it. I knew that it had come even before I got out of bed, because I could hear the ponies stamping around, trying to kick their way out of our dilapidated stables, in search of the few tiny shoots of grass that had pushed their heads out of the ground. The ponies were suddenly hard to control and lost interest in the dull dry winter food. It was the hardest time to keep them in good condition as they fussed and fretted after grass.

Gradually, the days got longer and I discarded my winter woollies. The hawthorn buds came to life, replacing the drab browns and greys of winter. So I stood on the top of the muck-heap leaning on my shovel and looking at the sea which always held a fascination for me. Sometimes it seemed so close, even though it was about five miles away, and I could see white crests and almost hear the roar of the spring tides.

So I would leave my mucking-out undone, pack Jester and Joker into my tiny wreck of a car, and trundle off to see what treasures the sea had washed up onto the beach at Morfa. 'Our' beach is how I always thought of it. The beach was bordered by two caravan sites that, in summer, disgorged their litter and happy loads over the sand and pebbles. In that early part of the year, the winter storms had cleared the debris and it was easy to forget the hordes that cram themselves onto it in summer.

The dogs raced up and down on the sand chasing sticks, and Joker usually decided to go for a swim while Jester occasionally put a cautious paw into the sea. Walking along the beach with the sun on my face, I felt completely free. Wars, nuclear missiles, and the misery that man always trails in his wake, didn't seem to matter on that deserted beach with only nature surrounding me.

Yet it does matter, because this beach, which is like so many others, is important and once destroyed cannot be recreated. The rock pools which border the point towards Llanon each have their individual life: shrimps, anemones, hermit crabs, limpets; the list is endless and varied. Occasionally, I was lucky enough to be there when the air was crystal clear and it was almost possible to take a bite out of it. Cardigan Bay spreads out to the north past Borth, with its lovely beach and the spectacular dunes at Ynyslas, and further on past Aberdovey with its edging of mountains. Further north still, the Llŷn Peninsula glistens, looking deceptively close, pointing towards Bardsey Island. On a clear relaxing day it is easy to see problems, perhaps, with more perspective.

Chapter 8

Testing times for Trefor

At nineteen I believed that hard work was the only thing necessary to succeed, but at twenty-seven I was considerably older and wiser, and as I writhed administratively in my bank's clutches, worrying over repayments, I wondered if I should have taken up computer science instead. Another problem was that we had little land of our own. Lluest would have floundered years ago if Trefor, our long-suffering neighbour, hadn't intervened.

We had just limped through our first winter, and had no money and therefore very little food. Trefor called in one morning with our milk, and mentioned in passing that he had a field spare for a while. He didn't want any money for it. I always hated accepting charity, however kindly meant, so I asked to work in return for the ponies' keep.

I arrived the next morning to muck out the cow shed, armed with a fork and spade. The cowshed door was a large rickety contraption made of wood and galvanised sheets. It was surprisingly heavy and, as the bolt was stiff, I couldn't get in. Finally, after ten minutes of struggling, I admitted defeat and asked Trefor to let me in. He laughed as he did so, but a few weeks later he wasn't quite as amused by my inadequacies. This time I was bricklaying with large breeze blocks. The first course was OK, if a little slow, but the higher I went the more problems I had. The blocks got heavier and I staggered as I lifted them. Unfortunately, I knocked cement off as I dropped them onto the wall. Trefor, who was being patient, groaned and finally lost his temper.

'Why do you do it if it's too difficult?' he fumed.

I sighed. It was useless to explain that I wanted to do the job but that my frail body just wasn't capable of keeping up with a strong five-foot-ten male.

I carried stones to make culverts, mucked out, and stripped fencing posts all at far too slow a pace for my energetic boss. Sometimes I was exhausted after half an hour, but I tried not to show it. I am feeble, useless with machinery or tools, and very slow to learn physically demanding jobs, but I tried. In fact, I was very trying and I felt sorry for Trefor who was definitely getting the raw end of the deal. Then he decided to give me a job lambing. I was over the moon: *animals at last!* So I read the textbooks Trefor lent me, and a week later when Trefor was on his milk round I spotted my first case. The ewe had a lamb clearly visible, so off I trotted to the house for a bucket of soapy water and a towel. When I got back the ewe was nowhere to be seen, and half an hour later I met Trefor and explained the situation and we looked for her in silence. Trefor gave me a yell and I raced over. The poor ewe was hidden in a thicket. Trefor quickly pulled the lamb without waiting for the soapy water. Its head was swollen, but it was alive, and despite my idiocy it survived. I expected Trefor to be angry, but surprisingly he wasn't and very tolerantly admitted that everyone made mistakes. He teased me about that mistake for days.

As lambing continued, many of the oldest ewes were due to birth, and losses were inevitable. Trefor, who sensibly never gets emotionally involved, accepted these losses philosophically, but as usual the loss of a life left me feeling miserable. I was careful to hide my feelings as I doubted if even the tolerant Trefor would understand me sobbing over one dead ewe.

I suppose things reached an all-time low the morning Trefor and his father called me into the lambing pen.

'There's a small ewe here, can't bring the lamb,' Trefor shouted.

I hastily pulled on surgical gloves and knelt by the ewe talking quietly as I did so. There were two legs sticking out of the vulva. The head wasn't visible so I slid my hand inside the ewe. I fished around for a while but couldn't find a head. All the while Trefor and his father were talking Welsh. I still didn't understand the language, other than a few swear words and horsey phrases, and I wondered if the two men were getting impatient. Trefor evidently was, as he disappeared off, leaving me alone with his dad.

'Try pulling,' his father suggested. I leant even closer to the ewe and then the smell hit me – the unmistakable smell of gangrene. I wished Trefor would come back but, feeling that my lambing skills were on trial, I struggled on, regretting the egg on toast and two cups of tea that

69

I'd eaten for breakfast. At every pull the ewe bleated in agony. Finally, Mr P, who had noticed me wincing, decided to take over. I knelt by the ewe's head stroking her as he pulled.

'How is it going?' I asked, turning to look. I could see that things were not going at all well, and sadly the poor ewe and her lamb lost their lives. Feeling terribly upset I just wanted to make a run for it, but I still felt I was on trial and didn't want to be labelled as lazy or just another squeamish female. Unfortunately, I *was* a squeamish female, and I was still a little worried about my breakfast.

Luckily, Trefor appeared and his father explained what had happened. Trefor took one look at my face and instantly switched to Welsh, no doubt to save any embarrassment.

'Come and have some tea,' Mr P said. I walked unsteadily towards the house and sat down as quickly as possible. The tea was accompanied by bread and jam; the jam was a very strange colour (perhaps it was the way I was feeling), which seemed to bear more than a passing resemblance to afterbirth. I sneaked a look at Mr P's hands and heaved a sigh of relief when I noted that they were clean. I still couldn't manage the odd-looking jam though, and for days afterwards the sight of jam was enough to send me scurrying for fresh air.

Now, I like most animals, and once I get involved with an animal I hate to think of it being eaten, but I was soon to meet a cow that would change my mind. The bad luck that had hung over Lluest decided to move over to Trefor's place. Lambing is a hard job involving long hours, and together with milking and all the other chores on the farm it was all getting too much for Trefor. When you are tired you make mistakes, and, as all farm machinery is potentially lethal, Trefor paid for his minor mistake with a badly broken hand. Annette rushed him off to hospital while I rang his dad and tried to look after the farm as only a feeble squeamish female could! I washed milk bottles like a maniac, fed and checked the sheep and waited for the cavalry in the shape of Trefor's dad and brother to arrive.

Of course, while mending from the accident Trefor was unable to milk, so I volunteered. After all, it looked easy! I approached the cows somewhat warily as they were all horned, and judging by the swishing tails and stamping feet they weren't too keen on strangers. Trefor was directing operations with his arm in a sling. Unfortunately, putting the milk clusters on is a two-handed job and it is easier to show a person how to hold them correctly than to tell them. Finally, after a great display of patience from Trefor I was ready to put my unit on a cow.

Handling cows is extremely different to handling horses, as I soon found out. Strawberry was a quiet old Ayrshire cow with bold brown and white patches. She had seen it all, or thought she had until a small nervous female advanced on her.

'Have you washed her?' asked Trefor, his pressure mounting.

'Oh, no,' I replied and left the unit sitting behind the cow.

'Um, don't leave it there,' he said.

'Oh, sorry, why?' I asked.

His look said it all, and I suppose that after many years of shovelling horse dung I should have known. So I advanced on Strawberry again, this time clutching a bucket and a wet udder cloth. I rolled up my sleeves, dipped the cloth in water, wrung it out and started to wash the udder.

'Not like that,' Trefor groaned, and in seconds the unfortunate cow was washed and dried by his one hand quicker than my two.

'Now put the units on. Remember not to leak air. Yes, that's OK, well done – no you're leaking air again so that cup is on the wrong teat.'

After a minute or so of these and similar comments, poor Strawberry finally had her clusters in place and she heaved a large sigh of relief, and if a cow could smile a congratulatory smile then Strawberry did.

Unfortunately, not all the cows were as helpful, and the next cow was determined to cause trouble. She was a large brown and white Simmental with equally large horns and feet which she used to maximum effect. With Trefor she was as smug and saintly as a comfortable housewife secure in her weekly attendance at the local Church, but once her Sunday duty was over she reverted to her true self. She knew that I was an innocent with her type and that I didn't know what I was doing, so she waited for me to make a mistake. She didn't have long to wait! After a cow has been milked for about five or six minutes she has to be 'stripped'. The units move up and down on the teats to milk the cow, but after a while they climb up the teats too far, stopping the flow of milk. So you have to squeeze the cups to release the air and massage the cow to get her to release her milk. Strawberry was easy, so I approached the Simmental confidently. As soon as I touched her udder to see if she was milked out, I was nearly hit by a flying hoof that sent me within range of her horns. I approached her again murmuring encouragingly. She stood quietly so I squatted down beside her.

'Good girl,' I said as I touched her udder. Seconds later I was calling her anything but 'good' as I hopped around nursing a sore knee. The commotion alerted Trefor.

'Oh, you don't need to strip that one,' he said. Poor Trefor, I had a strong feeling that his patience was being truly tested.

Most of the other cows co-operated and soon we were all on reasonably friendly terms.

I hoped that the Simmental would behave in time, but I usually had to call on Trefor if I needed to go within bucking range of her. Of course, there were other problems too, as I discovered when I stood behind a heifer to wash her. As soon as I applied the wet cloth, she lifted her tail and sent a vile stream hurtling down my sleeve. Then there was Bridget ,who only had three teats that worked, and for a while I called her three tits, which I thought was an appropriate name. Then I remembered an acquaintance who was rather prim and prissy, and not, I'd decided, my type at all. So Bridget was christened. She was also a bit stiff, and because of this and the bullying of the other cows, she tended to lie in the yard, usually in the muckiest spot possible. Like me, she hated getting up in the morning.

Some of these bovines were also reluctant to come in to their stalls. Bovril in particular would never oblige me, and yet when Trefor went to fetch her she would swagger in.

'Well, if I'd known that incompetent neurotic milkmaid wanted me in, I would have come, of course I would, but I'm not a mind reader,' she seemed to be saying!

Cows are stupid...!

U

The uneasy alliance between Trefor and myself was always being tested by my ponies not realising that Trefor needed certain fields reserved for his own stock or to be reseeded etc. I have really lost count of the times when my herd made a bid for freedom and new pastures.

One of these occasions was heralded by the arrival of friends Barb, Brian and their children, but as usual at Lluest, disaster followed disaster and we seemed to spend most of our time working frantically against escaping animals, overflowing loos, and all the other misfortunes to which Lluest was subject. Luckily, Barb and family were used to the hectic and rather messy life at Lluest.

That day, I wasn't looking forward to meeting our next guest, a gentleman who, after nearly two years of riding lessons elsewhere, had only just managed to canter.

'Of course, he could be quite nice,' Stella said optimistically over breakfast.

I resisted the temptation to strangle her and turned the radio up a notch. Pete staggered downstairs demanding a coffee, P Brain did her best to drink the milk from anyone's unguarded cornflakes, and Barb and Brian started to look haggard. Then Stella shrieked from the bathroom.

'Now what's wrong?' I yelled above the radio.

'The loo is overflowing again,' shouted Stella.

'Well, use the bloody stable then,' I snarled back.

Brian grinned, Pete hastily disappeared or possibly lapsed into a coma in a handy corner, and I smiled hopefully at Brian. He's a good sort of chap really and soon did the honourable thing and stirred our hole in the ground, which passed as a septic tank. Stella cautiously flushed the loo (I hoped she'd put her wellies on just in case) and reported that it was now working. A few minutes later some very relieved people were sitting around the breakfast table again, as far away from Brian as possible.

'Do you really want to ride?' I asked Brian, hoping that the answer would be 'No'.

'Why don't we go to the beach later?' Barb asked her family, while Stella packed her case, said her goodbyes and went home to the relative sanity of Wolverhampton.

Meanwhile the rest of us cleaned tack, the house and the stables. By midday everything was neat and tidy, so following Barb's suggestion, we piled into the cars and headed off down to the beach. There's something very special about watching children and dogs playing unselfconsciously on an unspoilt beach. Soon a seaweed fight started which rapidly got out of hand. The dogs raced around, enjoying the freedom, the sand beneath their paws and the odd splash in the sea.

'You're lucky living here,' Barb said.

'Yes,' I replied, 'but I'm usually too busy to notice.'

'Never mind,' Barb chuckled. 'You'll have an easy week next week with just the one customer.' She was wrong!

Later that afternoon, as Barb and Brian were just leaving, I got a bad-tempered phone call from Trefor.

'They're out *again,*' Trefor said. 'Can you move them?'

I could hear that even Annette sounded fed up.

'Yes, I'll come now,' I replied and slammed the phone down.

'Barb, the ponies are out,' I shouted.'

'That sounds fairly normal. Come on family, work to do.' She smiled.

Just then Pete came in, and with a slight panic in his voice said, 'Our guest has arrived.' He was trying not to laugh.

'What's he like?' I asked.

'You'd better come and see for yourself.' Pete was still chuckling.

I ran out into the yard and almost collided with a tall thin gentleman. I guessed that he was about thirty-five, though I wasn't sure. He was wearing a frilly shirt and satin breeches. His beard and moustache would have been impressive, but somehow they didn't seem to go well with the face they adorned.

'Good afternoon,' he said, and bowed as he introduced himself.

'Oh, hello,' I said, trying not to laugh. 'Look, the ponies have escaped, must dash – Pete will look after you.'

The ponies, who always sense when I'm in a rush, rose to the occasion and legged it as fast as possible in the wrong direction.

'Damn you, ponies!' I yelled.

'Well, don't just stand there you lot, just grab them,' I shouted. Of course, they refused to be grabbed; they raced along pounding through the wet grass kicking up large chunks of turf. I hoped that Trefor wasn't looking as they headed for his silage field. Barb panted valiantly up the slope to head them off, but the little horrors accelerated and shot past her with triumphant bucks and snorts. Joker raced after them with me racing along by his side but Jester decided she would wait for further orders.

'Get 'em then,' I shouted, as she hesitated, making sure that I *really* wanted her to chase the ponies who had disappeared up the hill.

'You useless animal,' I shouted. She wagged her tail, then was off in the true Jester fashion, head down, racing and intent on getting her job done.

The ponies enjoyed their exercise around Trefor's land all the better because they knew they shouldn't have been there. The dogs no doubt enjoyed it too, but us humans were mostly worn out by the exercise we certainly didn't need. Pete was tested in his entertainment skills and poor Trefor fretted and worried about his poor silage field, which I could only hope survived the intrusion of twenty-four pounding hooves. Poor Trefor. This wasn't the first time, and I guess he had worked out that it probably wouldn't be the last. I don't know how he put up with us!

Joker and Jester

Chapter 9

I've always known that I've been slightly eccentric

I 've always known that I've been slightly eccentric, and I suppose that I have come to ignore the effect I have on unprepared people. We hadn't been at Lluest for long and I was in trouble again. The weather was awful, with the snow and blizzards leaving my food store perilously close to empty and my purse much depleted. So, as usual, faced with a distinct lack of cash I had economised on the essentials of life, like coal or means of heat and food for myself. It wouldn't be the first or last time that I had huddled out in a cold yard waiting for a chicken to do the decent thing and lay me my dinner.

Unfortunately, the blizzard had damaged the roof of the hen house and the intense cold had proved too much for my girls, all ex-battery hens, so I brought them into the only unoccupied bit of the house: the bathroom. Now every morning they greeted my efforts with a reassuring barrage of clucks and tried to sit on my lap and 'help'.

Gradually, the snow eased and our services were repaired and I phoned the feed merchant for a delivery. I was feeling pretty miserable with a nasty chill, and felt that death from frostbite was imminent. So I filled a hot water bottle, covered it with a body warmer, and tied it around my middle with a variety of baler twine. Then I put one of Peter's jumpers over the top and waddled about my daily business. I was mucking out when the feed lorry arrived, and by that time I had warmed up; in fact I was sweating. Jester jumped into action as soon as the driver jumped out of the lorry, circling and barking.

'Five bags of sugar beet, one of bran, one of layers' mash, four of oats and two of maize?' he queried.

'Yes,' I replied, wondering if the cheque would bounce.

He was looking at me rather strangely as I bent to pick up a sack of maize. At least, I would have picked it up if I could have got past my padding-induced lump.

The driver coughed. 'It's alright, *bach*, I'll pick it up. You shouldn't be working in your condition.'

I hastily agreed with him, surprised at this sudden boost of concern for the female of the species. Welsh women are as strong and tough as their husbands and are expected to be able to hump sacks of feed around. However, I was knackered and hungry and I was in no condition to work. On the other hand, I did feel sorry for the driver, who wasn't much bigger than me, so I picked up a sack and staggered into the feed shed with sweat streaming from my face. I decided to remove Pete's sweater before returning for a bag of sugar beet. Before I could get hold of another bag, the determined little Welshman shot past me carrying not one but two bags. I decided he was late for a lunchtime appointment with his local.

'Are you alright?' he asked.

He didn't look worried as much as terrified.

'Yes, of course,' I answered, thinking that he looked far worse than I felt. His face was red with exertion and his breathing reminded me of a broken and wounded nag.

'Come and have a cup of tea?' I asked politely.

He agreed, and fidgeted in our freezing kitchen while Jester eyed him watchfully. I actually only had one used teabag left, so I was squeezing out the last dregs from it. I don't drink milk, and Tiger, one of my cats, had drunk the last milk that morning so I offered the unfortunate driver a pale brown brew with one spoonful of sugar, as that was also rationed. The tea soon warmed me up further and, chatting happily to the driver, I began to undo the zip of my body warmer. That was as much as the neurotic little man could stand and he leapt out of his chair.

'Well, must get back,' he muttered.

'You haven't finished your tea,' I replied, hurt.

'You sure you're alright?' he croaked worriedly.

'Yes, fine,' I said, extracting my cold hot water bottle and leaning over the sink to empty it.

The driver's face was a picture and I couldn't think why. Then when I looked back, and knowing the Welsh as I now do, I realised the horror on his face stemmed from the horrible feeling that I was either going to give birth or seduce him, and of course there was the fact that he'd carried a lot of bags of feed for a 'pregnant' woman who could easily have carried them herself.

'Um, can I use your... er?'

'Yes, of course. It's in the tack shed through there and turn right.'

I'd found that hot water disguised as tea did have that effect on people. Of course, I'd forgotten about the hens, or rather I knew that they were there and didn't mind. There was an outraged squawk as the lorry driver walked into the bathroom, and a yell as Road Runner, my most impish hen, drummed her usual tattoo with her beak on some part of his anatomy. I hope it was his feet! He staggered out glowering at me.

'You've got a flock of bloody chickens in there, and they peck,' he shouted.

'Oh, yes, it's because of the cold outside,' I explained.

'I'd rather they froze, than be pecked liked that,' he grumbled, and walked out slamming the tack shed door. His exit produced a triumphant cackle from the bathroom as Road Runner, no doubt overcome by the unfriendly intruder, produced my dinner. Life was looking up.

I'm surprised that any delivery men called at Lluest, because if the owner is nuts then the animals and birds are nuttier. I was waiting for the post bus one morning, sitting on the bank with a cat on my lap, Herbie the crow on my shoulder, Jester at my feet and Joker playing with the sleeve of my blouse. The post bus lumbered around the corner and I was surprised to see a new driver. I waved and yelled as he came level with me. He turned and waved back, did a double take and then drove straight into a ditch for some reason.

'Oh dear, you're in the ditch,' I greeted him, smiling sweetly.

He muttered something in Welsh that I don't think should be translated.

'Do you always have a crow on your shoulder?' he asked.

'Oh, yes, Herbie is quite tame. Here, would you like to make friends?'

The postman stretched out a cautious finger, and quick as a flash Herbie swooped down, pecked it and returned chuntering to my shoulder.

'Bee, bad boy,' I scolded.

'Somebody will shoot him for you – here's your post,' came the cross reply.

Postie was obviously unhappy, and forgetting his predicament he tried to zoom off. The wheels of the post bus spun and dirt flew at us.

'Hey' I yelled. 'You can use our phone to get help if you pay for the call.'

The postman gave me an evil look and somehow freed his vehicle. I wondered how he would explain the dent in the bumper, and what Jasper Carrott, in his insurance comedy sketch, would make of the accident report – maybe: '*I was proceeding along the road when I was accosted by a woman and an old crow'.* Or would he just put: an old crow and her crow?

Speaking of the crow, I should explain that I had always wanted a parrot, but somehow I never got around to getting one, much to the relief of my cats and dogs. However, one day during Whitsun a small black crow with an ever-open beak came into my life. Mair found him lying injured in the hedge and brought him to me. When I returned exhausted from a hard day's trekking, he was sitting under a bush, looking as unappealing as my husband's dirty socks. He was surrounded by a ring of expectant faces, belonging to teenage girls who were waiting for me to work a miracle. I didn't particularly want to, but luckily Stella is an expert in these matters and soon had us all digging up revolting wriggly worms and filling a conveniently shaped salt pot with beaten egg and milk. The crow ate the lot, as well as part of my nervous finger. He was found a box which was lined with straw. The next problem was a name. He had ice cold blue eyes, a large beak, and was already showing signs of a sense of humour. I named him Erbert, which later became Herbie or Bee, and within two hours he seemed to have learnt his name.

Most young birds go into shock when faced with humans, but not Herbie; he loved them. Kitty, our mother cat, was a very good hunter, so he had to spend his nights outside the downstairs bedroom, which at the time was occupied by half a dozen noisy children. Herbie was unperturbed by the shrieks, and the next morning he was cawing for a feed as they were demanding breakfast.

Soon he was clinging onto people's fingers, and then he progressed to exploring the kitchen. Unfortunately, little birds tend to leave deposits everywhere, and soon he was competing with P Brain for the title of 'messiest creature of the year'. His wing healed gradually, and soon he was mobile enough to make friends with Joker, who behaved well. Herbie never pecked me, but usually amused himself by pulling my hair out of my hair net.

He was growing quickly, and soon realised that he could terrorize our three cats by creeping up on them while they were asleep and pecking their tails. His favourite victims were Tiger and P Brain. Herbie would creep up and seize a tail, giving it a sharp peck. The result was always the same. The cat who had been pecked blamed the other cat, then spat and swatted it. Inevitably, a fight would develop, accompanied by much spitting and fur-flying. Herbie, of course, would be nowhere in sight, but if you looked closely he would be hiding under the table cawing happily to himself. Kitty, who had a very short fuse, was much respected by Herbie at first, but inevitably he grabbed her by mistake and, much to my surprise and Herbie's, she fled. By now, no cat was safe from Herbie, who dive-bombed them, swooping from our roof onto the cat and back again in seconds. His next target was the dogs; good-natured Joker was an easy target and was once pecked in a very delicate place. He had just been on a courting trip so got no sympathy from me! Jester hated Herbie; she would have loved to bite him, but because I was fond of him, and she was a loyal dog, she ran for cover.

I decided to take my first holiday for five years, and when I came home, Herbie was the first to greet me. That night he decided to play me up, refusing to come down from the caravan roof. I told him he could stay there but, as I marched away, there was a flapping of wings and he dropped onto my shoulder, cawing gently and apologising as best he could. He could be stubborn and, though intelligent, was completely untrainable. One evening, as a treat, he was watching television with us in the front room. I decided it was his bedtime but he had other ideas. He did a lap of honour, splattering my chair on the way. He refused to hop onto my hand, and when I tried to pick him up his angry caw sounded suspiciously like NO. A further attempt was greeted with a 'get off', until psychology in the form of bacon rind was applied. I thought I had got the better of him that time until Stella's laughter confirmed my worst fears – a direct hit!

He would try and follow me, whether I was in my car, on horseback or on foot. Several times I had to stop cars, so that a pedestrian crow could cross the road in safety. One motorist decided to introduce himself. We both thought Herbie would show some gratitude and use an appropriate gesture to thank a motorist. He did, and I had to waste ten minutes dealing with an injured finger. Some of his pranks were quite funny; others I could do without. He sensed if people didn't like him, and then either kept away or decided to drive them away. My Mum hated crows; Herbie retaliated by attacking her shoes with a vigour that any boxer would admire.

His various tricks included flying onto our porch and dropping stones on visitors' heads; thank goodness he was a small bird. Or he would hurl a full dish of water on some neatly permed head. After a few of those tricks he was only allowed water on the ground. Sunbathing was a nightmare with Herbie around, as he picked up dirty straw and muck and tried to stuff them down personal items of clothing. He also pecked if you tried to resist that procedure.

People often asked if I was frightened of his beak. I wasn't - it was his other end that worried me. He had a good aim and could produce ammunition to order. Herbie was completely free during the day but could be summoned by my feeding call. I can still remember his first flight. I had been wasting my time, together with Pete, trying to persuade Herbie to fly between us with raw meat as a reward. He would only perform short flights and couldn't take off from the ground. He had worked out that lots of short flights meant more meat. One morning I realised he was missing, and despite an intensive search of the ground he remained missing. I was heartbroken and in tears as I mounted Prince and took the trek out. I was later told by Mair that about five minutes after I left he flew down from the tree he must have been sitting in. Out on the trek I imagined the worst. By the time I had got back home he had disappeared again. Perhaps he had planned to keep his flying a secret, but as I came into the yard, he swooped to me - a proud bird in his natural environment. His flying improved and, although there were crashes, he was airborne more frequently. I expected him to leave any day, but was glad that he didn't. I had got too fond of him for my own good and his. I had no regrets. I knew him better. If and when he decided to leave, he would, without a backward glance, but I had a feeling that if he was hungry I would hear that call again, and my heart would beat a little bit faster as once again I would have a crow on my shoulder.

Of course, one day Herbie met his match, and surprisingly it was good natured Joker who finally lost his temper. Herbie tried to steal his bone and Joker snapped at him, damaging his wing and, more seriously, his confidence. The rest of that day Herbie was very quiet and sat on my arm feeling very sorry for himself. For days afterwards he was a shadow of his former self. He crept around with scarcely a squawk, and ran for cover if approached. He couldn't fly anymore, and I had the feeling that his days were numbered. Joker was also crestfallen and had been crawling along on his belly, conscious of my sadness and disapproval. Finally, he crawled too close to Herbie who snapped his beak to test Joker's reaction. Joker looked at me appealingly. With Herbie triumphantly revived, Joker just lay there, head between his paws, while Herbie attacked his tail. He was quickly satisfied, and with a cheeky squawk he flapped to my wrist. Confidence seemed a major part of Herbie's life, and any setback, however minor, would affect him. If I ignored him when he asked for attention, he just had to persist until he got my attention. Herbie had become part of the eccentric mishmash of life at Lluest, and his company, intelligence and humour will never be forgotten.

I do realise that not everyone is as animal crazy as me, and I know they must find it very hard to come to terms and understand my life and the way I lived it. There was a lovely old lady who hated animals, but dutifully brought her three young grandchildren along for a ride. We sat Mrs Jones down in the front room, evicted the cats and Joker, who was in training to be a bag snatcher, and gave the lady a cup of tea. So there she was, looking down her nose at our untidy front room, probably thinking that someone should dust the mantelpiece; and then we all just simply forgot about her. All except the animals, who I'm convinced dislike animal haters and enjoy livening up their animal-free existences. Jim wasn't used on that ride, and feeling bored, he opened his stable door and sauntered over to the garden. The garden gate was no problem for wily old Jim, and neither was our front door which I obviously hadn't closed properly. He walked in, his hooves no doubt muffled by our dog-eared carpet.

Mrs Jones probably didn't know he was there until she felt his warm breath on the back of her neck, and a grey, whiskery muzzle removed a digestive (his favourite biscuit) from her hand. Her shriek brought Pat, a trekker, to her assistance, and Jim was tempted back to the yard with the remains of the packet of biscuits. Mrs Jones was mopped up and settled down with a fresh cup of tea, as the other had splattered down the front of her dress and over the settee. Pat suggested she sit by a window and rashly opened it, as Mrs Jones was feeling rather warm. It's never a good idea to open a window at Lluest, as you never knew quite what would come in. It didn't take long for Lottie, one of our extrovert hens, to spot an opening to biscuits, cake and anything else she could steal, and no one should have been surprised when Mrs Jones threw another cup of tea over our furniture. When Pat came into the front room, Mrs Jones was standing gibbering in a corner, while Lottie demolished another packet of biscuits. When I arrived back in the yard, I innocently asked Mrs Jones if she'd enjoyed her tea and biscuits. Pat and the other trekkers dissolved into hysterics and Mrs Jones stomped off. Her grandchildren had enjoyed their ride and were back the following day. Their granny stayed in her car with the windows wound up. Thus was life at Lluest.

Chickens

Chapter 10

Can you take a party this evening?

'Can you take a party this evening?' asked Stella.
I'd just got back from a hot dusty day-ride to be greeted by a yard full of expectant faces waiting to be thrilled by an evening's riding.

'Yes, pack 'em in,' I replied. 'Where's me tea – oh, and get the next lot mounted, will you?'

Stella, who was used to my complete lack of manners, did as she was asked, then carried on with the cooking of dinner, answering the phone and coping with the occasional loose pony, and soon the next ride was ready. Someone, probably one of the guests who had been roped in as a groom, led my stubborn Prince out, and I mounted and rode off with yet another party of trekkers.

Although I only had about four half-day ride routes, the job wasn't boring because each party of trekkers was different. This group were all beginners, and they were a little nervous. So I ambled up and down the line chatting about their life and work, asking where they came from, and telling them about 'their' pony's history.

I couldn't help smiling when I remembered the last group I had taken out. The husband and wife were, on the face of it, the perfect couple. He had the obligatory hairy chest peering out of his shirt and battling with a rather large gold medallion. She somehow had managed to wedge her overweight body into a tight pair of jeans and a very blousy blouse. Stella was having problems persuading her to discard her flimsy white sling-back sandals in favour of more sensible riding footwear.

'But they go with these jeans,' she muttered, and 'the last place let me wear them.'

Not being persuaded to abandon my safety rules for the sake of glamour, I handed over a pair of scruffy but sensible boots. What I didn't know was that the boots had a lodger. The unfortunate lady screamed as her foot touched something furry and squidgy. The poor old mouse was quite dead and had been for some time, so the boots went out for an airing and I revived the lady with a cup of tea.

The two children, both replicas of their mother, preened and admired their reflections in our mirror. One was expensively kitted out in boots and jodhpurs. Stella and I exchanged knowing glances. On impulse I asked to see her hat, as somehow it didn't look quite right. It wasn't; the hat had no British Standard kite-mark, and in small print on the label there was the inevitable 'Made in Korea'.

'This hat is unfit for use,' I said bluntly, thinking that they were just the sort of family who went in for the external look of things, without a real care for the child's safety.

'But it must be,' chorused the indignant parents. 'We paid £50 for that hat.'

Yes, I thought, not much more than you paid for that elaborate whip that I'm going to confiscate before your child gets on any of my ponies.

But I am a businesswoman and, despite my thoughts about silly parents and spoilt kids, I believe in rider safety.

'A proper kite-marked hat – here, look at mine – will cost you around £13. Now please, when you get home, go to a reputable dealer and not a market stall. Also, remember not to buy a second-hand riding hat, because if the owner has fallen off, the hat may be damaged and therefore useless. A good dealer will measure your head for you.'

Neither parent looked very convinced while I explained all this, and their daughter was aggrieved that our hats didn't look shiny and new. Luckily for her they were all in perfect condition.

As Stella led them out into the yard, I could see why some trekking centres just give up. Perhaps people put their brain out for a rest when they go on holiday, but why can't people see that they need boots, jeans and a good hat before they go anywhere near a horse?

Mounting up was not going well because the youngest girl didn't like her pony.

'I want a black one,' she screamed.

Bluey, her white pony, stood quietly and miserably, realising his rider didn't like him. The eldest girl mounted Blackie, who is an iron grey, and pouted too.

'I bet he's a slug,' she said, kicking his sides.

I smiled tolerantly at her.

'Don't kick him,' I instructed. 'Just say, "Blackie, walk on".'

She did, and then lost her balance and heaved on Blackie's reins to regain it. After a quarter of an hour I decided that she didn't just need a decent hat, so much as glue to keep her bottom in the saddle and weights to keep her hands in position.

However, I politely agreed with her parents that the expensive lessons had paid dividends, as they obviously had – to the riding establishment that had had the unenviable job of teaching the child. Meanwhile, we were also trying to cope with the wailing Susan who wanted a miniature Black Beauty.

Blackie soon sussed out that Sally was useless, and he ignored her and her confusing aids. Mum and Dad were getting sore, but were determined to get their money's worth, and Susan was still wailing.

'I want a trot,' whined Sally.

'Yes, she can gallop,' enthused her proud mother.

'OK,' I said. 'Blackie, trot on.' The long-suffering pony snapped to attention and stepped out at a brisk trot. Sally, who was obviously used to the typical shambling riding-school pony trot, promptly started screaming.

'He's bolting,' she yelled.

'Hang on, darling,' yelled her father. Macho Man in his prime, rushing to the rescue. Unfortunately, Macho Man couldn't ride, and as he attempted to gallop into the setting sun, he caught a very personal part of his anatomy on the pommel of the saddle. By this time, I was beginning to have my doubts on the wisdom of running a trekking centre. But Blackie stopped as soon as Sally started to lose her balance, and Jadine stood still while her rider fought back his tears and tried not to hold his damaged pride. I didn't carry a truss and decided against offering him a triangular bandage, and very properly kept a straight face while the wounded hero regained his composure.

I patiently corrected Sally, reassured her mother that Blackie only did exactly as he was told, and tried not to listen to Susan, who, because no one was looking at her, had started howling again.

I returned them all safely to the stable and fled, after politely expressing my thanks for their custom. I went off indoors, leaving Stella in charge of taking money. With the job done, she came inside too – grinning.

'Had a good ride?' she chuckled.

'Bloody great,' I replied sarcastically.

'Oh, good.' she replied. 'I've just rebooked them.'

'Oh, bloody hell,' was all I could say.

'Now, now,' she said. 'After all, it's all money. Oh, and your next ride is here.'

I'm going to go nuts, I thought as I marched out to meet the next crew, smile fixed in place as soon as I entered the yard.

'We're all experienced except Judith, and she can trot but not canter.' I smiled but ignored their assurances. Years of leading treks had taught me never to trust what a person says about his, or her, or anyone else's riding ability.

Seconds later I was smiling genuinely as each rider patted their pony, tightened their girth, and adjusted their stirrups.

Judith, it turned out, could canter, but was nervous of doing so on a strange pony. But the easy-actioned Katy quickly put her at ease, and soon seven happy ponies were galloping the tracks with seven happy riders. As I swung round the bend, wind in my face and the fading sun on my back, I thought how wonderful my life was. Judith laughed and I whooped and we cantered on with not a care in the world or a thought of tomorrow's problems.

Those fast rides were great, but I got a lot of pleasure from taking the average novice family on a slow ride and watching them gain confidence in their ability to ride, through to developing a relationship with their mount. This relationship is important, as it makes a difference between sitting on a horse, which in some cases could justifiably be wooden, and learning to respect and understand a living creature, who despite the fact that he or she cannot talk to man, communicates in so many other ways.

∪

Roy wasn't the sort of person that you would normally expect to come trekking. He had spent his whole adult life working in a mill, and I suppose you would have expected him to be a typical townie. Appearances can be deceptive though, and as soon as he mounted Jerry I had a feeling that he was just what a jaded trek leader needed.

'Now listen to the instructions, girls,' he said to his two children, Gillian and Julie, who were instantly all ears. It was easy to see that they respected and loved their dad. Quickly, I explained how to hold their reins and then Mair and I clipped them onto leading reins. Both girls had grins nearly splitting their faces, and their ponies, Jim and Bluey, stepped out cheerfully. By the end of the ride we were all firm friends, and by the end of the week we presented them with a certificate for their achievements. We were all a little moist-eyed as their car pulled out of the yard.

The following year they were back as keen and attentive as ever.

Being polite to difficult customers should be second nature. They come in all shapes and sizes, and from all walks of life, but their common problem is that they must always be right. This can be dangerous.

Instinct warned me to steer clear of the Wilson family, but greed and the necessity for money got the upper hand, and I welcomed them with open arms. They were an hour or so late arriving, the children were showing signs of travel sickness, and Mr Wilson leered a condescending greeting at me. I watched in amazement as his wife struggled with the children and a heavy case. Mr Wilson was obviously a good organizer, and although he had probably had every opportunity, he didn't immediately strike me as being very bright. His smiles on arrival were as false as mine. He reminded me of a reptile, with his weak chin and wimpy personality. A man amongst men he certainly wasn't, although he had managed to produce three kids. His wife was actually quite nice and seemed genuinely interested in the animals. The eldest boy was the sensitive type. The sisters however were something else again. As they sat at the table hunched over their meal, I imagined them as toads set to devour a plate of worms. They hardly ever spoke and showed no interest in their surroundings or their mounts. Normal children swarm all over the stable as soon as they arrive, and have to be forcibly restrained from sneaking down to the ponies' field.

The Wilson children retained their upper crust detachment. I wondered what sort of father could breed children who had no natural joy in life. I couldn't help comparing them to the rough scruffy town kids who weren't afraid to laugh if they felt like it, and not afraid to cry when they left the pony they had come to love. I wondered what it would take to get some reaction out of them. Unfortunately for all of us I would soon find out.

The morning ride had been OK, if a little hard on my nerves. After lunch prepared by the cook, our own one-armed bandit Stella, we set off again. Stella had, uncharacteristically for her, taken a dislike to our family. Perhaps it was the fact that although they showed little respect for me and my Gloucestershire accent, they showed even less for Stella.

What they didn't know, or bother to find out, was that the down-and-out cripple-fisted cook taught special needs children, and was happy enough to be conned into working for me for nothing during school holidays.

Anyway, the second ride started easily enough, and all went well until we got partway along the gallops, when suddenly a dog jumped out of the hedge and rushed at us barking and snarling. Prince leapt in the air and I turned him, trying to protect little Bluey and his rider. Then all hell broke loose.

Mr Wilson yelled, 'Hang on! My God!' And he started screaming.

The children then found their vocal chords, which obviously hadn't atrophied, and suddenly I was caught in a maelstrom of panicking kids and barking dogs; and then Jadine, dragged around by her panicking rider, hit me. I remember falling and fighting for breath as Jadine landed on me and then I fainted. Luckily, I wasn't out for long. Presumably I was revived by the screams, or perhaps it was the rough hands and the booted foot that the generous, gentle Mr Wilson was using to see if I was still alive.

'Save the children,' yelled his wife.

'Do something,' yelled their father, oblivious to the fact that I couldn't get my breath.

The ponies had disappeared back down the track pursued by the dog. I struggled to my feet to survey the carnage. Mr and Mrs Wilson were unhurt but one of the girls had an obvious broken wrist, and the other girl seemed to have hurt her back. Her father, who I had decided was definitely stupid, rushed to pick her up.

'Leave her!' I shouted. At least I tried to shout but it isn't easy with broken ribs.

Mr Wilson turned to me 'Get an ambulance,' he ordered. 'Is there a decent hospital? You can never tell in these backward communities.'

I turned to walk the three quarters of a mile to the nearest farm.

'This is the finish, you know,' Mr Wilson yelled furiously. 'I'll ruin you. You'll have your licence taken away, and you'll never get another one – I've got connections.'

I groaned and tried to reason with him.

'It wasn't my fault. You saw the dog.'

'I don't care about the dogs. Who owns them, anyway? Are they from this farm?'

The pain in my side was getting worse but I struggled on.

'Have these people got any money?' he asked.

Then I made my first mistake.

'No, they haven't,' I muttered, and instantly knew that I had said the wrong thing. This greedy weak-minded little man with his pocket calculator of a mind decided in that instant to sue me for every penny I had.

Once we reached the smallholding, the dogs returned to the attack, and I wasn't tremendously surprised when my weedy friend dodged behind me and waited for one battered female to leap to his defence. So, considerate as ever, I left Mr Wilson standing outside the house...

Mrs Jones summoned the ambulance and lied about her dogs. Her daughter asked Mr Wilson where the ponies were.

'Damn the horses, they can go to the devil,' he replied.

He will never know how lucky he was that I had broken ribs. The customer is always right, but in this case the least he would have got is a right-footed kick into where it hurt.

Luckily the horses had been caught. They were returned home by a man who is taciturn and who has been moulded into a hard man by the harsh countryside that we all scratched a living from. This gentleman popped his hatless five- and seven-year-old children on the ponies and returned the 'dangerous' creatures to Lluest. Despite their fright they marched home in good order and looked after their tiny charges.

Meanwhile, we were all taken to hospital by ambulance. Mr Wilson took the opportunity to have his bruised shin examined, and later in hospital this believer in equality took his bruised leg off to X-ray while I struggled to breathe as I waited for a doctor to attend me. Mrs Wilson came to see me and told me not to worry as it wasn't my fault, but I knew that I was in deep trouble. Legally, I wasn't responsible for what had happened, but fighting our rich lizard would bankrupt me anyway. We both knew that if any bad publicity didn't finish me, the financial worry would.

Pete came to the hospital and drove us all home. Mr Wilson ordered his wife to pack their suitcases and harangued me on the doorstep of Lluest. He spent the next forty-five minutes threatening me and demanding immediate financial settlement. By this time my head was aching, and I was pretty well in shock. Stella was seeing to the ponies, but her diminutive shy, gentle mother pulled herself up to her full height of five foot, stood in front of this bully and told him in no uncertain terms what she thought of him. As she led me into the house,

I wondered if I had heard him right, that he was going to set his lawyer onto me.

Two months passed, and my insurance company had refused to pay out to the bully, because technically they could find no fault on my part; it had been an 'accident' and the accuser should have taken out his own holiday insurance (which he hadn't). I wrote down my thoughts:

I'm waiting to lose my business. I don't think I can do much to stop this bitchy little man fighting me, partly because poverty can't fight riches and win, but mainly because at twenty-seven I'm tired. I feel like an old woman. Life has been fairly hard and this last year has been too difficult even for me. Someone I respect and care for said that 'there is someone up there who cares.' I envy her that comforting vision.

So, when Mr Wilson and his associates go for the jugular I doubt if I'll be ready for them or able to take the pressure. If I lose Lluest, what will I do? I'm no good at anything else, and anyway I couldn't face life in a town without my rag-taggle army of rejects. I suppose I could return to Gloucestershire, dejected, and become a suburban housewife immersed in coffee mornings and good works, but I wonder how long such a society could withstand the onslaught from a very eccentric Ginny.

No one will know what I went through with these thoughts and grief. Also, I had to cope with the long recovery from the physical injuries from that awful day. But someone or something must have been looking out for me; in the end any case against us was dropped. I know that some think I am over-fussy when I yell at people on the rides who ease their hard hat off, or I refuse a rider in flat shoes, or endlessly care for and inspect the tack. These were the things that saved me and kept my reputation.

Chapter 11

P Brain and other related problems

Poor P Brain. Such a pretty puss with such a tiny brain. I often noticed her mother Kitty, who was a brilliant hunter, throw her a despairing look as she yowled and cuffed her for the umpteenth time.

P Brain, originally called Bella, spent most of her time asleep either on my lap or in some comfortable corner of the tack-shed or front room.

Occasionally, when she did wake and stretch, she would go hunting as far as the kitchen, and we would hear crashing saucepans and broken plates as she made her progress across work surfaces and into cupboards. Unfortunately, once she got into a cupboard she was usually unable to find her way out, and her yowls for help often ended in a cry of misery as she was evicted out of the nearest door or window. When P Brain did exert herself enough to jump, she usually landed on a slippery surface and ended up on her back on the floor.

One winter, Pete and I got bored so we borrowed a giant jigsaw puzzle from my Mum. Pete found a large piece of hardboard and put it on top of the coffee table which had castors. I did express my doubts at the time. When, an hour later, I heard a thud, the sound of moving castors, a yowl of terror and a lot of bad language, I hardly dared poke my head around the door.

'She's ruined my sky,' shouted Pete, pointing at the offending puss who was hiding under the desk.

'Never mind,' I said, laughing.

'B***** cat, you've ruined it, you should be out hunting,' he said. 'Too many cats here,' he continued. 'All they do is steal.'

P Brain and I had heard it all before, so we both ignored him. Still muttering, he returned to his shattered puzzle.

P Brain didn't earn her name for nothing. About an hour later, there was another crash, and this time Pete's grass was destroyed. Before I could stop him, he yelled at the cat, who jumped onto the window sill, slipped, crashed into a cup and broke it, and then lived up to another aspect of her name – all over the place!

When she was a kitten, I had made constant attempts to house train her. Finally, in a fit of temper, I realised I was wasting my time, to say nothing of air freshener, when I screamed at a helper to get the 'P Brained' cat out of here. The name stuck, and now I summon her at feed times and attempt to avoid the accusing stares of any shocked customers. Pete never did finish the jigsaw, because every time he completed a suitable chunk, a tortoiseshell bomb would fall on it, jump on it, or suddenly catapult on to his lap, making him knock it over. Tiger (P Brain's brother) was as intelligent as his sister was stupid, and although he was a dreadful thief, he was rarely caught; he encouraged his sister to steal and then waited for her to dash outside with her prize and promptly took if off her. When P Brain returned for more, one of us was usually alerted, and if was Pete, she had to run for cover to avoid a quick shower. Actually, throwing water at a cat is quite a good deterrent, because although it doesn't actually hurt, the wet pussy has to adjourn to a quiet corner to wash and recover its poise. This in turn means a cat-free hour or so, for the owner to continue the chore he or she started on before chaos took over.

Unfortunately, messy cats weren't the only problems faced by residents of Lluest. All our hens were friendly and could all use the cat flap, so it was quite common to find Road Runner helping herself to a packet of biscuits. I wouldn't really have minded one hen, but when she gave a squawk and summoned the rest of her preening, pecking companions, I had to leave whatever I was doing and race around catching the hens. They had no intention of going back out through the cat flap, so I had to open the door, remove the barricades that were supposed to be hen-proof, and lure Road Runner and her companions back into the garden.

Sometimes, as I shooed them away, I remembered the bald hens that I bought two years before. All the girls were ex battery hens and spent the first year of their lives cooped up in tiny wire netting cages with only their own feathers to peck at for amusement. Their strong yellow legs, meant for scratching in the soil, were bent and lifeless, too weak even to support their bald bodies. The local battery was selling off their old hens and I was watching in horror as the unfortunate birds were grabbed by their legs and carried upside down to their execution. What a life! So I stood gasping for breath in the stuffy, smelly atmosphere, while six birds were selected for me. I wondered what kind of man could work there amongst so much suffering. The man, round faced and smiling, looked as if he was a family man, and I could easily imagine him bouncing children and grandchildren on his knee. Yet there he was amongst shit, blood and feathers, going about his daily work without a thought for the birds in his care. He wasn't unkind, at least not deliberately, but I doubt if he ever even realised that the birds had feelings. I don't know how many birds lived in that revolting shed, but it's hardly surprising that the birds could not be treated individually; after all, how could you make up names for a thousand hens?

Every day hundreds of puppies and kittens are born all over the UK. I had always condemned the careless and callous pet owners that allowed this to happen. When I inherited Kitty, Tiger and P Brain, I dutifully rushed them off to the vet who returned them minus their 'naughty bits'.

Unfortunately, despite my good intentions, Joker, my beloved Jester's son, remained in possession of his 'naughty bits' because I wrongly assumed that training him would also keep his carnal desires under control. But about nine weeks after he had disappeared for a few hours, Trefor's dog Fly had four puppies. It was my fault, so I took the responsibility, and Jester and I brought four weaned puppies back to Lluest. They soon settled in; not so long after, Duke, Dovey and Jack had homes. I cried when they all went, but I still had Gypsy, a nervous runty little bitch. The smooth-haired little tricolour collie bore no resemblance to Jester, and yet in her she carried her grandmother's genes. Nobody liked her, and I realised that she would not be welcome in any normal household. She couldn't control her bladder even at twelve weeks. Gypsy was perpetually in motion, always rushing away from her fears and searching for somewhere to rest and someone to belong to.

At this time, there was a tragedy developing at Lluest. The vet and I were fighting to save Jim, but Gypsy played on, enjoying her puppyhood. She missed her brothers and sister, but Joker was a good father and Jester had become the only mother she would remember.

The last afternoon that Jim was well enough to walk to the field, Gypsy raced around him chasing Joker. Jim paused for a moment and stood looking at the puppy. She was three months old and he was over thirty years of age. He knew that he was dying, but he accepted his fate and enjoyed his last afternoon. Unlike Jim, I couldn't accept what fate had in store for us. I had a sick feeling, dreading life without my old favourite. The finality of death frightened me and I had no doubt that when I lost Jim he would be gone forever. I couldn't help wondering if I could have prolonged his life. If only I had been alert to his sickness earlier or tried a different treatment. There were endless mistakes that I regretted.

How I envied Gypsy as she revelled in her youth and speed. Jim sighed. He had spent almost six weeks struggling for life and he was tired. Even had he recovered, he would never again have galloped across a field bucking and farting, or taught a nervous young child the joy of her first canter. Jim nuzzled me, trying to comfort me because I was crying. He must have known that I couldn't face losing him, and I think he struggled on for that reason.

That night, Jim said goodbye to Pepper, who had been a faithful friend to the last, and then he collapsed and died in my arms. Even Gypsy was quiet as I led Pepper out of the stable away from Jim's body. For a long time, I couldn't think of him without thinking about the wreck of his body that lay in the stable. It wasn't just his death that distressed me but the manner of it – but out in the field that afternoon he had finally made his choice. However much Pepper and I loved him it was time to go. The life of an invalid did not suit Jim and he didn't want my pity, and to exist as a wreck of his former self was unthinkable. So, when his body was taken away, I hid in the house holding Jester. I had a duty to try and remember Jim as he was, not just that last day in the field when a very old man resigned himself to the inevitable.

Now I can almost see Jim as he was when we first met. In a way, Gypsy helped me to understand my grief. Jim did not suffer long and I don't think he had any pain, and whatever or wherever he is now, he is free. I wished that I could believe there is a horsey heaven and that Jim is causing havoc careering past angels and their harp music, which I am sure he would find very boring. I also wished that we could meet again, but at least I understand his attitude to approaching death a little better now.

It is hard to see the overactive Gypsy as an old arthritic dog, able only to laze in front of the fire, and I know that independent Kitty will disappear silently rather than accept any pity when she is dying. Some animals like Pepper or Jester can accept old age gracefully, but to other lively independent spirits, it is hell. Until the start of his decline, Jim was a lively wicked pensioner determined to die with his shoes on. He gave me so much, and when I tried to prolong his stay with me, he understood.

It may seem a lame excuse, but I couldn't help feeling that Joker's escapade had a purpose. Duke went to an owner who had just lost her old dog, also called Duke – surely not just a coincidence – and Bonny, re-named as Dovey, also replaced a well-loved pet.

As for Gypsy, well, her neurotic temperament kept me occupied, and watching her playing tag with Herbie the crow, I couldn't help laughing at her antics. But then another tragedy happened soon afterwards: Herbie the crow died too, and I came close to selling all of the animals. It nearly broke me. I don't think that any outsider could understand my grief. I suppose most people would have seen it as excessive, and think that I am more than a little crazy. Perhaps I am. I am beginning to realise that I take life and my responsibilities to my animals far too seriously. Like Jim, I'm not good at demonstrating love; but it's there inside me. I can't accept failure and I can't change my feelings that to lose an animal is the ultimate failure.

I doubt I would have gone on holiday if Herbie had been alive. He could be temperamental and resented my deserting him. When I got back it was to learn a much-needed lesson. Gypsy had driven friends and neighbours Sue and Dave mad, and I almost detected a nervous tick in Sue's eyes. Jerry had lost condition and confidence for no reason that I could see. Of course, I blamed myself. Things hadn't been going well before I went away for a break, and whether I was to blame or not, my presence had seemed to be more of a hindrance than a help. But on my return, I wondered if it was just my imagination that my ponies seemed a little lost. Even the hens were pleased to see me and came running at the sound of my voice. So I decided to give Lluest one more try – but how I longed for bygone days when I would drive into the yard and hear a fart from Jim's stable and a squawk as Herbie landed on my shoulder.

Gypsy's welcome on our return home was typical. She had been trying to do a greeting dance but unfortunately it had turned into a rain-dance and Pete was not too pleased. An argument followed, and Pete dared to suggest that Gypsy should be re-homed. We already had two dogs and three cats, and he knew I wanted Jester to have another litter the following year – and yes, he knew I would want to keep one of the puppies. But Gypsy had aroused some deep protective instinct in me, and I tolerated her idiosyncrasies simply because she knew no better and was unable to learn. The next day we decided to take the dogs for a walk up a valley near Strata Florida Abbey. The entrance to the valley is guarded by a small farmhouse and a chapel. It is a valley like many others in this part of Wales, and its empty ruined cottages tell of the shepherd no longer needed to work the sheep. The family that once lived in the farmhouse overlooking the waterfall have all gone now. Perhaps they are dead. Perhaps it was their restless spirits that gave the valley its unearthly silence on the day that we walked up its ancient track. Sitting on a boulder, high up in the valley, I tried to imagine what Wales was like before modern times ruined it. I thought of Druids and the simple peasants, and the sturdy Welsh ponies that carried their packs and helped the shepherds care for their flocks. Despite the disease and the continuous presence of death, life must have been easier then. They had a faith, admittedly very different from ours, but at least it bred a respect for the land they lived in. I wondered how much the coming of the Normans had affected the valley. Maybe Prince Llewellyn had passed this way before travelling on to his death. I wondered about Henry Tudor. His mother, Margaret Beaufort, had loved and felt deep emotions, but he was cold and hard. He visited Strata Florida before he took the English throne. Had he ventured into this valley, would its serenity have distracted him from his murderous ways and attracted a distinguished man to be a hermit amongst its rocks? The valley seemed made for hermits, and even today, five hundred years later, it offered a quiet corner for someone who was troubled by her life and its problems, to rest and daydream about the valley's inhabitants of long ago.

A buzzard called, and Gypsy rushed up with a stick, breaking the spell. I threw the stick and wandered into the cottage. I couldn't resist closing my eyes, trying to feel the essence of the ruin. Some people believe that stones can hold images, particularly stones in an old Druid stronghold. I'm not sure whether these stones held any secrets, but in my 'mind's eye' I had a picture of dark sturdy children following their wiry father across the mountain, and a tiny woman wearing a red scarf.

What I did feel for sure was peace and tranquillity, and when Pete and I reluctantly left the valley I carried a little piece of it back to Lluest. Of course, tranquillity always seems to slip through my fingers and rush back to secluded valleys high up in the mountains, which is where it belongs, far away from the noise and bustle of humanity which would destroy it.

Back at Lluest, Gypsy, probably with a reaction from travelling and an exciting new walk, vomited over Pete's briefcase and best coat. He was cross and we argued again – his eyes questioning the point in keeping a dog like her. I cleaned up his coat and brief case and mischievously sprayed it with lily of the valley perfume, wondering what his colleagues would think if the perfume lasted until he got back to work. Then the dogs and I wandered into the sitting room where Pete was stretched out on the sofa. He put his arm around me, and Gypsy put an apologetic paw on his knee and brushed his shoes with her wagging tail. Pete forced himself to smile tolerantly and cuddled me, and I forgot about the perfume and knew that life had to go on.

Chapter 12

Tribute to Jim

Jim: A short story by Ginny

'**G**et that animal out of here! What's a pony doing in the sitting room?'

We never needed to ask who the pony was, and we could be sure that if the other ponies had also escaped then my delinquent thirty-year-old pony would be in the lead. Jiminy Cricket must have been beautiful in his day, but when I first met him he was twenty-four and already past his prime. At least, a selection of judges at local shows thought so, but we knew better; when Jim got the inevitable rosette because he knew how to behave, unlike his better-bred rivals, we felt rather smug. Jim was smug too, and of course he always let off a series of burps as he trotted around the ring with the other rosette winners. One day the showy chestnut blood pony who had won the coveted first place was turned into a rodeo pony on his lap of honour by a well-timed explosion of burps from Jim. Of course, he didn't laugh – not much, anyway.

Then there was Judith: an expert rider who could pilot Jerry over any jump, usually at breakneck pace. Unfortunately, she had one minor fault – she knew everything about every horse, at least she thought she did. It was wicked really, but after watching her racing Jerry around as if he was a machine, I decided that she needed a little expert tuition.

'Why don't you ride Jim bareback?' I suggested, knowing that Jim hated being ridden bareback.

'OK,' she said, and marched over to Jim who was dozing by the side of the school.

'He's a bit slow,' Judith grumbled and vaulted on. Jim bucked her straight off without even opening both eyes. Judith used some surprising language as she sat on the floor. Jim went back to sleep.

99

'Want to try again?' I asked.

'I'll kill him!' she shouted.

'If he doesn't kill you first,' laughed one of Jim's favourite girls, and jumped on and cantered Jim around the field. Sue returned Jim to Judith, and all the customers gathered around to watch the fun.

'Horrible pony, I hate you,' muttered Judith and leapt on. Jim cantered sensibly up the field and I could see Judith relaxing, thinking that she had won.

Sue and I knew better and tried not to laugh. When they reached the boundary hedge Jim whirled around, unseating Judith for a second, but she stuck to him somehow as he hurtled back towards us. There were whoops and shrieks of encouragement as Jim neared the school fence. Judith was grinning until she realised that she couldn't stop him. He did finally stop dead about two yards from us and shot Judith over his head. She questioned his parentage for a bit while Jim nuzzled his admirers. Judith didn't ask why she couldn't ride Jim when Sue – a younger and less experienced rider – could, but I noticed that Jerry got a lot more pats and plenty of consideration. He also won her a great deal more rosettes than he had previously. Judith never admitted that Jim was responsible for those rosettes, but then no one is perfect.

Judith wasn't the only one who suffered from Jim's irrepressible humour either. In the early days before I broke in Mystic Prince, Jim was my only means of equine transport. Like most nineteen-year-olds I thought I knew it all, and didn't bother to wear a hard hat on a quiet pony unless my Gramp was around. I was sure that Jim was quiet, and as I rode him down the main road, clad in fading jeans with my hair blowing in the wind, I admired his new red headcollar. No, I didn't have a saddle or a bridle. I didn't think either were necessary.

Jim wandered quietly past the parked cars and ignored the heavy lorries that rattled through the village. I knew some of the lorry drivers who hauled animal feed to the local farms. Most slowed down somewhat nervously, as they were used to Prince who disliked any kind of vehicle and was inclined to attempt to race any lorry back to the farm. Jim had no intention of jeopardising his valuable body by dancing a pas de deux in front of an articulated lorry, so he walked demurely along. That is, until he heard the chimes of a Mister Softee ice cream van. He stood proudly trying to judge the direction. I leant forward and patted him vaguely, not even bothering to shorten my improvised baler twine reins. Jim waited for a break in the traffic, whipped into a U turn and bolted with me the wrong way up a one-way street. I tugged on the reins, praying that they wouldn't break, and grabbed a large handful of mane. The side street, normally quiet, seemed to fill up with traffic all hurtling towards us at an alarming rate. It wasn't so much the on-coming traffic that worried me, as the fact that I had to risk a collision with it to avoid the cars parked on both sides of the road. I'd always enjoyed bending[25], but I did have my doubts about playing dodgems with drivers impatient to get the routine Saturday morning shopping over with. Jim, however, had no doubts at all as we careered along in hot pursuit of Mister Softee's ice cream. We were heading towards the junction with the main road. I was still hauling on the baler twine, which didn't seem to have any affect on my 'safe' tiny mount. Jim, although eager for an ice cream, had more sense than to drag me under a car, and I was relieved as he slowed down to his now famous piledriver trot. I leapt off and tethered him to a lamp post while I recovered my poise, and decided to wait for a while until the temptation in the shape of Mister Softee was as far away as possible.

Barbara remembers

When Ginny announced that she intended to enter my daughter Shelley with Jim into the showing class at the local village show and gymkhana in Kingswood, we were a little apprehensive – a whole new experience for us.

We went off to our first gymkhana, having been up very early to prepare Jim. He was washed and groomed until he shone, and his mane and tail were plaited. He looked very smart and very proud. Shelley and Jim were sure enough entered in the show class. With Shelley on a leading rein, her Dad led them into the ring. Rosettes first to fifth place were handed out, and then we waited for the sixth place. I heard someone standing nearby say (referring to the Judge), *'Oh don't say she's going to give sixth place to the leading rein,'* referring of course to Shelley and Jim. Well, it was given to the leading rein. It was a purple rosette that many years later, in 2023, is still a treasured possession, and recorded on the back as '1st rosette, Kingswood, Jim 1978.'

---

[25] 'Bending' is a gymkhana game that entails weaving between poles.

Stella remembers

When I first became embroiled in the world of Lluest, Jim was already a bit of a legend. To say that he had a mind of his own was an understatement. That mind could be mischievous, self-seeking if the opportunity arose and biscuits *inside* the house were left unattended, and with a keen sense of humour! But the main adjectives I respected most were 'wise' and 'kind'.

My other life was teaching children with special needs, and one of my memorable charges was a boy I will call Simon. I became close to him and his family, well beyond his infant years with me at school. Briefly, Simon didn't have a good start in life, contracting meningitis as a baby. His language delay and subsequent mobility problems were attributed to this, and it wasn't until he was nearly six that he was diagnosed with Duchenne Muscular Dystrophy, a life limiting and disabling condition, that saw Simon wheelchair-bound by the time he was seven years old. But, like Jim, Simon had humour, kindness and character with a big C. By the time he was fifteen he was totally dependent; he controlled an electric chair with his hand, but couldn't lift his arms to scratch his nose. During a chest infection at that age, he told his mum that he didn't want to die yet as he was enjoying life too much!

During school holidays when he was about ten years old, he and his parents came to Lluest. We gave his younger sister a ride, and then came the time to see if we could give Simon a turn. Jim was led out to meet Simon. He walked up to the wheelchair and sniffed it, looked at Simon and gently nuzzled his hands and then just stood quietly with his head close to Simon. All I can say is 'they communicated'. We saddled Jim up, showing Simon what we were doing. Then, while Ginny held Jim's head, four of us lifted Simon into the saddle and supported parts of his body to keep him sitting upright and secure. The reins were placed into weak hands and we were set to go. Ginny urged Jim forward, and very gently he moved off. Every ounce of Jim's concentration was directed towards his fragile rider, ears flicking and feet placed carefully. Ginny then instructed Simon to use voice commands to tell Jim his directions: 'walk', 'stand', 'turn'. There wasn't a dry eye in the yard as we all paraded up the track, with Simon becoming more confident and issuing these voice commands to an attentive and responsive Jim. There was such a look of triumph and joy on his face, as he felt that he was in control of this pony and it's movements, and that for once he was looking down on his carers. Jim nursed Simon up and down the track. He knew the fragility of his burden, and he gave Simon such a sense of joy and us a respect for Jim's intuitive wise nature.

It was a day to remember for Simon. He was seventeen when he made the decision to turn off his life support during his last illness in hospital. He comforted his family and friends, planned his own funeral as a celebration of his life and, like Jim, left this world a better place for those that knew him.

Ginny remembers

I had watched a little girl try to ride Jim for about ten minutes and I'd had enough. She was always well dressed, but she never listened to anything I said. She was not the most light-handed child I had met, and it didn't endear her to Jim, who didn't think much of the sore mouth he suffered as a result. He was beginning to lose his temper with the little girl, and he was showing signs of dumping his burden in the nearest muddy patch.

'No, not like that,' I roared, after the rest of the group had successfully guided their ponies around the bending poles. She jerked Jim around with no concern for his mouth and kicked him sharply in the ribs when he wouldn't move. I asked her to dismount, and marched over to Jim. I didn't pat him or observe the usual civilities, and just mounted. I was in a bad mood too and I was fed up. I turned Jim towards the poles and sent him on at a brisk trot.

'Look, it's easy,' I yelled, quickening our pace as we dodged in and out of the poles. The rest of the class, all breathlessly keen on riding, watched us with admiration as we demonstrated. Most could hardly trot in a straight line, and what I was doing was way beyond them. It's always nice having an appreciative audience, so instead of allowing Jim plenty of room to turn at the end, to complete the return journey, I whirled him around in a tight circle. Jim slipped, but regained his feet and rocketed back towards his friends. I was enjoying myself until I tried to stop at the end. Jim gave a snort of rage, stuck his head between his legs and bucked and bucked and bucked. I stayed on for the first dozen or so and then landed at the feet of the little girl's father. I was about to leap up and sort out my delinquent pony when I noticed his mouth. I was in an ideal position to see it; Jim had made sure of that. I looked a right fool – Jim had made sure of that too, and I deserved it. I staggered to my feet. My ass hurt like hell and I felt as if he'd broken my back, but as I was still in one piece I remounted, and explained to the little girl what was wrong with Jim and why he had been forced to throw me: by my bad riding and his sore mouth.

Sadly, I didn't know it then, but it would be Jim's last summer, and soon I would have to rely on Screwy Bluey and another small pony called Folly for my little beginners.

However, I didn't need to worry; Jim must have known and began to take care of things. In those last weeks and hours, with his wise old head over the stable door, he passed on all he knew to his successors. Then, with his job done, he passed out of my life forever, leaving me and the other ponies to sort out our own lives. He had given me seven magical years and the confidence to carry on, but on that sad March day it seemed as though my world had fallen apart. I was full of self-doubt and blamed myself for Jim's death. Nothing comforted me and for weeks I cried as I sat alone in the house. I dreaded the new season: a season without my faithful Jim. I didn't notice the cautious arrival of spring, and I didn't even enjoy riding. I was working far too hard, trying to push the thought of Jim's death away from me, as if it hadn't happened. I couldn't look at his photo and tried to avoid thinking about him. He had loved life and lived it to the full, but I had lost interest in the very thing he had fought so hard to keep.

One day, I let Bluey and a few others out onto a field, one part of which had been reseeded. Trefor had quite sensibly decided to keep them off that patch, so I erected the electric fence, moving like a downcast robot. The job finished, I walked home without a backward glance, ignoring the dogs who played around me. A few hours later I checked the ponies again. Bluey was on the wrong side of the fence, and I swore as he ran up and down cutting the turf. He strutted along, arching his pathetic neck and flinging his legs out. I noticed how much his action had improved, and smiled when I remembered the cripple I had bought. Then I heard that saving voice again as I watched Bluey duck under the wire and gallop off to freedom. I had seen that cheeky action and that attitude before. I knew that the wise way he had with children, coupled with the inability to suffer fools quietly, was partly an innate character trait, but was part knowledge passed on by a wise old mentor.

Now Jim is no longer with us, but I have never forgotten the lessons he taught me. We've all missed him bringing us to heel with a series of loud smelly burps or a few well-timed bucks.

Yes, Jim had gone forever and I would miss him. He could never be replaced and never should be, but there had to be others like him. I couldn't save Jim now, but somewhere out there in my future there would be other rejects who would need help, and the best reject of all would be very cross if I failed them. There was a trekking season to prepare for, and although I still couldn't feel happy, I hoped that the peace and tranquillity that had surrounded Jim would come to rest on me and give me the strength to face 'Another Lluest Morning'.

Stella's songs

Ginny's mention of 'Another Lluest Morning' above refers to a song especially written about Ginny's Lluest Trekking Centre by friend and helper Stella Gratrix. The song was written to recall, reflect and try to convey the special atmosphere that could be felt at Lluest. It was often hard work, and Ginny could be an exacting master, but she could also transmit the special quality of a life devoted to animal welfare, and she greatly encouraged all who came into the special Lluest world to see and develop that special bond with animals and nature.

Stella also wrote a song about Jiminy Cricket's life, called 'Just Jim'. The words of both songs are included here, © Stella Gratrix.

Another Lluest Morning

See the mist roll from the hills, once more the sun breaks through,
The magpie's shrill, sharp cry insists that morning time is due.
Smell the fresh sea breezes blowing softly o'er the fields,
The rain-washed land reveals itself on cue.

Chorus: It's another Lluest morning, and another new day dawning.
Hoof-beats drum the ground, dogs bark at the sound,
And I know that life is good when they're around.

Riding out in convoy down the lanes and on our way,
Chestnut, bay and skewbald, shining black and dappled grey,
Horses' manes toss freely, they are glad to be alive,
And glad to ride the tracks another day.

Moist green turf springs gently under four sure-footed feet,
And mountainside reflects itself where slopes and lakeside meet.
The young red kite dives swiftly on its prey by tumbling stream.

Time drifts swiftly past just like a dream.

In the distance framed by pine, the sea, like spangled gold,
The shadows' line grows longer and the evening breeze grows cold.
Soon the sun's last rays betray that day-time's nearly gone,
And then we'll have to wait until the night-time hours have gone.

Chorus: And there's another Lluest morning, *etc.*

Just Jim

Jiminy Cricket, that was his name,
He was wicked and wise and certainly game.
He'd carry small children with care when he could,
But land a big know-all, with a buck, in the mud.

Chorus: Jimbo, Jimbo, come for a ride,
Jimbo, Jimbo, step right inside.
He was boss of the house, and lord of the yard,
With Jimbo around, gotta be on your guard!

When entering gymkhanas, he'd win his rosette,
By standing on toes of the judge or the vet.
He looked so demure and then so benign,
They gave him a prize instead of a fine!

When moved up to Wales, a sad tale was told
Of a poor old pony, stuck in the cold.
Some firemen and Ginny pulled him out of a bog,
They sneezed all night, *he* slept like a log.

Jim also likes Guinness, the truth I now tell,
And when he'd imbibed, you'd know it right well.
Great trumpeting echoes burst forth head and tail,
The wild winds of Wales can't compete with his gale.

For thirty-three years, he gave of his best,
Till death's cold, stark hand laid his old heart to rest.
To those who were lucky to meet with our Jim,
His memory is special and never will dim.

Chapter 13

Mick

I met Mick at a local sale shortly after moving to Lluest in 1981. I was looking for a pony for a large school party due to arrive in five days, and time was running out. Personally, I hated the sales, with the noise and smell of frightened horse flesh. I just hope that one day councils will implement much needed rules on the indiscriminate breeding of ponies.

So, as I leant on the rails, listening to the auctioneer describing a bay gelding in the ring in front of me as a dun mare, I tried to ignore the pathetic creature. The auctioneer belatedly corrected his mistake and there were knowing glances as the young pony, no doubt bought on impulse two years previously, was dragged around the ring with a large child kicking at his sides.

'Quiet to ride', said the auctioneer, as the two-year-old staggered around the ring trying to adjust his legs and back to the unaccustomed weight. His eyes were rolling and seemed to be pleading with me for health and life. I ignored their pleading and watched as one of the meat men who isn't known for his kindness bought him. Poor little pony, I thought; if only I had the money. He was no use to me now, but possibly in three or four years, with a lot of love and good food... I stayed at the sale until late afternoon, watching the procession of doomed ponies. Occasionally a 'good' pony would appear and be snapped up at double the price I could afford.

Finally, I left the ring, deciding to give up for the time being. And then I saw him. A tiny bay pony with an even tinier rider designed to show how quiet he was. His feet were appalling and his eyes rolled as he was led into the ring. He wasn't guaranteed and I suspected that he was a 'bad 'un'. But at least he was rideable. My mouth was dry as I bid for him. Luckily, his wild eye put everyone else off and he was mine. His ex-owners, who dealt in ponies, said that his rider had lost interest, and as I tried to find a lift home for me and my new pony I wondered if his rider's sudden loss of interest was due to the pony throwing her.

He was certainly very frightened. His small ears were constantly active and he jumped if a man came too close. I spoke to him quietly. I had found that buying ponies was largely a question of instinct and I instinctively liked him. As I borrowed the money to buy him from my father, who wanted repaying, I decided that it might be wise to call him 'Mick'

The auctioneers finally put out my request on the public address system for a lift home, and a few minutes later I was relieved to meet a man who could drive Mick and me within a few miles of Lluest. Mick quivered as I led him up the ramp and into the lorry. As we drove along, I chatted to the driver and time passed quickly. An hour later we drew up at a turning four miles from Lluest and Mick was duly unloaded. The lorry trundled away leaving us standing on the deserted road.

'Oh well,' I sighed, 'best foot forward, Mick.'

Mick's ears flicked and he matched his step to mine. The slightest command brought instant obedience, but this was accompanied by an immense amount of eye rolling. Back at Lluest his stable was waiting, together with a full hay net, and we covered the miles easily. I chatted as we walked and Mick gradually relaxed.

Ideally, a pony should have several days to settle in his new home before being asked to work, but time was pressing so the following morning I planned to take him on a ride. That night Mick whinnied constantly, and by morning we were both shattered. To my surprise he went beautifully as I trotted him out in the early morning mist, and once again I wondered what his problem was. He was certainly nervous, but no more than any other pony would be on the first day at a new home. Jester trotted at my heels and a curlew called and I relaxed and enjoyed my ride. Eventually, reluctantly I took Mick home. He was a saint with the school party, and as soon as they left I turned him loose in a twenty-acre field.

The next morning, I found out why Mick was unwanted. 'Hello Mick,' I called, walking towards him offering a carrot. Suddenly his expression changed and, ears flat back, he charged. I just jumped sideways in time, slipped and landed in a pile of 'you know what'. What

I said isn't printable, particularly when Mick returned to the attack. There was no doubt in my mind it was meant. I have seen a great number of ponies pretending to be fierce, but this one was no actor. Right, I thought, and leapt up, running at him and yelling for all I was worth. Mick was thoroughly confused; humans were supposed to run when you charged them, not charge you back. It was quite obvious that Mick would not be caught, so I rang a few friends and, together with Jester, we chased Mick into the stable. It only took us two and a half hours! Once he was caught, he was a saint once more and his gentleness surprised everyone, but every morning when I tried to catch him, he attacked me.

'He's just crazy,' said one friend.

'Get rid,' said another.

I had to admit they were probably right, but I liked him and could see that he had potential. If only I could find a way to make him come to me. I tried buckets of pony nuts, and swore as he flattened me and stole the nuts. I spent hours sitting on damp heather talking to him, but if I went any closer than ten yards he raced to the attack.

He seemed to enjoy work, and once he was rounded up his temperament changed completely. Something or someone in his background had made him neurotic about being caught, so next month I went back to the sale. His ex-owners were very wisely not there. So I went back home, equipped with a pair of running shoes. Early mornings were no longer peaceful, and all my neighbours were greeted by a 'Ginny Chorus' instead of the more familiar dawn chorus. The problem wasn't just that Mick charged me, but that I never knew quite where he would be.

Once he realised that his charging tactics didn't impress anyone, least of all Jester, he decided to get me fit in other ways. The secure field that contained the other twelve ponies just wasn't equipped to deal with a limbo dancer. Somehow, Mick wriggled underneath any fence including several layers of electric fencing. Trefor, always so generous with his grass, was beginning to get cross as the inevitable tiny bay pony hared across his silage field, closely pursued by a panting swearing female and a very cross Jester.

Unfortunately, Mick wasn't just difficult to catch, he was also very difficult to shoe. Bob, our farrier, hated Mick, and Mick responded by rearing and kicking. He was definitely a pony of habits, and he was in the habit of refusing to be shod, just as he was in the habit of refusing to be caught.

'You know, Bob,' I said, 'that's it'.

'What is?' came the grumpy reply.

'His vices,' I said. 'They're just a habit. He doesn't know why he is scared. In fact, I doubt if he remembers the actual source of the fear. He just knows he should be scared.'

'Sod it,' yelled the farrier. His hand was covered in blood.

'Oh God, you haven't hurt him, have you?' I asked politely!

'No, I * * * * haven't,' he swore.

Just then a car drove into the yard. Customers! I gave Bob the leading rein and dashed to help them. Mick probably didn't see me give the leading rein to Bob, and he tried to follow me, jerking Bob's injured hand. And then he panicked. Somehow Bob held on to him, tied him up, and struggled on with his shoeing.

The 'customers' were only religious types after a quick conversion. They tried hard to convince me of the wisdom of their creed, but were halted in mid platitude by an outburst of questionable language from an enraged farrier. They went very quiet. Then, murmuring excuses, they quickly left. I was chuckling when I returned to Mick and Bob, but soon stopped when I realised that Mick was still only wearing one shoe and breathing fire into the bargain. The next three shoes were pure murder as Mick pranced, cavorted and tried to throw himself down. I could feel his terror mingled with hatred and yet I was powerless to help him. I had tried all the gentle techniques, and although he was quiet enough with me, he would panic if a man tried to touch his feet. Someone had really beaten that little pony, probably in a vain bid to break his spirit. But why was that? He wasn't difficult to ride, and he would respond with gentleness and concern to any child. He was intelligent and willing to learn, but he had no trust in humans, and although I had not hurt him so far, he had no intention of giving me the opportunity to do so in the future.

Somewhere in that neurotic pony there was a reasonable, sensible pony longing to be liberated, and as he watched me catch his fellow ponies he looked on, always suspicious but in a way waiting for me to help him.

All the other ponies disliked the weird maverick I had introduced, and unless they were also in a wild mood, when the urge to gallop seized them, they flattened their ears and ignored his antics. They were only too eager to be caught and start another working day.

One morning I overslept. Of course, Mick had taken the opportunity to escape from the field.

Trefor looked unhappy as I followed Mick's example and ducked under the fence and raced to freedom. When I finally caught up with Mick, he was grazing belly deep in his favourite silage field. As soon as he saw me, he started edging away. I didn't have my usual two hours to spare, and anyway, chasing him around the field would probably lead to my immediate eviction. I sent Jester off to my left and walked to the right, ignoring Mick. He was far too bright for that basic ploy and gathered himself for a rapid exit.

'Oh, stand still you stupid * * * *,' I roared. 'STAND,' I roared again.

He did. And, as I slipped the lead rope on his head collar, he looked at me as if to say, 'whyever didn't you say that before, instead of murmuring words I didn't understand?' He was quite right. I should have seen it: give him a definite command and he will obey instantly.

It was still impossible to walk up to him in a field, even three years later, unless you first yelled 'Stand'. But why, oh why, wasn't 'come' the magic word. I often wondered that, as I tramped the fields in search of a little bay pony that was lost in a sea of grass.

Mick gradually made an uneasy truce with the farrier. He was always wary and twitchy though – and that description applied to both Mick and the farrier! He never really gave up his air of superiority when loose in a field either. The wild attacks stopped, so I felt that I could send other people to catch him. However, he found that it was then great sport to seemingly ignore their calls and entreaties from the gate. Grazing nonchalantly, he would wait until they were almost by his side and then, with impeccable timing, take a couple of casual steps forward before racing like the devil for the other side of the field and waiting to repeat this scenario! He also never lost his 'Houdini' ability to escape from most fields if there was the slightest possibility of dodgy boundary fences or sagging hedges!

As time at Lluest progressed, Mick, when caught, became one of the most reliable and lovable trekking ponies. He was highly intelligent and dependable. Stella built up a particular friendship with him. I always had Stella leading the ride so that I could bring up the rear and observe everything and everyone in front of me. It was useful that Stella was light and slightly built, as she could ride Mick; as a team they would look out for each other and any potential hazard that might threaten the ride.

Eventually, Mick joined up with Pepper in taking over from Jim. He had reformed from the uncatchable pony I first bought, and had more than his fair share of beginners, but was always calm, patient and kind. Occasionally, he got a real rider and could enjoy the gallops, but, even then, he was alert to any sign that his rider may be getting into trouble. Harriet, just seven years old, was an excellent rider but had never galloped. She had ridden out on several day rides, one of twenty miles, and had finally persuaded her father and myself that she could go to the gallops. She had always ridden Mick, and we were all sure that he would take care of her. In spite of the trust I have in all my ponies I do tend to fuss, so I made Harriet ride behind me and kept Prince at a steady canter. Harriet and Mick were not, however, fooled into thinking that they were galloping and soon got bored with 'plodding' behind us. I heard a whoop, and a bay pony complete with grinning rider shot past. Prince and I raced after them, but Mick was determined to teach his rider to gallop. I was worried about a bad S bend ahead and the effect on Harriet's young legs if taken at speed, but Mick slackened his pace, ignoring the heels drumming at his side, and cantered sedately around the bend and then zoomed off again. Harriet was unaware of his concern for her, but Mick had no intention of letting his rider know who was really in charge. He knew that I would do that at the end of the gallop. Of course, I explained to the young rider why Mick had slowed down, and I noticed that Harriet gave him extra pats on the way home. Eventually she graduated from Mick's careful and loving supervision and rode Folly, who was as green as Harriet once was. The fact that Harriet rode her with sensitivity and determination when necessary was a tribute to Mick's ability as a teacher. New pupils soon came along for Mick, and there was no doubt he was waiting for his next trip to the gallops. Like Jim, Mick didn't show his age, and it was easy to forget that he was twenty-two years old.

Mick, of course, joined us all in the move to our new home, Beili Bledw near Llandovery, where he continued to be an excellent trekking and riding school pony. However, a little while later Mick was going to experience one of the most traumatic periods of his life and, inevitably, mine. That story deserves another full chapter on the life of this remarkable little bay pony[26].

Mick

---

[26] The story of Mick's injury is told in Chapter 26.

Chapter 14

Birth of The Lluest Horse and Pony Trust

People often said they couldn't do my job: a job in which they would get too emotional. How could I choose one foal at a sale and leave hundreds of other little foals to their fate? they asked. How did I sleep at night? The answer to that last question was that I didn't sleep, not until physical and mental exhaustion took over. I hated going to sales, I hated seeing so many foals that I couldn't save, and I often wished I could just forget the sales before they wrecked my health completely, as well as my marriage. But then when I was feeling very sorry for myself, I remembered who I should really be feeling sorry for. The foals and their mothers suffer because of human weakness, whether it is greed for a quick profit or the apathy that allows indiscriminate breeding, followed by the excuse I hear constantly: that sales and the slaughter trade are there to clean up the 'rubbish'. I tried to get this point of needless cruelty across through various means, but it was not easy, and I just ended up getting labelled as a cranky female and a troublemaker.

I found the strength to go to the sales for the sake of the ponies. I felt driven to do it, as though I was travelling a road towards something that I had yet to realise. I also found that I could grit my teeth and deal with radio and TV work, although I hated it and felt very awkward on camera because my voice is too high and I'm nothing to look at. I would always be nervous, but would always grab the work eagerly. Even if I only reached one or two people who would then go on to reach another two or three people, then I considered that the interview had 'paid off'. I even allowed journalists to write the standard 'dotty female' bit, and if that was what a producer wanted, then fine, as long as I got the message across.

This chapter is dedicated to all those ponies we cannot save; it is not for the squeamish but is for those who do not themselves have the courage to visit a sale. Please read on, and remember that what you read may upset you, but it is nothing compared to the suffering of the wild ponies, old discarded family favourites, and thousands of foals killed annually. Their eager gentle faces are only a few little souls in the hundreds that form a cavalcade that will always haunt me. And the hundreds are only a few of the many thousands who suffer; all once had the same spark of life.

I never liked sales, wherever they are, and even though some of my best – if most delinquent – ponies were bought at a sale, I still dreaded going. Conditions were very often appalling, with floors slippery and soaked with urine and muck, the unnecessary use of sticks, and the brutality of men who punched and kicked. Like so many before and since, I condemned conditions at the market for the wild ponies, and then I went home, not to pick up a pen and protest, but to get on with my life and try and make my business profitable.

However, fate stepped in. We needed a new saddle, so Pete suggested a visit to the sale and I reluctantly agreed. It was a cold day just after Christmas 1983, and if Pete regrets any one day in his life it will be that day. We were standing near the entrance to the sale, saddle forgotten, watching a group of thin foals who were chased past us. One limped along with a front leg held up. The leg was broken. A welfare officer was on duty and ordered the foal to be removed. I watched in disbelief and anger as he supervised the foal's progress across the sale to a pen out of sight of the crowds. Every step must have been agony for the youngster who was already weakened by malnutrition. The knacker-man arrived an hour later, yet a veterinary surgery was just a few minutes away. As the shot released the foal into the next life, the stench of burning flesh drifted across the sale. Not that everyone was worried; many chomped away on fish and chips. The foal's companions were sold on for meat and faced a long journey to the slaughterhouse. It was too late for all of them. The only one who mourned the death of that particular foal was the owner, with the loss of fifteen or twenty guineas. At least he had the money from the sale of the other foals to console himself.

Pete tried to cheer me up and told me to forget it, but I couldn't rest or sleep and was finally shocked into doing something. I'd always wondered if it was possible to rehabilitate wild ponies but never got

115

round to buying one to find out. Now, looking back on that day which completely changed my life, I realise that I was exactly where I was supposed to be. At first, I had no idea how I was supposed to help the ponies, but I did have friends who made suggestions, so I reluctantly considered founding a charity. I knew that it would change my life and wondered if I had the strength and commitment to give up the rest of my life for this cause. It was tempting to walk away; the previous ten years had been hard, and now finally I had scrabbled into a reasonably secure position. The trekking centre just about supported myself and my family of dogs, cats and ponies. But would it support more ponies, especially if those ponies could not work? More ponies meant more reliance on Trefor's grazing, and more pressure to feed the ponies I rescued. A charity founded on rented land was not ideal, but then these ponies had nothing to look forward to, not even life, and I knew it would be useless to ask for money to set up a sanctuary. I'd just have to start a sanctuary with what I had. I didn't have enough, but I did have time and energy and I cared. I was also naive enough, then, to think that caring would change things, and that once everyone knew what was happening they would all want to do something about it. Of course, they would only know what was going on if I could interest the wider world through the press or the media, and as a small charity run by a 'cranky female' I had little chance of doing that!

Luckily, I did have friends who also couldn't have realised, then, how much being involved would change their lives. Lluest Horse and Pony Trust would not have been founded without long-suffering friends Barbara and Brian, who until then lived a reasonably normal life in a suburban semi – even if the semi was a bit over-populated with daft dogs. Barbara came with me to the sales while I lived in Gloucestershire, and on more than one occasion had lent me her housekeeping after I'd used all the cash I had on the latest scruffy equine nutcase. Barbara and Brian agreed to be trustees, and Barbara also took on the job of secretary and treasurer, and over the next few years my attitude to mundane things like receipts drove her nuts and turned her hair to a distinguished grey. My exploits didn't always amuse her hubby Brian either, who was permanently worried about the health and safety of his car and his wife when they were in my company.

Stella agreed to be Chair of the Trustees. Stella lived in Wolverhampton, but had been visiting the area for years since childhood, and began coming to Lluest to go pony trekking. We were about the same age and got along well together. As she worked in special needs education, she ended up coming down to assist every school holiday, helping and supporting me in many ways. She seemed to have endless patience with the demands I often put upon her, and my faithful Jester loved her. She loved the animals, she could ride, cook, drive and – importantly – muck out my house when we were about to welcome paying guests! Another bonus was that her parents, even in their seventies, would also lend a hand if they were in the area, with her dad Bert, an old country man, mucking out stables and mending things, and her mum Joan sorting the kitchen out and washing up. Luckily, Barbara, Brian and Stella all got on well together, and with my often-bullying presence the hard work of officially creating a new charity began.

A great deal of paperwork and protocol has to be worked through and adhered to when creating a charity, and there had to be a lot of liaising with the Charities Commission. This seemed to be an endless process, when all I wanted to do was rescue ponies and educate whoever would listen to me about the cruelty. But eventually, The Lluest Horse and Pony Trust was formed officially in May 1985, with a registered charity number 516674[27]. Our aim was not only to rescue, but to rehabilitate and then where possible rehome. We wanted to be able to receive horses, ponies and donkeys who were victims of neglect, abuse, cruelty and abandonment, whatever their age, temperament, behaviour or condition. I knew that some of the wild ponies that I wanted to rescue from horse sales would be unhandled, terrified and have health conditions that would need treatment. Some of these might not be able to be rehomed because of their medical condition, and then they would have a home here for life. None of the trustees took any payment for their service, and I, as manager, would not take any income from it. My motto was always going to be *'Every Penny Possible for the Ponies'*. Already rescued were Smokey and Jaws, and they were officially taken over by the Trust; Smokey was a Shetland, with overgrown hooves, hardly able to walk, and Jaws an unwanted foal born to a local mare. I named him Jaws as he used to take anything in his path, including clothes from my washing line. Ironically, however, when he was required to hold something for a magazine photographer, it took

---

[27] With the re-structuring of the charity in later years the registration number was changed to 1150948

117

some persuasion before he held a bucket between those infamous teeth. Following on from Smokey and Jaws came Dancer and Phoenix, whose stories follow.

∪

It was 27 December 1984, and Barb and I spotted a brown colt huddled in the corner of a pen at a local sale. He was undersized, thin and obviously wild, but underneath all the dirt and neglect we could both see a beautiful gentle pony waiting to be found. We were all agreed about 'Phoenix', but I did have my doubts about another pony, a bay mare who looked as if she had totally given up. Her thin backbone pointed an accusing finger at the owner who'd let her starve on an exposed mountain. Her eyes held no promise as Phoenix's had; rather, they showed emptiness and the resignation with which animals greet death. I leant in to try and touch her and, weak as she was, she reacted. I could feel her hatred of me and every other human being, and I realised that getting the pony to trust me enough to eat was not going to be easy. I voiced my doubts to Barb, but she was insistent, and because I used and trusted my intuition it seemed logical to trust hers. While we waited for the mare and Phoenix to come through the ring, we wandered around until the auctioneer's bell rang, and then Barb and I took up our positions by the ring. As usual, the meat men were inside the sale ring, able to bid amongst themselves and poke at all the ponies as they came in. Eventually 'our' mare was chased into the ring. She stumbled along, eyes wild, flanks heaving, not hoping for mercy or for her life. She didn't care and had stopped caring a long time ago. It probably wasn't her first sale, and she had no reason to expect it to change her life for the better. The bidding quickly reached £60. I groaned but kept going. At £64 our rival bidder lost interest, probably because the mare was thin and therefore had little meat on her and the profit would have been minimal. She walked out of the ring to freedom. She was ours, and Barb, myself, Shelley and friend Sarah were laughing and crying and rushed off to take care of the charity's official first rescue pony.

We left the girls to guard our mare in case she was mistakenly loaded into the slaughter lorry. Meanwhile, Phoenix hadn't been numbered, which meant only one thing: he was already sold to a dealer or meat man. So I wandered off to speak to one of them with an ingratiating and I hoped sexy smile in place, and I asked who'd bought him. Shelley posed as my sister and I explained how I'd promised her a Christmas present and she had set her heart on Phoenix. The owner of the colt was eventually found and persuaded to sell for the inflated price of £85. I knew it was too much, but my instincts told me Phoenix was going to be very important to our work, and I just couldn't ignore his eyes.

We moved the mare and Phoenix to a separate pen and waited until the meat men had loaded their ponies. The large lorries backed up to the pens and the horses and ponies milled around looking for an escape. People shouted, swore and hit out with heavy walking sticks. Barb tried to photograph the scene, but as usual she was elbowed out of the way. There were notices (usually ignored) forbidding the excessive use of sticks, but I wondered if management would prefer to ban the cameras, which cannot lie and which show the misery these sales cause. The lorry rocked as its cargo struggled to get a foothold on the metal floor – a floor designed for ease of cleaning not the comfort of the occupants. Big money always had its way; the slaughterer who took the life of so many was just doing his job and can't be blamed for that.

Barb was shaking when she came back to us from her attempt at photography. I knew how she felt and could understand the agony in her face. No one who has any feelings at all can go to the sales and come back unmoved.

'We'd better get these two home,' I said, thinking we'd better go before everyone burst into tears. 'Where's Pete and Brian?'

'Probably still in the pub,' answered Shelley. 'You did want to get them out of the way.' She smiled.

'Well, now I want them back.' I grinned.

Pete was not amused by the fact that eight little legs greeted him from the pen, but Brian was more resigned and seemed to half-expect it. Our lorry had arrived, so without the use of sticks or shouting we quietly walked our 'wild' ponies out to the lorry and their new lives at Lluest. Even the mare managed to walk out. She didn't know or care where she was going, but Phoenix, hoping for the best as youth always does, knew and he led her home. He wasn't afraid as he bounded up the ramp and settled to eat the hay. The lorry floor was bedded deep in straw and our driver was slow and careful.

Back at Lluest, their stable was waiting, with helpers Julie and Yvette to greet them. Phoenix couldn't believe his eyes and fell on the hay and short feed as if he'd been eating it all his life. When he finished the hay, he was prepared to eat his straw bed or the wooden door, and even years later he didn't take the provision of food for granted and was a real gannet. The mare cowered in the corner of the stable. I had seen this before: a pony that had been starved for so long that it was unable to eat, even when offered food. Of course, the mare had one other great problem; she hated us, and we would have to win her trust before we could save her life. We left them for an hour to settle down and had our tea. Brian filled our glasses and we drank to the success of the charity and a long life for our two newest arrivals. When Barb and I were on our own I pointed out that the mare might not live, but Barb had faith and was sure she would. I'd asked Brian how he thought Barb would feel about me calling the mare Dancer, after a beloved dog of Barbara's that had died a few years earlier.

'I think she would like that,' Brian replied.

So Dancer was named. She would have liked to have stood in the stable and eventually die, but Phoenix had other ideas, and he nuzzled her and bullied her into trying to eat. Gradually, she tried wisps of hay, although she was just as likely to try to eat her bed, and so the long process of rehabilitation began. Getting a headcollar onto Phoenix wasn't that difficult because, although nervous, he was prepared to put up with anything to get at his food. And so our work began.

Chapter 15

Rehabilitation of Dancer and Phoenix

P ete and I were not expecting too much trouble with Dancer as she was so weak, but weak or not she hated us and was prepared to fight to the death if necessary. We dodged front feet as she reared and struck forward, and back feet which could kick forwards and sideways as well as backwards. When we finally got the headcollar on, she stood sullenly in her usual corner. Our long-suffering vet arrived soon afterwards to check on the new arrivals.

'Well,' he said, looking at Phoenix. 'He's very poor, but he's eating and should be OK, but I'll worm him and give him a shot of B12 multi-vitamins to buck him up a bit.'

He soon found out that injecting wild ponies could be an interesting occupation. He should have dumped us there and then, but continued to do our vetting with his usual dedication. He never seemed to mind the early-morning calls, the difficult if not impossible patients, and the panicking female who always wanted him to attend on the double. Phoenix reared and plunged, dragging Pete and the vet around the yard, but finally had both his injections and wormer.

Dancer summed up the situation as Mr R and I came back to the stable. She didn't know what we were going to do, but whatever it was she wasn't having it, and with ears flat back she struck out with her front feet, just missing the vet. I hung on to her headcollar while she swirled around and tried to lash out with her back legs. Pete raced over to help, and between us we held her while she had her injection. We spent ten minutes trying to worm her but she was far too angry to allow it. She wasn't just a bit panicky, as Phoenix had been; her violence was calculated and evil and again I realised how much she hated us.

121

'Well, we aren't going to manage this. She's not going to give in and I don't want to make matters worse,' said Mr R.

I agreed.

'Look I'll give you some wormer in powder form,' he suggested.

'No good,' I replied. 'She won't eat short feed.'

He didn't look hopeful, as we both knew that the circle of worms, shrinking stomach, and lack of appetite would soon kill her. I could see that Mr R felt as we did; this little mare should never have been allowed to get into the state she was in. His bill probably didn't even cover the cost of the drugs. Dancer had her first friend – a friend she would hate for the next eighteen months. Her difficultly in distinguishing between friend and foe was something we all had to live with.

'Look, try to quieten her down a bit and I'll come back, but it's not looking good,' he said.

'Well, she's got the energy to fight,' Pete interrupted.

Yes, I thought, she might be OK if she'd fight to live as well.

Pete turned to me as the vet's car disappeared up the drive.

'Come on,' he said. 'Let's worm her and get it over with.'

For someone who hadn't wanted her, he had been good at helping me to look after her. So Pete grabbed her again and hung on while I squirted the wormer in her mouth. Dancer was now very tired and angry, and again I made the mistake of leaving her – or was it a mistake? With any 'normal' pony I would probably have stayed put and the pony would have accepted me and understood that I was doing what I had to, but Dancer was different. She was so stubborn that my instincts warned me again that if I pushed her too far, she would give up and die – if that was the only way she could win her fight for freedom.

'She's beautiful, though,' I said to Pete. 'And you can understand why she's so bad tempered.'

'She's crazy,' Pete replied. 'Be careful of her, and don't go in with her on your own.'

Easier said than done, I thought, as I mostly worked alone. 'Thanks Pete,' I said.

'You be careful,' he replied.

I knew he was thinking that Dancer was mad and Phoenix was almost as bad.

'Mind you don't get kicked,' he warned.

Of course, I didn't take much notice, and I did get kicked, usually two or three times a day. Phoenix wanted to be friendly and was soon taking an active interest in everything that was going on in the yard, but if frightened he would kick without thinking. I had to learn to walk quietly and very slowly, always keeping an eye on Dancer who lashed out without warning or provocation. Gradually, though, she copied Phoenix and began to pick at her short feed and hay. Success, I thought!

However, my optimism came too soon. During the next few weeks I despaired over the buckets of food Dancer refused to go near and the hay she only picked at. I rang Barb to give her news, but I wasn't happy. Phoenix never stopped eating, and he was so greedy for bucket food that he was dangerous to feed as he lashed out to try to reach both buckets. Finally, I gave up guarding Dancer's bucket. She was alive and eating a little hay, so I divided Phoenix's feed in half and put the two buckets side by side. I didn't see Dancer take her first mouthful but noticed Phoenix was crosser than usual as I put his next feed in. He finished first, and part of him wanted to barge in and take Dancer's food. Most ponies would have, as the stronger always dominates the weaker, but Phoenix was special, and he never tried to eat his friend's food over the next few months. By March she was eating as much coarse food as I would give her, and although not enjoying life as Phoenix did, she was beginning to thrive.

Then, because of Phoenix's improving condition, I had to make a decision. He was a colt, and she was a mare not in foal: maybe barren, but I couldn't take the chance. I had to separate them. Dancer sulked and went off her food and was evil towards all the other companions I offered her. I tried to introduce Katy, an elderly coloured mare, but she was ignored, and Della the palomino, who had been ill, was received with horror. So Dancer moped on her own. She was still unreliable, and although she was willing to come when called for her food, she reacted angrily if I touched her. Any attempt to train her was met with a hunger strike, particularly if I won. She hated me and hated everyone else, both equine and human. She had tolerated Phoenix, but then no one ever disliked him. Sometimes she let herself go to give a plaintive whinny for her 'friend', but to a pony who had been hurt so much there couldn't have been any further agony. Underneath her grumpy 'I hate you' exterior I was sure there was an honest kind little mare who could give love. Some days I thought I had made progress with her, and then, for no reason that I could understand, a kick would send me flying across the stable. I was covered in bruises and beginning to wonder why I bothered.

Then one spring morning she turned on me as I tried to retrieve her empty feed bucket. One hoof caught me in the stomach, and as I grovelled in the straw again, thinking of possible failure, I realized that I couldn't get up. I covered my head and rolled into a ball as best I could. After a few moments, I also realized that Dancer had returned to her hay and not attacked as I had expected. I was at her mercy. If she had wanted to, she could have killed me. Somewhere in her crazy mind there was a developed reaction that had kept her alive and as far away from mankind as she could get. She wasn't going to wait until she was hurt before she attacked; that wasn't how you survived the misery of a market. All her 'mad' attacks were just a reaction (over which she maybe had little conscious control) to half-remembered threats. No matter how often I reassured her and how hard I tried to love her, she couldn't forget her early life. Mankind had just taken too much from our little mare.

'Right, you stubborn old bag,' I gasped as soon as I could speak. 'It's war, and I'm twice as bloody-minded as you.' Dancer smirked as I lay in the straw. But that night, when I arrived in her stable with blankets and hot water bottle, she had hysterics. I lay down, wondering if I'd survive and if I was right that she wouldn't attack me if I stayed on the floor. The next morning, I was fine except for being stiff, cold and very tired. I managed to go and muck out quickly and then returned to Dancer's stable. She was very cross. Why hadn't she been let out? I knelt in front of her before she had a chance to box my ears and wondered which one of us was craziest. She was undecided, but as I leant forward she stretched her head down to me – not in a gesture of friendship, but as if to say, 'Well, I suppose I'll have to live with the silly cow'. Pleased even with such a small step forward, I rewarded her by letting her have her own way in going out.

That evening she accepted my presence in the stable, and the next evening something woke me. Luckily, I'm not afraid of rats – after all, it could have been a rat that brushed my face. I managed to wait quietly and not move quickly in panic. Then I realized that the 'rat' was a nose: an enquiring nose that belonged to Dancer. I was too cold and sleepy to be elated; there had been too many false starts in our relationship and this was probably another. Perhaps she'd run out of food. Wearily, I crawled to the door and got up to switch the light on. Her hay net was nearly full, and caught out by the sudden light she revealed an almost benign expression. As I walked back towards her, she gave her first

124

wicker to a human and then warned me to keep clear. 'Bloody mare,' I muttered and took myself into the house where a normal bed and electric blanket awaited.

Over the next few weeks, I spent a lot of time grovelling around her feet, and gradually she allowed me to touch and groom her. Dancer still had her off days, and if she was in a mood then I didn't bother to work with her. It wasn't worth the effort, because if it came to an argument I had to win, and as that could take me all day I didn't have the time. One of the reasons I didn't have the time was that we saw the return of Smokey the Shetland pony. He had first come to us with neglected hooves and laminitis, and I had made him as well as I could and then returned him to his owners with instructions for his wellbeing. But he had been returned to me, and now he could barely walk; his acute laminitis had progressed so far that putting him to sleep was a real possibility. Getting him fit would take years, but he was so loving it was worth the effort. I put Dancer into the stable next to him as he needed company for the long hours of fasting that lay ahead of him.

Dancer tried to ignore the black nose that strained to reach over the wall to introduce itself. She was still intrinsically an unhappy pony, though she was now quite happy to let me groom her. Perhaps she gained confidence from watching the patience that Smokey showed as he endured painful foot trimming and injections. Until then she had only seen humans as beings to be feared and distrusted. Maybe she was able to understand that I was helping the pony to get better. Most likely, I felt that it was the telepathy that binds a herd of horses together that was at work between Smokey and Dancer. Gradually, she spent more time close to the wall and occasionally leant over to Smokey. Two months later he joined her in our rough paddock. They sniffed each other. Dancer threatened, but the Shetland temperament took over. She could be as miserable as she liked, but he was going to try to eat the whole field in the next fifteen minutes. She then understood that Smokey was no threat, so she just joined him. They spent all of that summer together. Neither could go out to a good field, because Dancer could not digest normal grass, as her stomach just wasn't used to it, and any rich grass would have reignited Smokey's laminitis, which by then was back under control. So our rough paddock was ideal.

Summers at Lluest were always chaotic. As yet another minibus pulled up, I could see Dancer preparing to run and hide. Smokey was already in the stable to do his bit for the charity. One of the children in the group was very disturbed; his early life had been worse than Dancer's. I warned the teachers to keep the children away from her and closed the gate. We took the children for a ride which is best described as organized chaos. All of the ponies were brilliant, as usual, but I hadn't expected Dancer to rise to the occasion too!

After the ride the kids played football. Unnoticed by the adults, Dancer had walked up to the gate. The child that had attracted her was fair-haired and looked angelic, but, as I already knew from working with Dancer (now a pretty bay mare), looks can be deceptive. She stood at the gate. Most of her instincts warned her to run, but the vulnerability of the little boy held her. Maybe she was trying to work out why humans harmed their own young as well as the young foals of her herd. Perhaps the presence of another soul in torment worried her. Or was she offering comfort and reassurance? Like Dancer, I was torn between responses. The practical side imagined the loss of life for the child and a livelihood for me. The emotional side – the instinct I rely on – told me to introduce them, so that at last our little mare could prove that she was ready to love. I walked over slowly and opened the gate, while Julie, my helper, scurried off for a bucket of food in case a distraction was needed. Dancer didn't come to me; she stretched out to the boy and allowed him to stroke her. The other children stood around quietly and gradually moved forward. Julie arrived with the food, and Dancer ate from a stranger's hand. The children were too young to understand what had happened, but Julie and I were too choked to explain. For the first time I knew for certain that Barb had been right: Dancer was a very special pony, and one day when she had forgotten all of the pain, she would be one of our best ponies. She finished her food, nosed the little boy gently and then walked back to graze. I often wondered if those five minutes in a field with a mad bay mare had transformed the child's life as it had Dancer's.

We allowed her more visitors, and her behaviour improved as her trust in humans grew. Although still wary of all adults, she liked small children and never pulled an evil face at any of them, even if they were noisy or made sudden movements. She seemed to realize that they were no threat; Smokey had taught her that, but one of us was always on hand in case she forgot her manners.

By the autumn we trusted her with any small child, and as she often lurked while we saddled Smokey, I decided to try her with a saddle. She had no reason to fear it because it didn't hurt or frighten her, and as her friend was always close she accepted being saddled after only two lessons. I always rewarded her with a handful of food at the end of each lesson, and if she started to get bored during the lesson she would smack her lips, demanding her reward and an end to her 'work'. I didn't always give in to her, but the first time she did it I was so amused that I gave her a tit-bit straight away. She hated people laughing, so I had to keep my amusement to myself. She was still touchy about her head, particularly on the side where her previous owner had attached an ear tag. I spent at least ten minutes of her training every day just stroking her forehead. She stamped her feet, pulled faces and would rear if I tried to touch her ears. She wasn't the kind of pony that you cuddled; she would allow you to do what was necessary and no more. So I decided on a sensible approach. I made sure that she could see Smokey and the other ponies bridled without fuss and left a bridle hanging in her stable to get her used to the smell of it. I knew that I wouldn't get the whole bridle on in one go, so I took off the cheek pieces, bit and reins and approached her with only the headpiece and brow-band[28]. She sniffed at them suspiciously, but brightened when I offered her a handful of feed. So far, so good. I then took a firm hold of her headcollar and tried to put the headpiece behind her ears. She reared and lunged away from me. I held on to the end of the rope and tempted her back towards me with some more feed. I tried again and managed to lay the headpiece further down her cheek. Gradually, I inched it up towards her ears and very gently put her undamaged ear in its right place. I didn't want to walk in front of her to reach her 'bad' ear, as that always made her rear, so I leant over, and much to my surprise she let me put that into place too. I rewarded her with feed again and gently attached both cheek pieces. I wondered whether to stop or to attach the bit onto one side and then try to get it into her mouth. I didn't want a bit banging about if she reared and I had to let go, but I knew now that I might be able to bridle her normally. She was standing quietly, so I showed her the bit. Attaching it to the right side was easier than I thought, but as soon as I

---

[28] A horse's bridle consists of a headpiece running behind the ears with a throat lash underneath, a browband, a cheek piece each side, and a noseband. The bit is attached to the check pieces and the reins.

127

tried to open her mouth she reared and struck out in temper. Luckily, she somehow reared into the bit; it was in her mouth and I had hold of it and her. She ran backwards into the wall and then leapt forwards, but I hung on and attached the other cheek piece to the bit. Dancer twisted, shaking her head. I patted her and prepared for another pitched battle. Smokey whinnied to her. I talked to her quietly and set about her normal grooming lesson. 'Foot' I said, and she obliged, almost knocking me over. Gradually, she calmed down. The bridle wasn't so bad, nothing terrible had happened, and she heard Julie mixing her feed. I took her bridle off the normal way and immediately rewarded her with 5lbs of coarse mix[29].

Every day for the next week I had a fight on my hands. Once she had realized that the leather work, even in pieces, meant that the thing appeared in her mouth, she refused to allow them near her. Each time I 'won' and Dancer was bridled, she then was rewarded. After another two weeks I could bridle her without any trouble, as long as I undid one of the cheek pieces as well as the throat lash. I led Dancer around wearing her tack. She was ready to back, but I didn't dare risk it. I was far too heavy, as were the helpers. She loved children, but I wondered if she would panic if one sat on her. I thought about it for a few days. She had been difficult about her bridle because it meant having her ear and mouth touched, which had caused her pain in the past. She had never minded the saddle, and unlike most 'wild' ponies she wasn't afraid of the cars in our yard, as she had been following Smokey, who wasn't afraid of anything, when she saw her first car. Smokey looked forward to his little riders, and all the other ponies always left the yard cheerfully and took care of their riders. Dancer's first introduction to riding had been by leaning over the fence watching the gang earn a living. It hadn't worried them, so maybe it wouldn't worry her. Choosing her rider was easy; the child had to be seven or eight at most and as light as possible. She also had to be known to Dancer and reasonably sensible. Young Jenny fitted all of those criteria, but at that point her riding left a lot to be desired. However, she was a trier and eventually would be an excellent rider. I waited for a calm day, as like most ponies Dancer hated the wind and rain. After Jenny's normal lesson I casually asked her if she would like to help me back a pony. I was pleased with her

---

[29] Coarse mix is a type of prepared feed for horses, with ingredients typically including cooked flaked cereals and vitamins.

enthusiastic response. We tacked Dancer up and led her out into the yard. Smokey seemed to sense that it was Dancer's big day and waited quietly by his stable. Jenny walked over to Dancer, who greeted her, ears pricked.

'OK, Julie,' I said. 'Lift Jenny on, but hold on to her and lift her off again if Dancer objects.'

I held on to Dancer's neck and stroked her. As Jenny was lowered into the saddle, I used the 'stand' command. Dancer's ears flicked back and then forward again. Jenny was sitting on the saddle and Dancer was relaxed and happy and I think a little proud. Smokey looked on, and his presence reassured Dancer. I warned Jenny to keep still and hold on tightly to the front of the saddle; we were going to try a walk-on.

'Walk on, Dancer,' I whispered.

She moved forward at a steady walk – not in fits and starts. We had done it.

'OK, stand, and dismount please, Jenny,' I said.

If it had been any other pony, we would have cuddled her, but this was Dancer and she was one in a million. Andrea, Jenny's friend, looked on. She was a little heavier than Jenny, and maybe it would be pushing our luck to let her try Dancer. But Dancer stood by me as quiet as any trekking pony, so Andrea was hatted, introduced and lifted on. I led Dancer across the yard; her step was light and confident. Our crazy little mare had come good!

Andrea dismounted. We praised Dancer and crowded around. She accepted our praise and enjoyed the fuss. Smokey slipped quietly out of the yard, his job done – none of us noticed him go, we were too busy making a fuss of his friend.

Dancer's story wouldn't end there. I hoped she would learn to work on long reins and the lunge. She trusted me. We were friends at last and I had so many plans.

Chapter 16
Rhona

W hen Stella handed me my Christmas present I almost burst into tears. The framed photo of Jim, which has now sat on my mantelpiece for many years, renewed all the grief I thought I had forgotten. Jim had been dead for six months, and as long as I didn't think about him or look at his picture I could cope. This picture reminded me of death and of a year I would prefer to forget, but I cherished it. Gradually I got used to his wise old head confronting me, and I often found myself looking at him and even talking to him.

I hadn't really ridden much since Jim died, and I was far too preoccupied to notice that I wasn't the only one who missed a calming influence. Prince's behaviour deteriorated, and after the accident[30], he became almost unrideable. He had lost confidence in me, and there was no other pony that he respected or trusted.

Prince wasn't alone in lacking responsible leadership. Merlin and Della, both youngsters, began to misbehave, and even an old hand like Comet took to racing off at the slightest provocation. You need good nerves in my business, and I had definitely lost mine. Now that Jim was gone, I had to put a nervous or difficult child on Pepper. Now, Pepper means well, but unfortunately he is daft enough to do what any idiot trekker tells him and is easily confused. Kate, although old, could be scatty, especially on windy days and on those heart-stopping occasions when the ride comes to a grinding halt because a pig innocently pushes his snout through the hedge.[31] Now there was no Jim to sigh and march

---

[30] The accident involving the dog that had escaped, causing the ponies to panic, was described in Chapter 10.

[31] Horses have a natural instinct to distrust and fear pigs.

to the front to show the youngest and, no doubt to him, inferior nags the way.

I didn't want to replace Jim, but then Sue shoved a piece of paper into my hand.

'It's a 14.2hh mare for £150,' she said, and grinned. I hesitated for about three seconds and then rushed into the house to telephone Sue's friend Clare. The mare sounded just right.

'She's bomb proof,' Clare assured me. 'She's a first-class trekking pony, but will go if you can ride.'

I'd heard that before and resisted temptation to ask if she had four legs that were in working order.

'Where is she?' I asked.

'Oh, on the Llanwyni mountain,' Clare replied.

'Where?' I queried. 'Look, I haven't got a car.'

'I'll drive you,' volunteered a very eager voice – too eager, I thought.

So we arranged to meet in two days' time. Lluest was an extremely difficult place to find, as many discovered, so I arranged to meet Clare and hubby Fred at Rhos-yr-Hafod pub, which seemed miles away as I struggled along, on my feet for once, through a windy, cold November morning. I hardly noticed the silver car draw up as I huddled on the seat outside the pub. The driver smiled and waved and I leapt up and ran over.

'Hello. I'm Clare,' the driver said.

'Oh, good,' I replied, shivering. Clare was a small grey-haired woman who said she was about fifty but seemed about my age. We were soon engaged in horsey chatter. I liked Clare and realised that for once I was dealing with an honest person. I wasn't sure how to deal with this rare phenomenon. Clare was only selling Rhona because she was moving with her hubby Fred to a new job. She had very sensibly decided that unless Rhona could be found a new home she should be put to sleep. I agreed; I've seen too many ponies, once well-loved and useful creatures, end their days doing the rounds of badly run auctions.

'She's not pretty,' Clare warned as we drove up to the club that her husband managed. 'Come and meet Fred and I'll show you some pictures.' Inside the club I could hear a dog barking. It sounded large.

'That's Heidi,' Clare yelled above the barking. 'Sadly, she has to go too. Hang on, and I'll shut her in.'

'It's OK,' I replied, 'I like dogs.'

'Alsatians?' queried Clare.

I grinned, confident that no dog would bite me. Heidi nearly did. As soon as she had dragged Heidi to a safer spot, Clare introduced me to Fred. I liked him, too. They showed me the tack, and I bought two saddles. Then they showed me a picture of Rhona. I agreed that she was no beauty and was extremely relieved when Fred suggested we should go to see her. She can't be as ugly as her picture, I thought, remembering the upright mane and varied strawberry roan appaloosa blotches. Then I remembered a certain other little pony, and hoped that he would understand why I needed another one like him.

The journey to Llanwyni across the mountain brought back memories of our search for a home and the wet windy March days that blew us towards Lluest. For a while I had feared that Lluest had a jinx, but today on a windswept yellowed mountain I knew better. Life was difficult, but nothing could last for ever, and if I wasted my life grieving for Jim and Herbie I would accomplish nothing. Jim and Herbie did not live to roam the forty acre farm we were soon to buy, but Prince would, and maybe by helping Rhona I would bring a natural end to grief. Lluest was meant to be a happy place, a haven for the weary traveller, and was failing because I had lost confidence in myself and my aims.

The trekking centre where Rhona was living made me shiver. It was sandwiched between a crevice in the rock escarpment and approached across a bleak mountain. The owners were very friendly and the man walked with me to catch Rhona. Her picture had certainly told the true story, and she was also unwilling to be caught!

'She sometimes does this,' conceded my breathless host. Eventually, Rhona gave in and allowed him to slip a halter on. We led her back to the yard. She stood placidly while we groomed her and put on her tack. At first Clare tried to put the wrong bridle on Rhona, who merely sighed and hoped that she would eventually get it right. Although it was freezing cold, I decided that it might be a good idea to discard my long flapping coat which was guaranteed to upset most ponies.

'Keep your coat on,' Clare shouted as she rushed back with Rhona's bridle. 'She's not scared of anything.' As if to illustrate the point, two RAF jets screamed out of nowhere just as I was mounting. Rhona ignored them, but I couldn't help hoping for an anti-aircraft gun for Christmas.

'You won't miss those when you go, will you Clare?' I said.

Clare smiled. 'They are noisy, aren't they?'

I decided that I had better keep my pacifist views to myself and asked Rhona to 'walk on'. She ambled out of the yard placidly and, much to my surprise, didn't try to rejoin her companions. I gave her every opportunity to nap, riding her on a loose rein and giving very vague aids, but she behaved beautifully. It was too cold to ride for long so I took her back to her friends. Clare, Fred and I celebrated her change of ownership with a cup of tea. I knew that I would never forget Jim, but at least now the stables had a new 'boss'.

Rhona was delivered to Rhos-yr-Hafod pub three days later at four in the afternoon – her driver was late, as many horsey people often are. I tried not to show how cross I was as Clare tacked Rhona up, then we set off at a brisk trot. It was already dusk, and we had a long way to go, mostly along an unlit main road.

I hope we don't meet a police car, I thought. Rhona didn't have shoes on, so I worried about her feet. I suppose that it would have been more sensible to worry about getting squashed, which was a distinct possibility as large lorries thundered past and honked their protest at my unlit horse. Rhona trotted on ignoring all distractions, although she did manage a disgruntled huff when an unlit tractor suddenly reversed out in front of us. The tractor driver shouted at me in Welsh, obviously thinking that I was daft enough to be a local. We exchanged words of abuse while Rhona stood placidly still and waited for calm, then she walked on to deliver us both safely to Lluest, her new home and new friends.

The Rhona who arrived at Lluest was a different horse in looks from the ones all our trekkers knew and loved. But she didn't mind the jokes and laughter; she must have heard them all her life, She was an honest mare in her later years, prone to girth galls[32], and no longer wanted *again.* She had been a trekking horse, bred two foals and worked hard as long as the seasons lasted, but then it was off to a loan home or maybe to a sale, where thankfully her gentle nature – and more likely her weight-carrying ability – kept the meat men at bay. She was just what I wanted: large, sensible and a worker.

She had only been with me a few months when the school party came the following spring. Her rider was an idiot whose idea of riding was admiring the scenery and talking to her friend on Pepper. Luckily,

---

[32] Girth galls are skin sores that develop due to friction between the girth (a band around the body of the horse used to fasten the saddle in place) and the body.

Rhona was too well mannered to object, and she ignored the odd tug on the reins and the bridle pulled carelessly over her ears. When the party left, the children shed a few tears. Much to our surprise, Stella and I did too, not because we were going to miss the children but because Rhona was crying too. She stood in the corridor of the main stables, nose pressed to the window, whickering – or was she crying? The noise she made resembled a human cry and the emotion was the same. She feared for her future, knowing that horses didn't last and that once the children left she would be off again. She was sick of a life lived in transit, her gentleness so little valued. Stella and I cuddled her, crying too because Rhona still didn't trust us.

That summer we took her to a show. She loaded perfectly but was thoroughly upset at the show, refusing to jump or enjoy any part of it. She shot into the box to come home, and the following days she worked hard with a collection of beginners. I understood then her behaviour that day; she had thought she was going to another home and was annoyed.

It had been an awful summer, and the only consolation had been the founding of the Lluest Horse and Pony Trust. Another ray of sunshine was when Jester gave birth to a long-awaited and much-wanted litter of puppies. I was to keep Gemma, and Bracken was set aside for Barb.

The following year, on a cold rainy October day, I was sitting in the front room writing the first charity newsletter – at least, trying to write it, but looking at my efforts I wondered what Barb, our long-suffering secretary, would make of it. My spidery writing hadn't been helped by the activities of Gemma, who had been chasing my feet and was now busily chewing my writing arm, putting her wet smelly paws all over the paper and then chewing at the pen. Luckily, Barb's Bracken was just as uncivilised, so hopefully our secretary wouldn't notice the smell.

With all these interruptions my mind started to wander. As usual, my radio was blaring Radio 1, and I had to laugh as I listened to the strains of 'There must be an Angel' by Madonna. This was because it reminded me of the last time I had done something to an 'angel' tune. That one had been by Eurythmics, and the lyrics hadn't really suited either the rider or that pony who rode into Aberystwyth one hot sunny morning...

That particular pony was Rhona, and by then she had relaxed and settled. She had become Carol's favourite pony, and in spite of comments about Rhona's lack of poise and beauty she was also one of mine. When I saw the poster in Aberystwyth advertising Janice Long[33] on the Radio 1 Roadshow I decided to go along and try and get some publicity for the charity. I was never in doubt who I would take. Prince had no patience and was terrified of crowds, heavy traffic and noise. Sam was too young, if better looking, but safe old Rhona was just right.

So my helpers, Carol and Julie, had to cope with getting a nervous Ginny organised and making Rhona look beautiful – a task that Carol attacked with determination but with a definite lack of success!

'Well, Rhona,' I said as I mounted, 'it's a twenty-four-mile round trip, lots of noise and you've got to carry three saddle bags as well as me.' Rhona burped!

We left at seven in the morning and arrived in Aberystwyth by just about eleven. I was amused at the open mouths that followed our progress through the centre of Aberystwyth. We were half a mile away and could hear the Roadshow already. A shudder of apprehension went down my back. Rhona trotted briskly, weaving in and out of parked cars and holidaymakers. We slowed to a walk and she marched happily past the pier and fruit machines. If Rhona was concerned she didn't show it, merely stopping to express her feeling about gambling with a small deposit on the road outside!

'Quite right, old girl. They should give the money to our charity – we'd like it, wouldn't we?' I murmured.

I soon realised that I had no chance of riding Rhona through the crowd, so I 'parked' her at the back and left her in charge of a kind gentleman. She was soon surrounded by well-wishers who were filling the tin on our saddle. I eventually found a lady called Lyn who suggested I come back in half an hour, so Rhona and I spent our time making friends and giving out leaflets about the charity. When the half hour had passed, I remounted and rode Rhona past the crowd and went round to the back of the Roadshow caravan.

The producer was very kind. Yes, they would like me to go on stage, but they wanted me to ride around the front of the stage, in front of the speakers, and ride past Janice Long. It was a small space, and what would happen in Rhona panicked?

'Can you do it?' he asked, taking me around to the front of the stage.

'Yes, of course,' I replied confidently and hopefully hiding my doubts.

---

[33] Janice Long was well-known as a radio presenter and Top of the Pops host

135

The charity needed publicity, and I put my trust as always in Rhona. So I mounted and waited for the signal. Their choice of music alarmed and amused me. I couldn't believe it when the producer signalled me to go on during an ear-splitting harmonica solo.

'Oh hell,' I muttered. 'Come on, Rhona.' We marched on, heads up and with my feet missing the speaker by inches. Rhona wasn't happy, but she tolerated the noise as if she knew we were on an important mission to promote the charity and help other ponies. Janice Long said her bit, and Rhona and I retreated thankfully behind the stage.

'Hold the horse,' the producer yelled. A large gentleman from the Roadshow looked doubtful.

'Where's the horse gone?' I heard Janice Long shout, probably thinking that Rhona had run off. Then a telecom engineer stepped forward and held Rhona while I raced up the steps.

I had never been on a stage before and I nearly froze as I saw all those people looking at me. Janice, probably sensing my near panic, was kind but could not quite get to grips with the pronunciation of my surname – Hajdukiewicz. Then someone shoved a large microphone nearly into my mouth and the noise faded. Help, I thought. I could see why everyone wore headphones; as I spoke the sound blared from the speakers. It was noisy and confusing and I had the feeling that the crowd were as bemused by the eccentric female in jodhpurs as I was by them.

'Great,' they all said at the end of the interview. We all knew it wasn't, but at least it was over. I asked Janice to come and meet Rhona, which she did, giving a donation on the way, slipped into my hand as we went off stage. She didn't know then, and neither did I, but that donation would help us save not one but two lives the next day[34]. Rhona lifted her tail again as I mounted, and I hoped that none of the Radio 1 people who had been so kind to me would step in it.

Riding home, I thought Rhona was tired as the sun reflected off the pavements and houses, but once in the country her step lightened. She was never a comfortable pony to ride, but she was floating over the ground at an alarming rate. We were nearly home when we met the afternoon ride. They didn't need to ask if we'd succeeded as I was grinning from ear to ear and Rhona pranced and danced, knowing she was the heroine of the day. We left them to enjoy their ride and trotted for home.

---

[34] Copper and Barley, whose story follows in Chapter 17.

Yes, Rhona had become relaxed and secure, but it took her a move to Beili Bedw (our new home) and another year before she allowed herself the odd naughtiness – but only if her rider really deserved it. She became an unlikely TV star when S4C came to film our work. There was a background shot of me grooming her while our vet spoke in Welsh. She tried her best to appear well bred whilst looking like an honest gentle plodder of doubtful parentage.

We all relied on good old Rhona who ended up with the nervous or useless riders because she could be relied upon to look after them. She was at least twenty-five but showed no sign of old age until the autumn of 1987. I had flu and knew the only place I should have been was in bed, but a booking for a man and his daughter worth £7, which I desperately needed, meant that I dragged myself onto a horse. I decided to ride Rhona as she could be trusted to plod along while I coughed and spluttered and tried to remain upright.

The ride was almost over when I noticed a sheep on a bank above us. As it leapt away, startled by our approach, Rhona wheeled around and tried to run back down the steep hill. I had no chance and landed hard in the road. My back protector took some of the impact but I was bruised and angry. I remounted with difficulty and urged Rhona on. She hesitated, so I used my crop and used it hard. She trotted forward. I was in a very bad mood. Rhona didn't do things like that – Rhona knew better. She was actually trying to cope with old age and the gradual loss of sight in her left eye. I have been suitably ashamed of my temper that day; I should have realised that the old girl didn't have it in her to dump a rider without cause.

She slowed up on hills, so we gave her lighter riders and even small children in the school. By spring of 1988 she looked like an old lady, although still in excellent condition and, if the mood took her, still game for a good gallop. One morning, Stella was exercising her when she shied and pulled up. She was obviously in a great deal of pain. Stella leapt off and I rushed over to check Rhona. The vet arrived in due course, and confirmed that she had pulled a muscle and ordered a few days' rest.

The weather was horrible. It rained and rained until we were unusually flooded, and we found Rhona and her friends standing knee-deep in water. We frantically bailed out the stables and tried to divert the water that the local council so helpfully had channelled off the road onto our land. Luckily, no one was any the worse for their soaking, and four friends and I set to work to dig out all the wet bedding and replace it.

I had decided not to use Rhona again, feeling that she was finally 'past it'. However, Rhona had other ideas and was thoroughly fed up with the idle life, so we arrived at a compromise. We used her if she seemed fit enough, but if in doubt she stayed at home. Rhona, game as ever, enjoyed her rides and the occasional gallop. She was allowed one gallop and then settled down to a steady trot. Even this proved too much for Rhona. It wasn't just that she was a willing horse; perhaps somewhere in her mind there lurked the suspicion that failure to work meant another home, as it had all her life.

Then a local lad rode her on a lesson. He was very good with ponies, an excellent groom and stable worker, and generally an asset to the yard. Unfortunately, though, his excellent qualities vanished when he actually got on a horse. Much as he tried, riding just wasn't going to be his forte. Rhona had him sussed in seconds and ignored his carefully correct aids. In fact, she ignored him through his half-hour lesson, finally putting in a few paces of trot to try and unseat him. I then suggested that he dismount before he fell off. Rhona smirked and accepted the pats as she swaggered back to the stable. She had finally found the confidence to say 'NO'. She knew, as I did, that the kind well-meaning lad would never be a rider. She liked him, but for whatever reason saw no point in carrying him around.

I watched her trotting back down the field to her friends. Her back legs were just a little stiff but she carried herself well. She enjoyed light work, particularly with any rider who was nervy.

We brought her out again for a special needs group. Her rider was a girl of about eight stone who lashed out at people but not at Rhona, who nuzzled her. She was lifted on, and a helper walked beside her as we led Rhona forward. At first, she refused to move. Her rider was sitting properly and secure, but Rhona understood what we couldn't. The girl's grunts and strange noises made no sense to us. We can only listen with our ears, not our hearts, but old Rhona understood and refused to move forward until her charge was less nervous. Our helpers understood too, and let a very heavy angel have her way as she plodded forward with her ears pricked. I realised that angels come in all shapes and sizes, and I was thankful for a spotty one called Rhona.

Chapter 17

Copper, Barley and Ben

T he day after the Radio 1 Roadshow, Julie, her Mum and I headed off to the sale. I was clutching the donation given by Janice Long, together with another donation of £40 saved in loose change from Melanie, Jane and Ruth, the three faithful supporters from Pates Grammar School in Cheltenham. We hadn't been at the sale long when Julie and I spotted a tiny bay colt, and I knew that this could be 'the one'. Julie guarded him while I found his owner. I bought 'Copper' for cash outside the ring, and then the fun started. He had not been handled or halter-broken and he was thoroughly upset by the fear and confusion of the sale. Julie went to buy a headcollar and carrots while I talked gently to our newfound friend – our fifth rescue. I was determined that Copper was coming home with us instead of with the meat men. A crowd was gathering, no doubt wondering how I would cope with this wild and frightened little colt. Some had already made a donation to the Trust, some were curious but several were hostile. One large meat man hovered, sensing a defenceless and possibly foolish female, then turned away as he recognised me. Julie returned, and I walked quietly towards Copper with the headcollar, but he shot off around the pen. I heard the gate to the pen clang and saw a man, complete with stick, stomping towards me.

'I can do it for you in two minutes,' he said.

'No, I can manage. Will you get out now, please,' I answered firmly.

He shrugged, ignoring the poisonous glares he was getting from Julie and me. I turned back towards Copper and cleared my mind of everything except my love for the little pony and his future happy life at Lluest. I advanced to his shoulder, dropped the head collar over his neck, did it up, then inched the noseband across his nose and did that up too. Copper was headcollared in under two minutes, and was calm and happy. As I turned towards the man and gave him a triumphant glare, I realised that a lot of people had been watching me. I cannot explain how I can reach out to a pony; perhaps it's telepathy, or luck, or more likely I think that sometimes when you most need help, you get it. How or where from I don't know, but help is often there when most needed, and it comes to Lluest. It comes from all those who care so passionately about our work. Perhaps Copper was aware of the girls from Cheltenham.

I believe in fate, and whenever I trust my instincts, things happen that I cannot explain. But these things always work out for the best, as I was to find only a short while after buying Copper. I'd gone to the Roadshow on impulse, and now I was walking down a deserted sale corridor just looking around. I knew why when I saw a tiny palomino colt being cuddled by a child.

'Is he yours' I asked.

'No,' she replied, scuttling off before I could find out more.

Perhaps she was afraid that I would reprimand her for messing with the foal. I smiled, remembering another small child crying into a pony's mane at a sale because it had been sold for meat. I knew myself as a woman, who often felt like crying late at night after a day at the sale. This small colt was enough to make anyone cry. He was dirty and thin, but so friendly and trusting. Sensing that I was interested in buying him, a couple who had befriended us at the sale found the owners. They had bought him from a woman who was overstocked. They were hoping to keep him but, as so often happens, later realised that they didn't have room or time.

'He's a lovely chap,' the man explained. 'Shame to kill him,' he continued. I agreed, through gritted teeth.

'How much do you want? Look, I've got £40. That's for the colt and a lift home,' I said.

'OK' he said.

I was amazed.

'Trouble is, he'll have to go through the ring,' he said.

I groaned. If *I* started bidding, the meat men might well push the price way over our £40 limit.

'Don't worry, you stay there. Don't bid. I'll go and put a silly reserve on him and withdraw him from sale.' The colt came out at £52, but thankfully I wasn't asked to make up the difference.

I was weak at the knees as I cuddled this friendly young colt which I had already named 'Barley'. Julie and her Mum were over the moon, and surprised to be going home with the *two* colts. It was like walking on air after a lot of champagne. We had saved their lives and they knew it, and the bond between us developed quickly. I could only silently thank everyone who gave us their time, money and love and made it all possible.

However, there always seemed to be at least one foal who lived in my memory after the sale, sometimes for weeks. The foal that day was just another scruffy brown colt, probably born somewhere on the marshes of the Gower coast. He stood in a pen at the sale with eight other foals and yearlings. The little colt was one of thousands born to a collection of scruffy mares; foals that had only one use – the horse-meat trade.

I didn't notice him again until he was standing in the holding pen behind the sale ring. The entrance to the ring is through a cattle crush which rattles and shakes as the foals are driven into it. As it was already occupied by another foal, the little brown colt hesitated and then tried to climb over the pen rails to get back to his companions. A stick and fist collided with his head and sent him reeling. Then rough uncaring hands threw him into the crush as the other foal was thrown into the ring and the colt stood quietly waiting his turn. The previous occupant was sold for meat as most, if not all, these ponies are. A man banged the crush gates open and a kick propelled the colt into the ring.

Then I noticed a young child, a little girl, leaning into the ring. The colt skidded to a halt in front of her. I waited, dreading the inevitable screams of an injured child, but I should have known better. The foal reached out an enquiring gentle nose and sniffed her hand. I turned away, swallowing hard, trying not to cry at the brutality of a trade that kills a foal with so much potential. The little girl was pulled back, a stick waved and the foal was swiftly the property of a meat man.

By the time I got back to Lluest I was shaking with rage at the unfairness of life because I did not have the finances to save the colt, followed by the inevitable depression as his gentleness haunted me. By now he would be crammed into a lorry racing towards the slaughterhouse, struggling to keep his feet with several dozen other foals.

All of these reminisces suddenly disappeared as I woke from my daydream with a start. The puppies had been playing, and the carpet was littered with chewed discarded papers and penguin wrappers. I began to pick up the pieces that had kept them amused whilst I had daydreamed, when I came across a letter that I had received that morning from Ruth, one of the Cheltenham girls. I had extracted the cheque enclosed and left the letter to read later. But one paragraph stood out.

'Oh, Ginny, I am so relieved that you bought that colt. I'm sure Melanie, Jane and I will work something out to help towards its keep. Those photos of the horse sale have really made me realise things I didn't realise before.'

It was so typical of those three girls, who originally had come to stay at Lluest with their school party and stayed closely in touch and given support. They had worked hard and donated their money to our cause, ridden on the sponsored ride, helping to promote Lluest as well as studying hard for their 'O' levels, but they still found time to care about the fate of a tiny foal.

Ben was the seventh pony to be rescued by the charity. I spotted him standing quietly behind his mother at a sale. His mother was sold for meat despite being in foal again. Her gentleness deserved better. Like her son she was a plain dun with an ugly head, but as she stood trembling on the weighbridge accepting the punches and blows without malice, I didn't notice her lack of beauty. Once the men left her alone, she walked into the ring and waited quietly, her whinny an acceptance of her own doom. I hope she knew that Ben was safe, saved because once again the same three girls cared enough to save their pocket money to rescue a 'no-hoper'. They accepted my choice of an undersized dun colt and clustered around as I went into the pen. Getting a headcollar onto a wild foal can be dangerous, particularly when it has been frightened by the noise of the sale. No one seems to care that these foals are wild; they haven't seen humans before as many live in isolated areas. Their first sight of the human race is hardly ideal, and even after only a few hours at a sale they associate humans with sticks and pain.

Ben edged away from me, but as I extended my hand I tried to block out the noise of the sale and the sticks. Ben was safe now. I moved closer until I was near his shoulder and tried to touch him, but he reared in panic expecting another blow. More quiet words relaxed him until I was once again standing close to him. Melanie passed my rope in and I gently put it over his neck. Ben flinched but stood still, so I held the rope and stroked his head and neck. Jane handed me the headcollar, which was undone. I slid the strap over his neck and fastened it, inching it towards his head, murmuring praise and hoping he felt the love we all felt for him. Experience had taught me that the most terrifying thing for the foal was the moment I tried to do up the strap which goes over the nose. Ben was no exception and reared again as I secured the headcollar, but it was a rear without malice and with no intention to kick or hurt me. I carefully played the rope out, and then as he calmed again I put my arm around him, speaking quietly. I could see Ruth brushing a tear away as Ben relaxed and accepted our love.

Somewhere in the chaos his mother whinnied a last goodbye. Ben answered. I hope they heard each other. Was she telling him to be good? That is perhaps 'too human an emotion' – but is it? His mother was kind, and although wild would have eventually made an excellent RDA[35] pony. I'm sure any lesson she would have taught him would have been that of kindness and gentleness; she could not have advised him otherwise.

Ben whinnied for two days, but at twenty past ten on Monday morning he stopped. His silence unnerved me, as the slaughterhouse would be killing then. Had his mother called one last goodbye? He was so placid: no bites or kicks from Ben, who accepted his injections and wormer with the same gratitude he accepted a carrot.

Ben grew into a rangy yearling. He wasn't pretty, but he had something special. The ugly head with the Roman nose was rarely noticed, because his gentle eyes and good manners held the attention.

As a two-and-a-half-year-old he was an unlikely TV star, standing quietly with our vet while the TV lights blazed above him. Their last meeting had been when he was gelded, but luckily Ben had borne no malice and even managed a shaky whinny as he struggled to his feet after the operation. Ben didn't look pretty on the TV, but he had 'something'. By the summer of his third year he stood at 13.2hh and was growing almost daily. The gawky legs occasionally showed grace, and he was a superb natural jumper, sailing over gates when he fancied a trip to see his friends in the next field.

Ben was always kind, so it seemed quite natural to bring him out to meet a group of disadvantaged children. One lad couldn't hear or speak. He wore callipers, and his random movements would have upset most youngsters, but Ben didn't see someone who looked and sounded different. He saw a child who needed love. Ben gently nuzzled his face.

---

[35] Riding for the Disabled Association. An RDA pony works with disabled and disadvantaged children and adults.

The lad laughed and clutched at Ben's head. His quick movement caught his teacher and me by surprise, but Ben just stretched down to the child, understanding that his jerky movements held no malice. The other children clustered around; Ben had a caress for each of them, gently blowing a kiss onto shy, nervous faces. By the time we led the riding ponies out, the children, none of whom had ridden before, were sure that ponies were gentle creatures. The children's happy faces, as they overcame their initial fear and learnt to enjoy riding, helped me to keep my sanity too. Then I remembered a brown colt who could have reached out to a loving hand. The next time that foal reached out to a human hand it had been to a man with a gun in his hand. I wonder, did he nuzzle that hand too, or did he finally recoil from the human race? The tragedy of this foal and thousands of others like him is that he could have reached out to another child's hand – a child who, just like him, needed us to take a little time to notice the love he had to offer.

I walked out to see our youngsters and was soon surrounded by sympathetic noses. Benjamin, by then a gangly three-year-old, did his best to cheer me up, racing across the field trying to keep his legs under control. As I sat in my field watching the youngsters graze, I realised that society was the poorer for the death of the brown foal. If he had lived, he could have enriched the lives of others who lived with suffering and difficulty on a daily basis. But so many of them suffer in silence in a world too busy with the scrabble for riches to notice the riches of a child's or a foal's love.

Chapter 18

She is an emotional bitch

Jester, my faithful collie dog, always trotted at my pony's heels on the rides, and all the ponies were used to her brown and white form running past them. We hardly ever met any other riders, mainly through choice, but when we met a neighbour and her son out riding it didn't seem polite to ride off in the opposite direction. The woman rode a chestnut Anglo-Arab gelding which cavorted about the countryside at great risk to his rider, himself and all other road users. I must admit to disliking Arabs – that is, I do like looking at them, as long as some other poor devil is in the saddle! I don't mind crazy ponies, as at least their head carriage is low enough for them to see the ground they are bolting over, but Arabs frighten the life out of me. Perhaps I've just met some very silly Arabs, but to me Arab means 'stargazer', added to which most of them dislike water, and Wales is full of the stuff! Her son's pony was much more my type: knock-kneed with an ugly head. She was supposed to be four and was being broken in, but looked much more like an under-developed three-year-old to me.

On this particular day, I saw that the hippy campers had come to our local mountain, the Mynydd Bach, again, with a variety of assorted vans and buses and even the odd goat. Our lot were used to them, and although my pony, Prince, expressed his doubts, we usually passed them without incident. However, the young pony wasn't at all sure and reared as a pack of dogs hurtled across the mountain. The Arab danced, and Prince, as ever eager to be at the front of a 'bolt', snatched at his bit. A yell from me brought the dogs to a halt and further insults sent them slinking back to their owners, but both our neighbours' mounts snorted and whirled around. I exchanged glances with Stella, and we both silently wished we had been impolite earlier and not encouraged their company. Poor old Jester was just doing her job, circling to check that we were all alright, and she didn't expect the Arab hoof that crashed down on her head. She shrieked and lay down on the track. I leapt off Prince to comfort her while our neighbour tried to calm her mount.

'She's OK, leave her. She'll get up and follow us,' the woman said.

'Not likely,' I snapped. 'Can't you see she's hurt? She could be concussed. There is no way that she can walk home,' I growled.

'Alright, I'll go home and ask my husband to pick you up,' she replied.

'Oh, God, how are we going to get Prince home? The kids can't ride or lead him, and neither can Stella – I need her on Mick to take charge of the ride,' I moaned.

'I'll ride him,' the woman said, giving her horse to her daughter to lead. I wasn't happy, but much against my better judgement I gave the OK, warning that she rode at her own risk.

I cuddled Jester and wrapped her in my sweater and coat as the others rode off the mountain. Looking into the distance at the fog muffling the glory of Cardigan Bay, I imagined the worst scenario: Jester must definitely have broken her skull; brain haemorrhage; death. By the time our lift appeared I was nearly hysterical. Jester groaned as I laid her in the car and didn't even revive when we passed the ride near to Lluest. Prince was behaving, though mainly because his reins were held so tightly he could hardly walk forwards. I was too worried about Jester to rescue him, principally because I thought he was more than capable of rescuing himself by depositing his rider! By the time the ride arrived home I had phoned the vet in a panic and arranged to take Jester over to him. Stella jumped off Mick and threw his reins to one of the girls. She leaped into the back of 'Pygsy', my decrepit three-wheeler van, and cradled Jester. I drove slowly up our bumpy drive. Once on the road I accelerated to Pygsy's top speed of forty miles and hour downhill, with the wind behind her... It seemed to take us ages to get to the vet's. In fact, it was a miracle that we got there at all, as I spent most of the time trying to watch Jester in the back, with only one eye on the road. The vet, Mr R, ushered us in with a pat for the 'poorly doggy'. Jester whimpered at the lightest touch. She must be in a bad way, I thought, as she made no attempt to bite the vet.

'She's not too bad,' he said. 'It is a nasty kick, but I think she'll be OK. Just keep her warm and quiet. I'll give her an injection to help her with any pain and inflammation.'

Jester's lip curled as she felt the needle, but she did not have the strength to bite her 'tormentor'.

'Are you sure she hasn't fractured her skull?' I asked.

Mr R smiled tolerantly – he was used to me panicking. 'No, I don't think so. She's just very sore. Ring me if you're worried.'

Both the vet and Stella smiled. 'Try stopping her,' Stella laughed.

'You're just as bad. What if it had been your dog, Dylan?' I retorted.

Jester whimpered as Mr R carried her back to the car. I drove home reasonably sedately, and we soon settled back into the normal routine of mucking out and feeding the ponies. Jester lounged in the house with an invalid's place of honour on the settee. I looked in on her every few minutes and soon realised that she was much *sicker* if she realised that she was being watched. I suppose that I did encourage her really, as every whimper resulted in an instant cuddle, and Jester isn't a dog who suffers bravely or quietly. She dozed during the evening and seemed almost normal by the time she went for her late-night constitutional at eleven o'clock. As she squatted to do the necessary, she suddenly gave a shriek of pain, ran a few steps, shrieked again and then leant against my leg quivering.

'Oh my God, Stella, she's got a blood clot on the brain, or maybe...?'

'You'd better phone the vet,' Stella interrupted, remaining annoyingly calm.

The poor long-suffering vet! I suppose, like most pet owners, I am completely incapable of being rational when my favourite is ill. Unfortunately, I am just as bad about all of the other animals too, and it is a very brave or silly vet who suggests that I should 'wait until morning!' I can't remember what I said; I doubt if any of it was relevant anyway, but Mr R told me to bring her straight over. Stella and I bundled Jester back into Pygsy and I drove over to Mr R again, none too sedately. I'm not a good driver at the best of times – in fact, I later gave up driving – but with a sick dog in the back and being in a panic, as well as it being dark, no one was more surprised than me when we arrived in one piece. Stella, who was of a more cautious nature than me, did well to even agree to come with me! Jester was duly carried into the surgery again to be examined. This time Mr R examined her back end more thoroughly and sure enough he found a fracture in her tail.

'It will heal on its own, but she may be a bit constipated,' Mr R reassured us.

'Shall I give her a little milk?' I asked.

'Yes,' was the weary reply. 'That should do it.' His look said – there really is no need to panic. He patted Jester.

'She's covered from this morning's jabs, so just keep her warm and quiet.'

I noticed a roguish glint in his eye as he looked from Jester to me.

'Of course,' he said. *'She is an emotional bitch.'*

We all laughed and I knew exactly who he was talking about. He ushered us to the car. It was nearly midnight. My conscience had finally started to bother me, now that I realised that Jester was OK.

'Sorry to make you work so late, and thanks for all you've done,' I apologised.

'It's OK. Don't worry, and give me a ring if you're worried.' He grimaced.

'Now, that is dedication to duty,' Stella chuckled.

'I just hope she'll be OK,' I wittered.

'Emotional bitch,' Stella chortled.

'Oh, shut up,' I muttered, laughing.

We started off making good progress homewards. But suddenly, Pygsy, who was not an enthusiastic car at the best of times, remembered that this was her second trip of the day. So I was not too surprised when we stopped abruptly and the headlights went out.

'Oh, God,' Stella groaned.

My first thought was to phone Mr R to come and help us, but then I thought that may be pushing our luck a bit too far, and anyway the nearest phone was over two miles away.

'Come on, you old bitch,' I muttered turning the key.

Pygsy shuddered into half-hearted life but we still had no headlights. A bit of fiddling with the switch brought a quick flash as the switch made contact with something. Unfortunately, that something was precarious, and it had to be held in the 'on' position. It was impossible to drive and hold it in place, so Stella had to hold it steady as we drove, very sedately for once, along the Welsh byways. There were lots of lumps and bumps on some of the old lanes on our route home, together with pot-holes, humpback bridges and corners. Any, or a combination of which, meant that she lost the contact, the headlights went off, and I braked violently to avoid hitting a bank. Well, as violently as Pygsy's brakes permitted.

'Hold the wretched thing in position, can't you, Stella,' I snapped.

'I'm trying,' she snapped back.

'Yes, very,' I agreed.

148

Then we both laughed – it could only happen to us. Luckily, I knew the road fairly well, so after a while, when the headlights went out, I just kept going – until I got just a little too close to the parapet of a bridge that had slipped my mind!

After that we pottered along at ten miles and hour hoping that we didn't meet a policeman, stopping frequently because Stella's hand was cramped. As for Jester, the cause of all the trouble, she fell asleep, obviously bored with the role of the invalid. Whether it was my driving, or the 'unstoppability' of nature, I don't know, but as soon as we got home Jester was able to walk, jumped out of the car, and then produced a smelly pile of poo, most of which got stuck on the tail that she couldn't lift. As I cleaned her tail, trying not to breathe, I glanced at the clock. It was 2:30 a.m. If the vet could see us now, he would definitely think that at least there was some justice in the world.

Continuing to recollect our dealings with this long-suffering vet, I mused that Mr R made a habit of bailing Lluest out. I was lying in bed at my Mum's, having just come out of hospital, and was recuperating from back trouble. The news was that Ben, the young rescued colt, wasn't picking up, that Mick was off colour and, worst of all, no one had time to go and collect Jester and reunite us after our three day separation. Mum finally walked up to Lluest to collect a very muddy Jester. Mr R had checked Ben, and, as Julie was worried and he knew a certain 'emotional bitch' would be worried too, he had a look at *all* of the ponies.

I thought I recognised the voice as I lay still trying to ignore the pain and frustration. Then a brown bombshell hurtled into the bedroom and landed on the bed followed by the vengeful cries of a decidedly put-out Mother.

'Oh, she's all wet and dirty,' Mother complained.

'Just leave her, *bach*,' a familiar voice laughed.

Mr R came in to join us. Jester sat by my side, the determination to stay there glowing in her eyes.

'How's Ben?' I asked.

'Fine – how are you?' Mr R replied.

Then we chatted about the animals, how well Julie and her friend Mick were caring for them and how all the ponies were fine. So were the dogs, cats and chickens. Mr R stayed for ten minutes or so and when he was satisfied that his two most emotional customers were satisfied and happy, he got up to leave.

149

'What do I owe you?' I asked.

'Oh, don't worry about that, see me some time, no hurry,' he answered.

He later charged me £14 for what must have been an hour's work at least.

'Tell Julie and Mick to call me any time and, as for you, go and see an osteopath. It will probably be what you need now,' he counselled.

Mum appeared with a towel for Jester and Mr R gave me a knowing wink. Then I managed to doze off, knowing that at least all the animals were OK, and at least I was getting better.

Chapter 19

I've been here three years now

It was St David's Day. Should I have been wearing a leek or a daffodil? I supposed I shouldn't, as leeks and daffodils are not suitable food for ponies, and one of them would be certain to eat even the most patriotic of buttonholes.

I had arranged to go out with Annette and Trefor to the local school. I have never been any good with languages, and Welsh is the most challenging one I have ever come across. Unfortunately for me, the whole evening was conducted in Welsh.

I was beginning to get very bored and, as I was sitting near the front, it was impossible for me to study my neighbours. The singing was impressive, and I wondered why it is that all the Welsh seem to be excellent singers. The school at Cofadail had been threatened with closure for some time, and this evening had been arranged partly to raise funds. I couldn't help remembering the dingy school I had so reluctantly attended. Cofadail leans against the foot of the Mynydd Bach and gives visitors a feeling of space and welcome. Perhaps that was why Eirwen was singing so sweetly. I knew her as a tomboy who was not afraid of any of our ponies, even Jim and his tricks, and yet here she was dressed as a Welshwoman should be, and with such a gentle voice. She seemed to sum up the Welsh nature - tough and impervious to the inclement weather, with all the misfortunes that the country could throw at her and yet with a deep understanding of the rhythm of things. All my life I have struggled towards my goal and I am still struggling. I will no doubt worry and fret myself into an ulcerous state while my Welsh neighbours will cope with far greater misfortunes without thinking them worthy of comment. There were, of course, some exceptions to this calm acceptance of life - rugby is one, holiday homes and water charges another, and a fourth is any threat to their way of life. Cofadail was feeling such a threat, and yet, compared to my school back in Gloucestershire, it was a paradise. It was friendly with (I was told) reasonable teaching standards and, most of all, it was part of the local community. So what good reason could there be for the distant bureaucracy to shut it? Thankfully, my attention was caught by several wrong notes by the pianist. The source of these notes was a two-foot-high lively toddler who had decided to 'help' Mum. I began to chuckle and nudged Annette, who also saw the funny side. The singers soldiered valiantly on while I tried very hard to control my mirth. Finally, someone grabbed the budding concert pianist, and the music continued in tune.

It is very disconcerting to be part of a close-knit group whose language is 'gobble-de-gook' to me, and it is asking for trouble to be unable to sing the Welsh National Anthem on St David's Day. Of course, with the arrogance that is common in many English people, I had expected it to be sung in my own language. Well, at least I stood and tried to look reasonably shamefaced at my lack of *Cymraeg*. We wandered into the eating area for tea and cakes. Understandably, there was no black tea, so I ordered some in my pidgin Welsh, much to the amusement of the tea lady. At least I tried!

I often wonder what brings trekkers to West Wales. The scenery, although beautiful, is not spectacular, and the gently rounded Mynydd Bach, with its liberal scattering of treacherous bogs, cannot compare with the gaunt beauty of Snowdonia. In North Wales, the stark mountains seem to rise out of fertile valleys lush with spring grass, but here, although the mountains are kinder, the valleys compensate by giving as little grass as possible.

At Lluest, perched on its plateau high above Cardigan Bay, we tried to exist on our acidic peat bogs and looked enviously down at our lowland neighbours. Yes, I think most of us loved our life, and of course we loved our mountains, but as we eked out our precious grass and worried about the condition of our stock, we all secretly hoped for a green valley of our own.

Life was easy in the valley; mistakes were less serious and the struggle for survival and the continuous war we waged against the elements was further away. Up here we were close to nature, and its rough edges were more likely to cut. The rain seemed to fall heavier, driven into our faces by the howling winds. The house suffered, and each winter the garden was patterned by slates.

'Will the barn last another year?' I asked Pete. He would shrug and groan, remembering how many times we had hauled it upright. Our barn (the Dutch variety), sited by the side of our stables, was exposed to the full fury of the south-westerly gales that battered us. So, after each storm, our leaning barn was hauled upright by chains attached to Pete's car. Sometimes I had to swing on chains to pull it upright. So why didn't we get a new barn? Simple, really. We couldn't afford one.

'But you must make a bomb on trekking – no tax overheads.' I often heard that comment, and I always resisted the temptation to scream. In a way, people were right; trekking can be very profitable, (a) providing you have your own land and (b) you have no old or retired ponies.

Of course, I noticed the harshness because I am soft, as only someone born into a green valley can be, but by nature 'Cardi Folk' accept all that their life throws at them, without finding it necessary to comment. They understand this area and squeeze each blade of grass for all it is worth. In their hardiness, they have learnt to exploit available resources to the last. Old fences are only replaced if neighbours insist. After all, why waste valuable grazing which borders the road, and if your neighbour is unlucky enough to have thirty-odd sheep descend on his overworked fields, then it is not you who lose. It isn't just the fences that are stretched to their limit. Lanes are filled with a variety of battered vans, cars and tractors. I wondered if some had ever experienced the rigours of an MOT test.

I suppose you expect a hard area to breed hard people, but their hardiness was sometimes more than I could take. The average farmer allows himself no emotion. Every animal must pay its way, and an old or sickly animal that will produce weak young (whether it is a sheepdog or a broken-mouthed ewe) has to go. I often despised their callousness as I saw their scraggy half-starved ponies on the mountains, without even a bite of hay to tide them through the winter. Yet those scraggy tough creatures often produced first-class riding ponies, cheap to feed, strong willed but highly intelligent. Perhaps the locals do have the right idea, because their sturdy flocks flourish with all the weakness culled out of them, while my crew of weaklings cost me hundreds of pounds in feed bills. It is a thorny question as to how much *duty* you have to look after old animals that have served you faithfully. Do you think only economically, and discard your expensive old pony as soon as the feed bills exceed what he can earn? Or do you keep him on as an honourable and valued pensioner whose appetite might just as well be eating banknotes. The odd passenger doesn't matter in a valley if you have plenty of land, but at Lluest we had to rely on a neighbour's land and a steady income to pay off our mortgage. Economies aside, is it kind to keep on an arthritic old pony who feels the cold, and at what point should you end a 'friend's' life? I've always believed that all life is precious, but inevitably there will be times when you must let go and let nature or a sympathetic vet ease the pensioner on his way.

There is no easy answer, and in all conscience I couldn't just discard a friend like old Jerry. But then my business could have failed at any moment, while the tough locals and their stock thrived. The cost to them is high, though, and despite the accumulated wealth of a lifetime there is no love or compassion for their stock. Or rather, there is no sentiment; all decisions are made logically with both eyes on the cost of any indulgence.

'Animal rights' people usually condemn all farmers as cruel, and yet on the whole I don't think they are. Let your favourite pet bitch have a litter and watch her kill or ignore a defective pup. She isn't being cruel, just practical and instinctively obeying an unwritten law of nature. Most farmers living close to the soil merely follow the same law. A beef steer is a valuable possession and has to be cared for if its full value is to be realized. No farmer wants to lose one single calf from his dairy herd, but experience has taught him when to ignore a new-born calf too sickly to survive.

I was born on the outskirts of a town, and although I learnt to understand the values of a farmer, I found myself fighting a succession of losing battles against old age with my own animals. I realized that my sentiment could result in the loss of my business and having to sell my ponies, but I struggled on, trying to hold all the animals together, hoping that one day I would succeed.

Although my neighbours were tough, I didn't dislike them. I knew that some disapproved of my way of life.

'A woman should live with her husband.' I heard that frequently, both to my face and behind my back. I often wondered if disapproving men who tut-tutted were not just a little envious, as their hard-working wives kept them to the pledge and to the 'straight and narrow way' of life.

U

Three years had passed since our move to Lluest, and I was gradually making friends. It wasn't that the locals were aloof; far from it, but I never allowed them to get beyond pleasantries. I ceased inviting people to Lluest, and I also ceased visiting their houses unless I had to. I doubt if any of them understood that I preferred the company of my cats and dogs to the more demanding company of the jam-making house-proud ladies. If you came to Lluest anytime outside the trekking season, you would find dirty floors and dust, and my possessions scattered untidily around the house. You would also find a cat in all the chairs, and possibly a saddle half mended on the kitchen table.

Houses and their appearance don't interest me and neither does polite conversation over tea and scones. I often think that I should have been a man, particularly when I am trying to move large loads of straw. I can't bake a cake; my cooking is appalling, and I have no idea how to organize a kitchen. What I can do is organize someone else to sort out such mundane problems for me.

Sometimes I think about how easy it would be to go back to life as it was before we moved to Wales, with Pete, my husband, coming home after work every day. But I often wonder if I could cope with a 'normal' life. It was easy to live alone at Lluest with no one to interrupt my thinking, or nag because I hadn't cooked any dinner. Animals instinctively understood my moods and adjusted their behaviour accordingly. Jester was an excellent judge of my moods; as she walked by my side through rain, blizzards and blazing sun, I talked to her about problems and fears that I could never mention to a human being.

She was so easy to understand and communicate with, and her loyalty was never in question. It is easy to get a close relationship with any dog, as they are usually only too willing to devote their lives to a master who, despite his faults, is a God to the dog at his heel. Jester was more faithful than most dogs I know. She was a small rough-coated brown and white border collie with a brown nose balanced by two pink bits that someone forgot to paint. At seven she was still perky, never too tired to romp with her son and grand-daughter or chase any escaping pony. And her expertise as a judge of character was second to none. I often wondered if customers were really as tolerant of my dogs as they seemed, when the three of them (often dirty) hurtled to greet their shiny new cars as they inched into our yard. Jester judged humans instantly, a fault she probably got from her owner, and it was interesting to see the people she ignored. Her judgement was rather better than mine, as I found out one day when a brand-new family car rolled into the yard.

The father seemed pleasant enough as he enquired about prices and times of rides, but I noticed Jester curl her lip and realized that she had taken up a defensive stand next to me. I edged further away from the man and grabbed Jester's collar. Mr Symonds booked his daughters in for a two-hour ride that afternoon, then left. They were back again at two o'clock, but instead of coming to the house they wandered around the stable. The children were really hard-looking city kids of about nine and twelve years old. I walked into the stable to groom their ponies and was annoyed to find that the brush I had left sitting on the stable wall had gone. 'That's strange,' I said. 'You didn't notice it, did you, girls?'

Both girls looked away and mumbled, so I went back to the tack-shed for another brush. When I got back to the stable, Mr Symonds handed me the lost brush.

'It fell down in the stable; the girls found it,' he said, smiling innocently.

I didn't believe him and tacked the ponies up in record time. Although I usually invited trekkers into the house, I decided not to invite them in and left them outside. On impulse I left Jester guarding my possessions as I took the ride out. At that time a saddle and bridle could be worth £180, and I didn't want either to develop legs. The youngest girl, who was called Susie, was riding Comet, who chewed fretfully on his bit, while the eldest was mounted on steady old Pepper. Both ponies followed me reluctantly out of the yard but soon took an interest in the ride which passed quickly.

I knew that something was wrong as soon as we rode back down the drive, because I could hear Jester barking. She was raving outside Mr Symonds' car while the terrified gentleman sat inside with all his windows wound up. It was a boiling hot day – he looked unhappy.

'Jester, leave,' I yelled, and she reluctantly obeyed me.

Mr Symonds cautiously wound his window down. 'That dog is dangerous,' he said, then he smiled an ingratiating smile. 'I was just going to use your loo, and I opened the back door and she attacked me.'

'Oh dear,' I replied. 'She won't let anyone in the house.'

The girls, meanwhile, had let their ponies go and were advancing on the car. I couldn't help wondering if they were planning a quick getaway, so I ignored the dangling reins and the fact that Comet was heading for the garden and leant into the car.

'Would you like some eggs, Mr Symonds?' I asked innocently,

He got out of his car and followed me to the hen house. I collected three eggs, keeping a watchful eye on the children.

'Well, the ride comes to £5,' I said.

'Oh,' he replied, edging towards his car. 'Won't £4 do? After all, there are two of them.'

'No, it won't,' I snapped. '£5, please. I'm not open to bargaining.'

'Well, I've only got £4,' he murmured, smiling triumphantly.

He obviously thought he was onto a winner, because he drew himself up to his full height and leered down at me. He should have remembered Jester, who had crept into position behind him. I gave a tiny nod and Jester gave a massive bark and leapt at Mr Symonds' backside. The poor man shot up in the air and dropped the eggs. Then, crestfallen, he fumbled in his pocket and brought out a bundle of notes. He selected a fiver and handed it over.

Jester growled once more on cue.

'Oh, I forgot,' I said. 'There is a £2 surcharge for taking rides with less than five.'

Mr Symonds hesitated until Jester sat in front of him and stared menacingly at his face.

'That's disgusting,' he fumed. 'It's robbery.'

'There's a lot of it about and these days. Even the most respectable people seem to go in for it,' I replied.

He ignored my sarcasm and nervously handed over a further £2. I had a feeling that I could have got more money out of him, but I decided to call Jester off and let him hurry to his car unmolested.

Jester watched our unwelcome guest drive away and calmly ate the smashed eggs, then, with a wag of her tail and a large doggy smirk, wandered off to play with her son.

157

Chapter 20

The power of the press

R uth and I were sitting by the phone waiting in vain for it to ring. 'Do you want a cup of tea?' Ruth asked.

'OK,' I replied.

What I really wanted was a lot of customers and some money in the bank, but as neither looked likely, a cuppa would have to do. Ruth clattered about in the kitchen. I turned the radio up and stared out of the window. So many worries – we had decided to sell the farm and look for a property with more land, but would we ever sell ? Did I really want to anyway, and how would the charity get enough money to feed all of the ponies? How much longer before my back gave out again, and the bank foreclosed on us? So many questions, but sadly, no real answers.

Suddenly the phone rang, stopping me in mid panic.

'Hello. Lluest Horse and Pony Trust,' I said hopefully.

'Hello. This is Jenny from Horse and Pony magazine,' was the reply. My heart sank. This was all I needed.

'Hello,' I replied cautiously.

'I've got some good news for you,' Jenny bubbled.

Yes, I bet. It was probably this week's special discount of advertising that I still couldn't afford, I thought to myself.

Jenny continued, 'Horse and Pony magazine is holding a National Riding Day[36], and Lluest Horse and Pony Trust has been chosen as one of the charities to benefit.'

---

[36] National Riding Day was organized by *Horse & Pony* magazine. It was a day when readers took part in sponsored rides, and the money raised was divided between seven UK equine charities.

At that point a shriek stopped her in mid spell. 'Ruth, we're going to get some money from Horse and Pony,' I screamed.

Ruth whooped, and poor Jenny was still trying to get a word in edgeways.

'Are you sure – we're going to benefit?' I asked fearfully.

'Yes,' was the reply.

More shrieks from both Ruth and me followed, when we realized it was true, and again we were both yelling.

'Oh, that's great, Jenny,' I managed to squeak. 'Sorry for shouting. I'm so excited – you've made my day.'

Jenny laughed and tried again. 'Do you want to advertise?' she asked patiently.

'I don't know... well, I might, yes, I suppose I should,' I dithered, and then I think I rattled on about the ponies. Poor Jenny, sensing that she was talking to a gibbering idiot, said that she'd phone again. I slammed the phone down, probably forgetting to thank Jenny and *Horse & Pony*, jabbered to Ruth who later said I made no sense at all, and phoned Barb. I doubt if she made much sense of my call either, but that was probably because she kept shrieking too.

When I finally sat down to drink my cup of cold tea, I couldn't help thinking that normal charity managers did not shriek on the telephone or jump up and down, but then I had to admit that I was no normal charity manager. The money to come from *Horse & Pony* represented security for the ponies and a cash injection that, with the best will in the world, neither the Trustees nor I were capable of providing.

My shrieks that day were nothing to my reaction when Sue, a journalist from *Horse & Pony,* phoned a few weeks later to ask if she could come and do a story on the charity, to give readers an insight into its work – who and what is Lluest? I wondered that myself too!

'Oh, God' I panicked to Barb. 'We'll never get any money. I mean, what is she going to think? She'll be used to all those gleaming thoroughbreds.'

Joker burped loudly in the background, reducing me to helpless giggles.

'And what about this house?' I wailed, as I carried on opening a window to let Joker's exploits out and some fresh air in. 'She'll be used to central heating!'

'Oh, don't fuss,' Barb interrupted. 'She'll just have to take us as she finds us.'

I had met Sue once before, when I went to the headquarters of *Horse & Pony* to collect some used postage stamps that readers and supporters had saved for us. She seemed nice enough, and Jester had liked her, but she was a journalist, and she looked as if she rode a lot and probably agreed with the rest of the horsey community that ponies such as ours were not worth bothering with. All of these doubts went through my mind, and of course, as usual, I was completely wrong.

I wasn't any happier as I got ready for the big day: the day when Sue was to arrive to start her story on the charity. The ponies gleamed in their stables, but I was a mess as the clock ticked by. I tried to make myself as presentable as possible, applying make-up whilst dropping the tube of mascara on the floor! I had already faced several journalists and had quickly realised that it didn't matter what you said in an interview; they would make up their own minds what to write, and nothing you said made much difference. Sue probably thought that the horse-meat trade was a good thing. Well, I definitely didn't. Barb was right – she could think what she liked. We were all proud of our work, and worked with wild ponies out of choice. Yes, we needed the money very badly, but we would manage whatever happened. I just wished I wasn't so nervous.

'She's here,' Barb yelled over a chorus of woofs and howls.

I rushed out, trying hard to be confident.

'Hello, Sue, pleased to see you again – have you had a good journey?' I asked.

She smiled and said 'Hello'. The dogs were saying 'hello' too, and Sue's clean jeans were soon covered with muddy paw prints. Jester looked at me, tail wagging, trying to signal her approval, but I was still too wary to relax.

The photographer arrived and wandered around while Barb and I chatted to Sue and showed her our photograph album. The photo session was going well, and better than I expected – that is, until Jaws decided to liven things up. His name always attracts journalists and photographers, but most tend not to make his acquaintance too closely.

'Will he hold something?' the photographer asked.

'Yes,' I replied confidently. I had spent most of my time trying to persuade him *not* to chew objects, both the animate and inanimate, but that day, perverse as ever, he decided to behave. That was not what I wanted, so I offered him a lead rope, then a bucket which he tried to lick out. Finally, I rammed the bucket into his mouth and he then posed with a wicked glint in his eye.

Phoenix rose to the occasion as usual, as did Ben. But Whisper (taken in from a local family, born as a 'mistake') and Barley were not in photogenic moods, so we tried Dancer. It was her first ever public appearance, and I wasn't sure of her reaction, so I warned everyone to keep clear and encouraged her to stand nicely. The result was an unforgettable photo of Dancer nuzzling me. This was going to be OK. The ponies seemed to understand that they were on trial and that their future and the future of other ponies and foals like them depended on their behaviour. Even naughty Trixie and Thomas, the two newest arrivals, were angelic and assured the world that neither had any intention of doing anything unpleasant.

'OK,' the photographer said. 'Now we'll have one of you two doing the paperwork.' Barb hated having her photo taken as much as I did, but we obligingly sat in our very tatty kitchen, as I sneakingly cast a furtive eye around to see if any more newts or slugs had found their way in.

Jester wanted attention, as she was thoroughly displeased at having been shut in so that we could get photos of the ponies without a leg or nose of Jester included. At last she managed to sneak up to me for a cuddle, just as the photographer did his stuff. Afterwards he left, but Sue was staying overnight. I let the ponies out and cooked dinner, and then afterwards answered questions from Sue. She was a veggie, anti-hunt, and no, she didn't *just* like thoroughbreds; in fact, I had a feeling that our scruffs had won her heart. If Sue had been a trekker, I would have taken to her in two minutes flat, but I was allowing my previous experience of a few bad journalists to blind me to the fact that the woman sitting in my front room was a woman who cared about her work and about all ponies. However, even so, to be honest I was relieved when she left the following morning and I could then relax a little bit.

Of course, I spent the next few weeks worrying about the article, but when Sue sent me a copy of the magazine I couldn't believe my eyes, or the note pinned to the magazine. It just said that she hoped the article was 'OK'!

It was considerably more than 'OK', and it was the start of a new life for the ponies at Lluest. It was accurate and compassionate without being sentimental. The response to it was tremendous, as more children

161

then realized what happened to the 'wild' ponies. They were eager to help and formed a nucleus of dedicated supporters.

I still couldn't believe what was actually happening for some time; sadly, even years later, I still read that other charities, with considerably more funds than ourselves, think that the horse-meat trade is a good thing. They see the 'wild' ponies as useless. Of course, I disagree! I do realize they are difficult and dangerous to deal with at first, but with work and love they are no different from any other pony. I proved my point, as our youngsters grew up and were broken in. Barley looked after his five-year-old rider as if he had been doing the job for years, and Phoenix showed tremendous promise. Gradually, they were finding good loving homes. When Sue first met me, what would she have seen? Probably a nutty woman with equally nutty ponies, and a charity which, however well meant, was small and badly undercapitalized. Yet she had the faith to support us, and her support made the difference between success and failure.

♘

We were to meet Sue again, as she had decided to join us at the forthcoming October foal sale. When she arrived at Lluest, I suggested a ride on old Rhona, who of course was an angel and seemed to carry her special rider with care and pride. I don't know why, but afterwards we were surprised when she offered to help with the chores. But, as she helped fill hay nets and water-buckets, everyone forgot that she was a journalist and chatted away happily.

We settled down to a meal and an early night, which was just as well because the big day turned out to be even worse than we had imagined. The Land Rover and trailer that we had arranged to borrow broke down, leaving us stranded, and we had a mad scramble to find other transport. Eventually, a neighbour agreed to pick us up from the sale, so Jane, Mel, Ruth, Shelley, Barb, Sue and I set off.

I had warned Sue what the sale would be like, but nothing can prepare a sensitive, caring person for a day at a foal sale. The stones and the corridors echoed with the screams of the foals as they were herded in, slipping and sliding on muck-covered walkways. Sue groaned as sticks prodded, poked and beat the ponies. Foals fell over each other as they tried to escape the noise or a sale sticker rammed onto their rump. Through all the chaos, children were laughing and eating hot-dogs while

162

their parents ate fish and chips, enjoying their day out, oblivious to the suffering under their noses.

Several times I noticed Sue or one of the girls retreat to the ladies when they could no longer contain their tears, but they kept coming back determined to do their job. Meanwhile, our 'intrepid' TV cameraman, too cowardly to film the 'wild' ponies, chose instead to film the soft option of 'quality' horses and ponies unloaded from horse boxes. Our record of that day would have been as biased as the cameraman, but for the courage of Harry (the *Horse & Pony* magazine photographer) who took the still photos. He ignored the threats that came his way to focus on the suffering. Unlike the local cameraman, he felt it was his duty to provide an accurate record, but then of course Harry did not have the worry that the TV cameraman had, which was of losing the work he did for local farmers. He irritated me, but I ignored him and concentrated on looking for two foals out of two or three hundred to rescue. We picked out two possibilities. One was a pretty, odd-coloured filly; we already had a name, 'Cariad', which in Welsh means both love and charity. The other was a grey colt in poor condition, lousy and wormy. He belonged to a couple I saw quite a lot. These 'horse lovers' bought – or rather, 'saved' – half a dozen foals, usually in poor condition, and then either turned them out on a marsh somewhere to grow up, or sold them on straight away. Their speciality appeared to be 'much loved, quiet to ride' two-year-olds, usually fairly poor, not wormed, and much-loved only when they were sold for a good profit.

The grey colt, who we would later name Davy, was driven into the ring twice, and each time he sauntered out, his progress unchecked by the auctioneers or the louts who were often to be seen waving sticks at the far end of the ring. Barb, Sue and I chased after the owner and agreed a deal of £40 cash. Unfortunately, our favourite cameraman, eager as ever to be in the centre of things, suddenly decided to do some work, and our vendor was more than a little camera-shy. I managed not to lose my temper with our media friend who reluctantly agreed not to film. Davy's owner, who had three other foals to sell, refused to give a receipt, which aroused suspicion that she was a dealer doing nicely from dealing in ponies on the side. We watched as she tried to decide between greed for the forty pounds, which I waved just out of reach of her hands, and the fear of being caught, as she actually pretended that it was an outrage that she was being considered 'cruel'. She loved horses and had 'saved' Davy. Perhaps she genuinely believed that, but I find it hard to feel any sympathy for a woman who had hawked Davy and his companions from Swansea to a Cardigan sale, and then back to our local sale the next day. I wondered if the foals had stayed overnight in a lorry, maybe without food or water. The sale stickers from the previous day were still clearly visible on their rumps, and they were obviously exhausted. I'm pleased to say that finally her greed triumphed, and Davy was ours and, for the first time in his life, surrounded by truly loving hands.

But now I was in trouble. The sale had already started in ring three, and I was afraid that I had missed Cariad. I forgot that I had a bad leg as I raced through the crowds, losing Sue, who is a little more polite than me. I wriggled and pushed my way into the stands in time to see Cariad being driven into the ring. Sue, who had caught up by this time, watched, heart in her mouth, as I outbid the meat men and dealers; then Jane and Ruth chased after Cariad to make sure that she wasn't driven into the meat pens. They dared any of the drovers to use their sticks, and the drovers wisely refrained, aware that they were being watched and photographed.

Harry sat quietly while I walked into Cariad's pen; the cameraman seemed to want to join us until he realized that Cariad really was 'wild'. I approached her gently and managed to get a rope around her neck easily. She trembled, too tired to resist, until I tried to do up the noseband of the headcollar, when she reared in panic, towering above me. She could easily have crushed me, but I was unaware of the danger of my unprotected head and back. All I was aware of was how special this filly was; her intelligence and her spirit were beautiful, and given time, love and good food, her body would be beautiful too. Cariad relaxed and came back to earth as I secured the noseband and held her. Harry was as emotional as everyone else until the cameraman shattered the mood.

'Can you do that again for me? Problem with the camera,' he stated blandly!

Ruth, Jane and I had all witnessed him put the camera into his pocket to hide the problem of what he should have done when he started filming. Lens covers do not help when you intend to record evidence for the posterity of TV stations. To my surprise, a polite voice that belonged to me explained why I wouldn't do it again. Cariad had faced enough misery and fear for one day, and I had no intention of letting her loose and making her face the ordeal of being headcollared again, just so that her fear could be recorded. We came to the compromise of me fiddling with her headcollar. She had relaxed by this time, so Mel led Davy into the pen to join her. He was calm and quickly settled into the role of 'Daddy', which he played ever afterwards to recently-weaned foals. Cariad was weak and vulnerable, which he understood, and he snuggled up to her, patiently enduring her attempts to suckle from him.

When our lorry arrived, Davy loaded willingly, eager to get away from the market, but Cariad hesitated and reared again. Davy turned to look at her and made encouraging noises. She didn't want to lose her new friend and followed him into the lorry and a new life.

Sue and the girls stayed to record the loading of the slaughter lorries, while I took Davy and Cariad home to Lluest. Later, they came home, saddened and angry by what they had seen, to find Cariad and Davy sharing a stable and tucking into the hay. In fact, Davy was tucking into anything he could find and ate his straw as well as the coarse mix and hay. We gently persuaded him that we really did have plenty of hay, and I put a little short feed into Cariad's mouth. She was really thirsty now but wouldn't drink from a bucket, sure that Davy could work a miracle and provide milk – he was so like her mother in every other way. I wasn't worried about either of them because Davy would soon teach her to eat and drink, probably overnight.

We fed the other ponies and settled down to a meal and rather a lot of wine! One moment we were happy knowing that at least two ponies had found a happy secure home with plenty of food, but we remembered all of those other foals who were cold and hungry while awaiting their unhappy ending the next day. What we had done was just a drop in the ocean; we felt that we had to try and help all the foals we couldn't save. Each of us brooded over the noise, the sticks and the injustice of it all.

The next morning, we faced another sale. After cuddling Cariad and Davy, who had now settled into Lluest quite happily, and a very hasty mucking out, we set off. This sale has greatly improved since that visit, and so I do not intend to dwell on the dreadful conditions that were there on that day. We left oppressed by the misery. One group of foals and youngsters bought by one of the meat men waited overnight in the lorry; we believed they waited without food or water but couldn't prove this. The stench from the lorry hit us as we walked over – our presence was noted and was not welcome. The following year, when once again we checked this particular lorry, our presence provoked the meat man's son to throw a bucket of cold water over us. I'm not sure what he hoped to gain from this childish, loutish action, but we just laughed and he retreated.

Sue later put pen to paper in a courageous article, condemning both the trade and conditions and also the appointed welfare officers, whose lackadaisical approach to their job allowed abuse to continue. Predictably, they were not amused, but it resulted in them doing their job a little more conscientiously. The market proprietors were not amused either – their replying press release, duly printed by *Horse & Pony,* tried to affirm their concern for equine welfare. However, an off-record quote to Barb and me at one following New Year sale is considerably more honest and sums up their attitude somewhat more succinctly:

'What are you worried about these little buggers for? They're only worth fifteen or twenty guineas apiece. We've had Shires through here worth thousands of pounds, and no complaint about their treatment.'

I don't doubt the veracity of that statement, as we have never received any complaints about the handling of *valuable* horses and ponies.

Sue's article was the beginning of an improvement in the conditions for the foals, and *Horse & Pony*'s stand on horse welfare was just what was needed. It was and still is easier not to meddle with the horse-meat trade, but meddle we must if we want to call ourselves 'a nation of animal lovers'.

Some time much later, Sue came to see us again, this time at our new home. She brought with her a cheque for £7227.86 raised by all the caring readers of *Horse & Pony.* Our cameraman reappeared to record the event – and this time he remembered to remove his lens cover! Cariad behaved exceptionally well, but Davy, who had now realised he was a little boy, was a pest and tried to nip the hand of his benefactress.

It all seemed to be happening, as only two days later a gentleman – I'll call him Mr L – arrived with a film crew for an interview with me. I naively led Davy and Cariad out of their stable, and then the chaos started. Firstly, the soundman didn't seem to understand that the furry microphone was an attractive 'toy' to a colt. So I was trying to restrain Davy, who, being thwarted in his attempt to chew the microphone, chewed my arm instead, while I tried to smile for the camera and talk about our work.

'That's lousy, visually,' the cameraman interrupted.

I chuckled, as that comment just about summed me up. Mr L was very kind and pointed out that it did look very funny, as I was saying how wonderful these ponies were as I was being savaged by one. He even suggested using it as a Christmas 'funny'. We decided to release Davy, but Cariad, who was a 'wild' foal only six weeks previously, stayed for the duration of the filming. She was a real professional – in fact more professional than a certain charity manager who still winces when she has to deal with journalists.

Sue, well-deservedly, later won a prize for her article entitled 'Foal Sale Horror', and kindly donated it to Lluest.

Ginny with Cariad and Davy

Chapter 21

Back injury at Lluest

I had almost given up. The house was cold and damp, my hot water bottle was cold, and I wanted to go to the loo. Finally, I struggled out of bed and tried to walk to the bathroom. It wasn't far – just a few yards – but my legs buckled again[37]. So I crawled through the kitchen and tack shed, crying in pain and disgust at myself for crying in the first place. It must have taken me half an hour to get to the loo, and the return journey just didn't seem worth the effort. The dogs clustered around, eager to help by licking my face, but I just wasn't interested. I think I fainted, or maybe I just fell asleep where I was. By the time I came round again, four dogs were snuggled into me. Gemma, Joker, and Gypsy were asleep, but Jester was awake and staring hard at me; her sharp little woofs were a reprimand. I could lie there on cold tiles feeling sorry for myself, and she would stay there by my side as she always did, but not for one moment longer than she had to. So, chided along by one very cross collie, I crawled back into our front room and tried to pull myself back into bed. As I lay there, I wondered what I was going to do. How could I go on living alone, relying on parents or friends to bring me meals and light the fire?

Pete was still working away from home. He always looked tired and, even when I was well, I never had time for him anymore; I was always too busy or worried. He was under pressure at work and hated travelling, and yet he was prepared to support me.

Outside, the ponies munched their hay in what I hoped were clean stables, properly bedded down. But I was no longer capable of looking

---

[37] Ginny's back problem probably stemmed from an old injury to her neck and right leg in a riding accident in 1968.

after them. The treatment I'd had wasn't working, and there was no prospect of any improvement. Life had thrown a few wobbles my way and I had always prided myself that I could cope with any of them, but here was the one thing I could not cope with: being a cripple. I just did not have the courage to adapt to life in a wheelchair, and to accept the help of others, however well meant, gracefully. I was jealous of the helpers, who could muck the ponies out when I so wanted to pick up a shovel, and I even found myself envying beginners, because at least they could get on a pony. Life without gallops was unthinkable. The alternatives to a life lived without my ponies was not an alternative either. What else did I know? What else could I do?

It was a sad and depressed little person who was carried to the car for the next appointment with the hospital. I didn't like the consultant, although I felt sorry for the man, who had far too many patients and no time to deal with any properly. I also felt that the man was a complete idiot who relied on pain killers as his only defence against my problems. The very movement of the car intensified the pain, and the long wait in sitting position at the outpatient's clinic was just too much. I just had to lie down. My back was aflame from my brain to my heel, and the kidney infection that I developed after the epidural, given to 'relieve the pain' while the consultant tried to put the disc back, didn't help.

When the consultant appeared, he chatted to Pete who he obviously felt to be more intelligent than a down-at-heel horsey type like me. I lay on the bed and fumed. How dare he, I thought, refuse to show me my X Rays on the grounds that I wouldn't understand them? It was *my* body, and I was fed up with other people ignoring my instincts and telling me I would not be allowed to ride. By the time the consultant dictated my case notes to his secretary, as if I did not exist, I was furious. I did exist, and I'd had enough.

'Why can't I see an osteopath?'[38] I asked again. 'I don't need you to give me the OK, as he can see me without it.'

The consultant hesitated. He was stumped, and, four months after he first saw me, he was no nearer finding out what was wrong with me. He could also see that I was about to have a massive temper tantrum.

He sat down and explained that he could not recommend that I see an osteopath as he thought it could be dangerous, but that he would not

---

[38] An osteopath uses his hands with a mixture of forceful and gentle techniques to manipulate muscles and joints, to help the body heal itself.

stand in my way if that was what I wanted. Pete agreed with the consultant, but could see that there was no point arguing with me. He took me along to see the osteopath a few days later.

The osteopath was also a highly skilled doctor who, rather than being inhibited by orthodox medicine with its rigid cures, used osteopathy as a tool to help whatever kind of healing he thought most suitable for his patient. He was a kindly man, rather round in shape and very jovial. I felt at ease with him straight away. I couldn't sit in the chair, so I lay on his couch while I answered his questions. He warned me that the treatment would hurt, and wasn't even sure if he could help me, but he soon discovered the trouble. My spine had twisted and was pressing on the sciatic nerve. Several times I almost begged him to stop, but despite the pain I had confidence in him, as each move was explained. By the end of the session I was black and blue, and had black felt tip pen marks up my spine.

'Could I ride?' I asked, expecting a very definite 'No!'

'Yes, if you want to,' he answered. 'But don't take any risks, and don't fall off.'

Suddenly, the pain was bearable. I could walk with difficulty, but if I could ride...

The osteopath smiled. He realised that my ponies were the only thing that kept me going, and had realised that the struggle back to fitness would be easier for me if I had an incentive.

Pete had no idea that I was going to try to ride. And our helpers, Diane and her boyfriend, didn't think that it was a good idea at all – particularly as they were the ones who would have to get me onto the pony, and be responsible for me once I was up there. Diane saddled Prince amid my mutterings and general protest, and then came in to help me out into the yard. Prince was standing quietly. I was shocked by his condition. Physically he was OK, not thin or run down, but mentally he wasn't the same pony. The boss's pony – proud, difficult, and full of trouble – was no more, and in his place stood a quiet old nag, so like any riding school mount.

'Prince,' I called as I limped towards him. He turned his head and whickered, surprising me with such a public display of emotion. Diane helped me up onto the mounting block and tried to lift me onto the saddle. Her boyfriend helped her to steady Prince as she pushed my right leg over the saddle and lowered me into place. She pushed my feet into the stirrups and turned a very worried face to look at me. I knew that I must be white. I was shaking, and tears were streaming down my face – whether from the pain or the joy of sitting on Prince again, I'm not sure.

'Do you want to get off?' she asked.

'No, I don't,' I muttered. 'Prince, walk on.' His ears flicked forwards and he walked forward, lifting his legs high and placing them gently but firmly, careful not to hurt me. His head came up as he carried me proudly up our drive. Diane was at his head, but I didn't need her because Prince, who could so easily have trampled us both underfoot, was happy.

'He's not the same pony,' Diane enthused. 'I wondered why you rode such an ugly little thing, but he's different when you get on him.'

I smiled. We had been together for ten years, and what years they had been – full of laughter, some tears, friends we'd met on the way, and latterly a fight to end the horse-meat trade that seemed a hopeless one. By the time Diane led me back to the mounting block I was almost unconscious but so happy.

Getting me off was even harder than getting me on, perhaps because I really didn't want to get off anyway. I had to be carried back to the house and bed, leaving a scruffy skewbald pony staring dejectedly after me, but it didn't matter because I knew that I would soon be riding Prince again.

My recovery was long but interesting. One morning I looked out of my window to see a bobble-hatted figure crouched over the well, teetering on the brink of the none-too-safe stonework.

'Oh dear, oh dear... shit,' he muttered.

'What's wrong, Mick?' I asked[39], wondering if he was seeing pink monsters in the well.

'I forgot to anchor the rope, man,' Mick replied, vaguely pointing to our only rope which was attached to a bucket twenty feet below us. I hobbled out to see him. It was all too much; I leant on the garden wall and laughed. Six months before I wouldn't have seen the funny side, but with a winter like 1985/86[40] our only means of raising water being out of action didn't seem important.

'That's it, then,' I said, between fits of giggles.

---

[39] Mick was Ginny's hippy neighbour, not to be confused with the pony Mick.
[40] November 1985 was the coldest November in the UK since 1922, and February 1986 was an exceptionally cold month, the coldest since January 1963.

'No, man, I'm going to go fishing.'

I couldn't wait. I knew that our well probably had nasties in it, but wondered if they were edible. Still chuckling, I limped in to fill a kettle for a cup of tea. I had been holding the kettle expectantly under the tap for several minutes before I remembered that we had no water, which was why our hippy friend had thrown a bucket into the well in the first place! I decided to check on Mick s progress and was amazed to see him triumphantly hauling the bucket out.

'Well done,' I said, thinking that he wasn't as daft as he seemed.

Lluest was obviously becoming home to another nutcase, which was probably just as well, because only a nutter would want a non-paying job with the real risk of injury from our delinquent ponies. You would have thought that the ponies would have been suitably grateful to Mick and Julie, our voluntary help. Some were, with Jerry in his vague way rather reminding me of an ageing Mick. Smokey was friendly to anyone, but of course the usual ponies refused to co-operate. Prince usually behaved the first day he met a new worker, but only to lull then into a false sense of security. It wasn't long before I saw a skewbald, ears flat back, being pursued by a mad hippy. So I dragged myself out of bed to watch the fun again. I'm still not sure who won the day, as Mick appeared moving rapidly, this time with Prince doing the chasing. Was it a strange new method of catching a pony? It was certainly an interesting one, but looked more like terrified self-preservation to me. Of course, as soon as I tottered out, Prince gave himself up with an innocent expression and a smile in his eyes. Chasing and kicking the help is fun, but it can land you in trouble, as Prince knew; I had a habit of administering a firm slap.

I found Mick almost dancing in temper – not an easy feat when you are well laid back.

'I've been trying to get Prince in for ten minutes, the bugger,' Mick complained. 'And he keeps trying to kick me.'

I have a way of walking when I'm cross but couldn't manage it at the time, so I limped up to Prince with a severe expression on my face. He put his head down meekly as I slapped his neck and told him off. His withering look said it all – after four months in bed, my arm had no strength, so my favourite pony let me lean on him as we walked back to his stable. I wasn't sure if I was laughing at Mick or myself. I wondered if Prince knew what he was doing – he hated other people handling him, but while I was too ill, he had accepted it, but now he sensed a recovery and he was going to make sure it was speedy.

The freeze of that winter eventually ended with several burst pipes. When Mick said he would mend them I couldn't believe my luck. I took him a coffee an hour later and was greeted by a hole in the ground spouting water, and a collection of what had once been pipes propped up in nearly a foot of water.

'Hey, man, do you have a stopcock?' Mick asked. I looked vaguely at him. 'I don't know. Probably not. I'll have to phone Pete.'

Pete sounded worried. Our plumbing was bad enough without Mick's help, and no, we didn't have a stopcock.

Mick seemed unperturbed as he cobbled together a pipe tap and bodged it all together into working order. I didn't like to criticize, but the tap seemed to be at a strange angle – or was it me?

Mick smiled. 'I can't get it on straight,' he explained.

'Oh well, never mind,' I replied. It was better than a fountain.

Gradually, I began to realise that Mick was an excellent worker. He was certainly different, but then I'd always preferred eccentrics.

And then, one morning a few months later – I heard the cuckoo!

Prince was in a fidgety mood. It was to be our first ride to the mountains since I hurt my back. I was nervous. I knew that I couldn't stop Prince if he really wanted to gallop, and I wasn't sure that I could stay on board if he did take off. By the time we reached the lake he wasn't walking at all, and as he bounced along like a demented kangaroo I wished I'd taken Pete's advice and ridden Rhona.

'Hey.'

I heard a familiar voice behind me and turned Prince to welcome Julie on Jadine. I was very relieved to see them. We talked as Prince joined Jadine at the front of the ride. Our canter back was getting closer. Nerves travel both ways along the reins, and we were both pretty wound up. Julie led us into the canter track, and the other riders stayed well back in case I fell. I don't remember telling Prince to canter, and I probably didn't. Luckily, he didn't do his usual leap forward and land galloping, but we were travelling fairly rapidly, and, in spite of a firm grip on his reins, we were too close to Jadine.

'Go faster,' I yelled as Prince tried to overtake Jadine. 'Bloody move!'

Jadine did, and as Prince and I flew up the hill, I realised that nothing hurt. I wasn't in control, couldn't stop, but I was galloping –

something I thought I'd never experience again. It was as if I'd never galloped before, as I felt Prince's strength of body and spirit. Julie was slowing down, but I couldn't. My arms felt as if they were going to fall off and I felt faint. Julie turned Jadine across our path, but Prince was already slowing. The track ahead was a steep, stony one, winding down towards the mountain road. Only an idiot would gallop down it, and Prince was no idiot. As I patted him and yelled 'I've done it', I realised that I was crying and laughing too. I could ride again. I knew I'd never be as fit, but at least I'd been given a second chance. Prince was so proud, and he was happy too. Head up, he matched his step to Jadine's and pranced on towards home.

I had ridden over the mountain in gales, blizzards, and on clear days when sky and sea seemed to meet. I'd watched red kites circle overhead, laughed as Bluey took yet another shortcut, cried over the loss of my dear Jim, and watched sunsets, but the day I'll remember for the rest of my life is that cold April day when Prince gave me back my nerve.

It was the beginning of the end of my days at Lluest. Julie was leaving in a few months. Catrin, Heather and Merin, who once relied on me to control their ponies, had grown up. While I had lain in bed they had mucked out, groomed, fed, and helped out. When Prince and I had raced off we could have put them at risk, but they had their ponies under control and were proud that they no longer needed me. Somewhere amongst the elation I felt a touch of sadness. Lluest meant so much to me, and this would be our last spring there.

That was when we heard the first cuckoo of spring. I laughed, looking forward to the warmth and security of summer. I couldn't help feeling that the cuckoo was making a valid point. I was mad to risk galloping, especially to gallop on Prince... but we knew better, Prince and I, and whatever our disagreements, and there were plenty, we loved each other. While I was in pain, he would take great care of me. He had probably planned it all. Doctors were not going to condemn his boss to a quiet life. Prince had to get me fit again, because no one else would ride him. As I looked forward to summer rides, Prince no doubt looked forward to the day when he could buck, rear, and do his demented beetle bit, and know that his rider was back in control. Or thought she was...

Chapter 22

Ceri

Now, then. Fifteen, sixteen... what the... *seventeen?* There were only supposed to be sixteen ponies, and even allowing for the fact that I'm not that good at counting, and that it was early in the morning, I only owned one chestnut and there were definitely two in the field. As I plodded over, I realised that the new arrival was Ceri, who belonged to neighbours Caroline and Mick. I knew that they had split up but hadn't seen either of them for weeks. I had wondered what had happened to Ceri and worried a little. Well, now I knew, and I had a feeling that yet another Lluest delinquent had come to stay.

Yet another pony was all I needed at that time, so close to our move to Beili Bedw, our new home. We were very short of grazing as it was, and I didn't want to buy another lorryload of hay six weeks before our move. It wasn't as if Ceri was even a likeable pony. He was around 14.2hh, a nutty chestnut with definite hippy tendencies and heavily into self-expression, man! Rather like his owners, really, I thought with a grin. The problem with Ceri was that he usually chose to express himself in the middle of the road, preferably in front of a variety of oncoming traffic, and his favourite form of self-expression was dumping his rider.

I was definitely not pleased with Caroline, and as I advanced on Ceri, who immediately trotted off in the opposite direction, I remembered that another form of his self-expression was refusing to be caught. Ceri looked extremely sorry for himself; he was 'ribby' and looked as if he needed worming and de-lousing.

Well, I thought, he isn't staying. And I stamped off down the track to Caroline's cottage to tell her to remove Ceri before he infected my own ponies with his lice.

Halfway down the track I stopped, thoroughly ashamed of myself, and turned around and went back to have a closer look at 'my new pony'. I knew that Caroline was short of cash. I owed her and Mick a favour, but more than that I owed Ceri a chance. I'd never turned a pony away before, even if I was short of cash at the time. Somehow, we'd always managed. We were short of grazing, but I supposed we'd cope, and our herd would just have to accept another new member. I'd deal with Pete, who would no doubt make his views known, and Trefor, whose land we used earlier. In fact, I thought, to hell with them anyway. If I ignored Ceri then I shouldn't be doing this kind of work.

The dogs and I ran back to Lluest to get some food and louse powder. Gypsy stopped at our postbox and sniffed at it, looking at me between the whines and tail-wags.

'OK, have we got some post?' I asked.

Her tail went into overdrive. I opened the box and found five one-pound coins and an apologetic note from Caroline. I knew how hard it must have been for her to spare the cash, but what I didn't know then was that this cash was the only money I would make for nearly two years out of one of the craziest ponies I ever met.

So I packed my wheelbarrow with two bales of hay, a tube of wormer, a tin of louse powder and some coarse mix, and puffed my way to the field three-quarters of a mile away. Ceri raced over with the others, most of whom hadn't accepted him. I spread piles of hay as quickly as I could, dodging flying hooves and trying to keep some kind of order. Two bales aren't much between seventeen, so I rushed back for another two bales. The water trough was getting low, so I would have to spend the rest of the morning refilling that. By the time all the ponies were munching quietly and their trough was full it was one o'clock and I was hungry. Ceri seemed to be used to me flitting around, so I sat close to him and offered a handful of coarse mix. Ceri wasn't sure, but he was hungry so he stretched his head towards me.

'There's a good boy,' I encouraged.

Prince wasn't impressed, sensing a rival who would challenge his position as leader of the harem of mares. He skidded into Ceri, knocked him sideways and then bit him on the back. Ceri ran off. He wasn't strong enough to challenge Prince yet, but he cantered over to Bluey and drove him away from his pile of hay. The field was in uproar again as Prince and Ceri chased each other around disturbing everyone else. Even normally quiet ponies like Sam and Katy seemed to sense that the old pecking order was about to change, and set about beating up the weaker members of the herd. Jerry and Bluey, the usual targets for a trainee bully, hastily took themselves off to the farthest corner of the field. I knew from previous experience that it was useless to take their food over to them, as Della, the next weakest pony, would leave the herd and chase Jerry and Bluey away from their piles so that she could eat in peace. So I pushed the wheelbarrow back to Lluest, and loaded two more bales onto it and two headcollars and lead ropes, so that I could bring Jerry and Bluey back to the stable. By the time they were settled and fed it was two thirty in the afternoon and time to top up the water trough again. I grabbed a couple of chocolate biscuits to eat as I worked, and my earlier charitable feelings towards Caroline had faded. Somehow, I thought that Ceri was going to be nothing but trouble. He certainly was!

I tried everything to catch Ceri over the next few weeks, including removing all the other ponies hoping he would follow, but the fact that he didn't was no surprise. I spent hours offering him his choice of titbits and lots of praise – hours that should have been spent packing and preparing for the big move. However, Ceri was not going to let me catch him, he liked his new friends and was determined to stay with them, lice and all. I fumed over the lice, while dousing them with a good dose of the precautionary powder. Ceri was so like Prince when I met him all those years ago, and like Prince he loved the mares. None of the mares were in season, so I had no chance to see how he behaved with them, but instinct warned me that Ceri was no normal gelding. He was as arrogant as Prince had been but as yet showed no sign of that Prince charm. Yet he did have that extra 'something' (as all the rogues of this world do). If only that something could be tamed without breaking his spirit, and channelled into a life as a riding-school pony. I chuckled again; he was no more a riding-school hack or trekker than Prince was. What Ceri needed was one owner, one person to love and respect. But that person would probably have to be a good rider.

Beili Bedw, the farm we had decided to buy, was a real tip, although in a good position in the Brecon Beacons National Park at the foot of the Black Mountains. The house was immaculate, but the yard was a mess and the land was largely unfenced. It had potential, though, because it had forty acres of good grazing and a sheep shed that would easily stable twenty-plus ponies, and other sheds which could convert to stables. I had decided to take Stella down to see the farm and see what she thought of the place. Stella, like me, could see potential for development, and yes, the location was lovely but it wasn't like Lluest. For one thing, the farm was close to the road and lacked Lluest's aura of calm and isolation. However, we agreed that a move was the only way for the charity to survive and grow. But as we drove away from Beili Bedw, it was with a feeling of driving back home. I wondered if I could ever grow to love any other place as I had Lluest, which was my first real home.

Back at Lluest there was more trouble brewing. The ponies were still on the top field at the farm. The field had no grass now and the ponies were completely reliant on the hay I carried up to them. Unfortunately, although I had left them enough hay to last until we got back at six that night, they much preferred good grass. It soon became clear that the school bus had arrived and left Caroline's children at the top of the drive as usual, but unfortunately they hadn't closed the gate properly. Stella and I must have arrived just as Trevor saw some of the escapees in his newly re-sown field that was intended for his cows. However, I noticed that the usual band of troublemakers was absent, and I ran across the field calling and waving my torch as Stella put out yet more hay. I heard Stella shout and turned in time to hear the sound of a lot of panicked hooves approaching at a mad gallop, followed by barking dogs and yells of Welsh abuse. Jadine and the rest of the troublemakers were heading straight up Trefor's drive towards the road.

'Stop them, Stella,' I screamed.

Luckily for Stella, she couldn't run towards them quickly enough. If she had been in front of them, they would have trampled her. We had a full-scale bolt on our hands.

'Get in the car,' I yelled, struggling to run across the field. I leapt into the car. 'Come on, get moving. We've got to get in front of them – it's our only chance,' I snapped. 'Robert's due any minute, and if he meets them on a bend there'll be a terrible accident.'

Stella drove as fast as she dared, only slowing down for the bends. Then we saw them: shapes in the gloom just beyond our gate. If only I hadn't closed it, they would have just gone home.

'Right drive past them,' I shouted. 'Now!'

Stella wasn't keen, but I knew that their training would take over and they would all move to the side to allow the car to pass as they did every day of their working lives. We edged past Kate and Merlin and several others. Things were going too well. Then I saw that Jadine and Ceri were in front, and Ceri wasn't traffic proof. If I got out of the car I couldn't get through the hedge, and anyway the hedge rustling would spook them further. I decided to take a risk.

'Drive on,' I said. ' If he tries to gallop away try and accelerate past him.'

Stella was about to dither. I could see her point but didn't show it.

'Go on, for Christ sake,' I yelled. 'Now!'

We shot past and skidded to a halt two or three hundred yards beyond the ponies. Ceri had shied into the hedge. I got out.

'Right,' I ordered. ' Reverse back past them, park your car across the road beyond our gate, open it and stand next to your car. Yell when you're ready and I'll send them back.'

Stella got past the ponies easily this time. They weren't happy. Once they had got over the fear and then the exhilaration of a mad gallop they felt lost and waited for us to sort things out and get them back home.

'Road block complete,' Stella shouted.

So I walked towards the ponies telling them to 'walk on'.

They turned resignedly and trotted back towards Lluest. But then Ceri galloped through them – as always, ready to panic – and by the time they reached Stella they were in a mad gallop again. For a sickening moment I was afraid that Stella and her car might be a novel jump for Jadine and Ceri, but a loud yell from Stella swept the herd down our drive. She leapt back into her car and shot into our drive. By the time I got there she was leaning weakly on our gate. We pottered down the drive and set about catching the ponies and checking to see who was missing or injured. I heard a car racing down the drive and peered through the gloom. By the time I had recognised the white pickup it had braked with a vengeance and Trefor had leapt out.

So Trefor was cross! Well, so was I. We'd had our rows in the past, particularly if my ponies escaped, but we had made it up with only the odd niggle on either side. We needed each other too much to fall out. I needed Trefor's grazing just as much as he needed me to wash bottles, strip fence poles or dig post holes, but this time he had gone too far and I was in no mood to forget and forgive. If he had walked over and apologised for chasing the ponies onto the road, I would probably have apologised for them breaking onto his newly re-sown and drained field. Not that I blamed any pony who took advantage, if some idiot left a gate open. Trefor had no intention of saying sorry and very little of our conversation that evening is repeatable. Insults were traded fairly liberally on both sides and I finally told him exactly what he could do with his grotty grazing. He stormed off, leaving me to re-calm the ponies, who had panicked again at the sound of his voice.

'How could he?' I fumed to Stella. 'They could have been killed.'

As soon as we had settled the ponies into their stables, we raced back to the field to bring all the other ponies down to Lluest. This time I was relieved to count to seventeen. Now we were really in the 'manure'! – twenty-seven ponies and four acres. Luckily, I had expected something like this and had arranged back-up grazing in Llanrhystud. The only problem was that it was four miles away. We ate tea in a tired silence. I was sure that at least two ponies would be lame by the morning.

I phoned the people with the grazing, and was relieved to hear that I could have the field as soon as necessary. It was a beautiful field with plenty of grass and its own water supply. The ponies were divided into those who had to stay and work over half term, and the young charity ponies and the old or non-working trekkers. The first group to leave were amazingly good as they trotted away from Lluest, each charity pony led from an experienced trekker. Luckily, they liked their new home. I had wondered how they would like living away from us, and although I knew that Carolyn would keep an eye on them, I missed them all. Back at Lluest we had the usual endless round of feeding, mucking out and watering, but at least I wasn't carrying the bales up our lane several times a day.

Ceri wasn't at all happy. He liked all this food – hay and coarse mix more or less on demand was a new experience for him – but he didn't like the stable and being shut in it. He was putting on weight almost daily. Worming him had been 'fun' as he shot around the stable, and when I approached with a tin of louse powder he really had hysterics. I offered it to him to sniff and see what it was all about, but he cringed away from me thinking the tin was a weapon of some kind. As I sprinkled the powder over him, he spun around and reared so that most of the powder landed on me or the floor. So I tried putting the powder onto a body brush as I did with the foals. Ceri was still a bit concerned but he accepted it. Poor chap, I thought. He looked even more moth-eaten now that he had white patches all over him. As for me, I thought that I'd gained a few new 'friends' and hurried into the house to change. At least Beili Bedw had a shower, but at Lluest it was a straight choice: have a luke-warm or cold bath in a cold bathroom, or sit and pick any stray lice out of your hair, because however well covered I was, several of the little devils usually found a way to make friends. Even after a change of clothes and brushing my hair I still felt itchy. Sue from *Horse & Pony* magazine was paying a visit the following week. I couldn't help chuckling to myself; there we were trying to be on our best behaviour, preferably with not a hair out of place, and here I was playing catch with what seemed to be a particularly athletic louse.

By the time Jane, Mel and Ruth arrived from Gloucestershire a week later, Ceri had settled down a bit and I'd stopped scratching. They piled out of Pete's car eager to see the new arrival. Pete was still grumbling, but then he always did as yet another new pony joined the herd. 'What use will it be?' was usually the first question. In most cases the honest answer would be that I hadn't a clue; most of Lluest ponies arrived because of their needs rather than mine. I often point out that Pepper, Jim, Mick, Della and Prince were all no-hopers once. In fact, so was every pony I owned. So, it was usually a case of *nil desperandum*, break out the liniment for all humans involved with the new arrival, and talk very nicely to the vet and farrier.

We were pleasantly surprised by Ceri's behaviour on his first ride out. Jane was thrilled. Yes, he was slow and didn't even seem to understand basic aids, but he was willing to follow his new friends and was fairly sensible. He was still unreliable with traffic, but given time we hoped that he would be OK.

'Yes,' I smirked to Pete, 'we've got a good pony here.'

The next few months proved how wrong I was. I suppose my mistake was to allow Ceri to go down to Carolyn's with the rest of the ponies. Good grass was just what he needed. Of course, Ceri thought so too! It was lovely, all this food, and he didn't even have to be handled by a human to get it.

I was too busy packing for the move to see the ponies more than once or twice a week and left Carolyn to keep an eye on them. She couldn't get anywhere near Ceri. When I did go down, all the ponies ambled over on the lookout for a titbit, except Ceri who raced around the field and refused to allow me anywhere near him.

Our new home was a lowland farm, particularly when compared to Lluest's gale-swept bogs, and as soon as we arrived at Beili Bedw, Ceri showed his real temperament. In some ways I was pleased to see him so full of spirit; at least it showed that he was fit.

'Fit for what?' Pete snarled, as Ceri galloped around, broke through fences and generally set about wrecking our new home faster than we could repair it.

Jane, Ruth and Mel joined us again at Easter. By then, Ceri was much easier to handle, but I didn't envy Jane her first ride into the mountains on him. And it was one of those rides that was a particularly Welsh one, because the bridleway was nearly vertical, rocky and crossed a river. Ruth dutifully came back to lead 'Granny Ginny' across. Prince had splashed through so easily that I wished I'd stayed on him. I hate water and this was knee deep and fast flowing over slippery stones. How I wished we were back at home at Lluest on the Mynydd Bach or heading up our special gallop. Ruth and I staggered onto the opposite bank and remounted, heading up the path towards the mountain. I spotted a rider coming towards us and recognised a local farmer. I wasn't too sure of the way, so after exchanging greetings I asked for directions. Half an hour later the track we had been directed to became impassable. Something upset the ponies, especially Ceri who plunged off down the ravine and nearly unseated Jane.

'OK, that's it,' I shouted. 'Everybody off. Let's go home.'

What was wrong with Ceri? He was being difficult, as he always was, but there was something more: the pony was obviously terrified. He wasn't the only one – Prince spooked at a rook and nearly threw me for no reason that I could see.

Once we dismounted, I understood. I could feel the streams under the ground. No wonder the ponies were in a panic; none of them had ever experienced anything like it. Neither had I, and I didn't want to again. We ate our picnic in a depressed silence. If this was all the riding country near Beili Bedw then we would have to move again.

Ceri's behaviour deteriorated even faster after the ride. Every morning I found one of the geldings with a bite or a kick. At first, I blamed Prince, but when I found him with a cut leg and wound on his neck I guessed the truth. An evening spent quietly outside the field confirmed my fears. Ceri was a rig[41], and as more mares came into season his fights with Prince grew more frequent. The mares loved all

---

[41] A true rig is a male horse that has either one or two testicles undescended (concealed in its abdomen), making it look like a gelding while it behaves like a stallion. A false rig is a gelding that displays stallion-like behaviour, even though it has had both testicles removed and is therefore not driven by testosterone.

the attention and flitted from Prince to Ceri and back again. Ceri was now too dangerous to ride – that is, if you could catch him in the first place – and any attempt to mount him was greeted with an impressive display of rearing. One day I did manage to sit astride him but dismounted hurriedly as he reared and tried to throw himself over backwards.

Ceri was unreliable in the stable too, crashing around and quite prepared to run over the top of any human silly enough to get in his way. I had already decided to ask our vet to do a blood test to see if Ceri really was a rig, and meanwhile I concentrated on keeping him away from the mares and tried to teach him how to behave in the stable. He was surprisingly good about the blood test and stood quietly while the sample was taken. The phone call to give me the test results a week or so later gave me the worst case of indigestion I'd had for years. It turned out, however, that Ceri wasn't a rig – he just thought he was; but, as usual, what was in Ceri's mind was a bit of a mystery to everyone else. At first, we tried to separate him from the mares, but Ceri was a natural jumper and sailed easily over all the fences we had. The real love of his life was Jadine, Pete's chestnut mare of similar temperament and as scatty as he was. I had removed Prince and his harem to another field, leaving Gerry, Jadine and Katy with a few geldings that could get out of his way. Ceri was a real bully and would attack anything smaller or weaker than himself.

I finally decided that Ceri would have to go. I had never sold any Lluest pony, but this one was too big and too mad, and I was too crippled to cope with him. I decided to have 'one last go', as Pauline was helping me muck out the stables that day, and I marched into Ceri's stable determined to get the better of him. I'll never know if I really would have sold him, as Ceri, sensing he'd met his Waterloo, gave in after a few rears and stood properly to be groomed and even allowed me to pick up his back feet. Over the next few months, we discovered another side to his nature. One evening, I was sitting on a lump of wood in one of our paddocks looking at the tadpoles in the pond. I felt a nose touch my neck and turned to see that it was Ceri. He stood for half an hour or so accepting a cuddle as sloppily as any of the other ponies would.

Just as we were about to congratulate ourselves on reforming Ceri, he started to toss his head. At first, he just moved it up and down, but after a week or so he was throwing his head so badly that it was impossible to

183

ride him safely. So I phoned the vet again and asked if he could suggest what was wrong. The suggestions varied from just a bad habit, which knowing Ceri as we both did was definitely possible, to trouble with his teeth or ears. An examination revealed nothing, although I suspected his wolf teeth were to blame. Reluctantly, it was decided to remove the offending teeth and give him a good tooth rasp as well. For a time, Ceri was beautiful. Yes, he was scatty, but he gradually learnt to stand still to be mounted, and obeyed the lightest aid when ridden. Perhaps that was his trouble; he only needed a light aid and was easily upset if the aid was even slightly different from normal. For whatever reason, after a month of good behaviour Ceri was at it again. I think I know what started him off again. He was ridden by a rider who should have known what he was doing. Unfortunately, this man was so impressed with his own ability that he tried to ride Ceri as he would a trained dressage horse, unable or unwilling to realise that he was riding a very immature little horse who needed to be treated very much as an individual. I still threatened to sell Ceri, but it was a half-hearted threat. In time I was sure that he would be a lovely horse for one or two different people. He would never make a school horse, as he could not take the pressure of dozens of different people. He loved children and became fond of us too. Perhaps, I thought, one day he would calm down. I hoped that day was not a too distant, and hoped that I would be able to afford to keep yet another passenger in the style that he had become accustomed to!

Ceri with Shelley

Part Three:

Beili Bedw

Peter and Ginny
with Jester, Gypsy and Joker

The foal Rhiannon, with Ginny and Morfydd

Joker tolerating Gypsy

Chapter 23

November 1986 and new beginnings at Beili Bedw

B eili Bedw wasn't a home to me, beautiful as it was; it was just a large transit camp, a place Pete and I bought because it was cheap and we thought we could do it up and sell it for a profit. I didn't really want to buy the farm. The sheds were a mess, nearly eighteen inches deep in muck in some places, and in the barn the heap was taller than I was. Mixed in with this mess, we found wood covered with rusty nails, scissors, carpet and other discarded remnants. And there was a muck heap that, when we began to remove it, revealed that it had been an obvious handy place to bury a sheep carcass. As I gagged, I couldn't wait for the day we sold Beili Bedw.

Kitty, one of our cats, had disappeared within three days of our arrival. I was still grieving for her when, three months later, Tiggy, another gentle old cat, also disappeared. The dogs and I searched every ruin in the area, we put advertisements in the local paper, contacted the local vets and the RSPCA, but no one had seen either cat. Finally, I gave up, vowing never to have another cat. But P Brain, the last of my trio, was lonely, and friends Lisa and Christine cornered me into going to see two tabby kittens at the RSPCA cattery.

'Has to be male,' I countered, trying to be difficult and wriggle out of the responsibility of owning another cat. Both kittens were male so, half-heartedly, I chose the bigger of the two. He looked the best potential mouser, but the other kitten demanded attention as I reluctantly cuddled it. Ivy, the cat lady, stood back – I'm sure she knew that I was making the wrong decision, but she kept quiet and let 'Perseverance' and nature take its course. P Brain still wailed for Tiggy every morning, and I looked for Tiggy too, knowing deep down that he was lost to us. When Pete came home for the weekend, we went to see the kittens. I showed him 'my' kitten while I tried to disengage the other kitten from my leg, back and hair! Finally, I gave in and saw sense. Perseverance was just what I wanted, and he was definitely affectionate! I felt he'd be a homely cat, and he was so like Tiggy it was uncanny.

When we collected Perseverance four weeks later and got him home to meet P Brain she took one look at her new 'friend' and had hysterics. She was terrified of the tiny kitten with just a squeak for a meow, but soon she was to be so much in love. At first, she ran away, but the smell of dinner lured her back. Perseverance advanced, clearly upset, and then P Brain launched herself onto the top of the settee. I picked her up to cuddle her, but Perseverance shot up my leg and P Brain yowled and retreated. Perseverance was well named and was soon tolerated. By the end of the week he was cuddled and washed, and P Brain never wailed for Tiggy again.

As Perseverance grew, so did the chaos. He chased the chickens, attacked dog tails (except Jester's, because he was not a silly kitten) and chewed human fingers. Typing became a very high-risk occupation, and answering the phone was difficult too, as Perseverance insisted on 'helping' with daily tasks. He was definitely a house-cat and rushed back inside if anything frightened him. His antics made me laugh, and though I still missed Tiggy and Kitty, he made sure I didn't have time to brood. As with all kittens, Perseverance grew; it might be fine to have a tiny kitten perched on your shoulder, but at six months he was becoming a lump. He was also discovering sex, so Pete and I took him to the vet to have his naughty bits removed. The advice was to keep him quiet for a couple of days after the operation, but that was virtually impossible; in fact he was quiet for only a few hours, but as he seemed none the worse, I didn't worry too much.

During this time, although Perseverance considered Beili Bedw was his home, I worried that the ponies showed no signs of settling down. We had managed to renovate the 'sheep shed' by the end of April, but we hadn't made a start on the building that was to be home for the charity's ponies, which was full of partly constructed cow cubicles and debris. What concerned me most were the solid piles and layers of muck. I wondered how many of the cows and sheep that had occupied the building had trodden on nails or other debris. Renovating the yards was not going well either. We had made the mistake of hiring a local lad with a JCB to dig the drains. Unfortunately, although the lad and his family were good people, the digger was permanently broken. The lad would arrive for work, dig a ditch and the digger would break down. I was very often left with a deep ditch, usually in front of the stables or hay barn, which had to be negotiated. The best ditch of all was the one he dug in front of the sheep shed, just before I was due to have an inspection for my trekking centre. It was supposed to be filled in but of course it wasn't, so the man from the Council (who had forgotten his wellies and therefore got muddy feet) and the inspecting vet had to leap over the ditch to inspect the ponies. Needless to say, that inspection was not a success. I was grudgingly issued with a provisional licence, and could only imagine what they thought of the farm, which was still a mess of polythene sacks, broken buildings and open ditches. I agreed with them, but could only remove so much muck and litter, in between looking after thirty-six horses and ponies, and youngsters.

♘

The charity had decided to rescue two more ponies, and returned from the sale in January 1987 with Sunshine, a 'wild' bay colt, and Sian, a grey mare in foal[42]. Sunshine was a real pain. Although weak and terrified at the sale, he soon recovered his spirit once at his new home. He was a natural jumper but easily frightened, and he spent a huge amount of time breaking out of his comfy stable and inciting the other ponies to join him. Between them they left a trail of broken fences and battered humans. I could only manage to squeeze in a small amount of time tidying up between dealing with these breakouts, but gradually Pete repaired the fences.

I breathed a sigh of relief when the JCB and its owner departed, but his swan song was a real epic. The JCB, as well as not liking work, seemed attracted to water pipes, and, to be fair, the idiot (whoever that may be) who had laid them in the first place had done so very close to the surface; not very good when yet another fountain of water decorated the yard, and I had to carry buckets of water from the house to the ponies who, of course, were trapped behind the ditch with a fountain in it. As I slithered along, clutching buckets and hay bales, I swore about diggers, men, the weather, and horses, but most of all I swore about this farm that seemed to be dealing me one blow after another.

---

[42] Sian's story is told in Chapter 24, entitled 'A Nose on my Arm'.

On the plus side, I had gained respect for our new vet - at least we have a decent vet here too, I thought. We started building the outdoor school, which was a bit of a funny shape but at least it suited our purpose, and anyway nothing was ever 'normal' with us. Several new friends became regular visitors, but I soon discovered that some were not 'friends' at all and were only prepared to support us if it involved making a profit. And then Eve arrived. I wasn't too sure about her at first. She was about ten years older than me, with a son and daughter. The daughter wanted riding lessons; she was a bit of a whinger but soon developed into a plucky little rider who, to her credit, cared enough about ponies to shovel up after them.

Gradually, I realised that Eve and I shared the same sense of humour and fanatical devotion to horses. Eve worked for me, drove me to sales, enduring the threatening looks and comments, helped me clean stables, and became a real friend. She never expected payment, which was just as well as I was too impoverished to offer anyway, but we both knew the other was just a phone call away. It was Eve I phoned when I came back from the sale one day after I saw a foal stretch out a gentle nose to a small child that he could so easily have trampled underfoot. His gentle action haunted me often, as I knew it would for all the years to come, but if I needed a reason to fight power and greed with love then that colt was a supreme example. Eve listened patiently as I poured out the pain of my day. She didn't tell me to forget it, or offer an easy solution, as we both knew there wasn't one, which was why I was upset in the first place. By the time I hung up I felt a little better.

Other new friends came to visit. Lisa and Christine were both very involved with the local RSPCA. I met Lisa initially when she worked for our vet, but she got involved with the Lluest Trust and soon found herself offering grazing to a permanently overstretched sanctuary.

Eventually, Lisa's lovely mare Jenna came into the care of the trust. The mare was originally rescued in poor condition at a local sale. She had then recovered well, giving Lisa five years of pleasure as a riding horse, but now she needed a home in a controlled environment. Jenna had ringbone (a form of osteoarthritis causing lameness), and would normally have been shot, but Lisa and her vet wanted to see how she would be if she was confined to a stable. Lisa's land was steep and marshy in places, and the lean-to shed, although more than adequate for a healthy horse, wasn't any good now for Jenna. Lisa's attitude to her horse should be an example to other horse owners who, despite maybe having considerably more money, would discard a sick animal without a second thought. Lisa not only donated to the trust for Jenna's keep, but also immediately offered free grazing for two of the trust's ponies. She had considered having the mare put to sleep, but only if it was right for Jenna. Her own emotional feelings were firmly ignored. Her vet's decision to give Jenna a bit longer was the right one. She improved slowly with regular checks by the vet.

Over time, other people came into our lives. I liked Tanya and her family as soon as they walked through the gates. The three children had impeccable manners, were very intelligent and great fun to be with. Tanya settled in quickly, and for some reason devoted herself to Comet, one of my original trekking ponies. Typically for Comet, he responded by throwing her at every opportunity. Tanya wasn't discouraged and progressed to helping to school Sony (one of the charity's newest residents) and eventually backing the smaller ponies for me. Sara and Tanya were firm friends and, despite being only ten and eleven respectively, were sensible mature helpers. True, it took the two of them to hang a hay net up, with a bucket to stand on, but they had more common sense than some twenty-year-olds who have worked for me.

One morning, after Folly (one of the youngest of my herd) was particularly horrible and had bucked Tanya off twice, Sara was busy mucking out. Eve and I were busy teaching when I noticed Sara sitting quietly watching us. Sara wasn't a lazy girl, so I smiled as Eve went up to see what was wrong. I smiled even more when Eve came back. Sara, afraid that Folly might seize any excuse to dump Tanya, had waited for the lesson to finish before wheeling the wheelbarrow past the ménage to the muck-heap.

I suppose all of these things were gradually making me realise that Beili Bedw was home, as 'home' to me depends on the teamwork of dedicated friends. So as Gillian, one of my new found friends, shovelled her way cheerfully through another day's mucking out, or teased me about me teasing her about her accent, we laughed our way through one crisis after another. Gillian's parents actually made four journeys of twenty miles each way, so that Gillian could work for nothing and help make sure that the motley collection of ponies could live in comfort.

That first summer at Beili Bedw was a time of exploration as we tried to get to know the maze of lanes around us and got used to the chaos. Rides were never on time as I lost one ride after another on the mountains.

The Trust's open week was in August, and this meant a panic of hard work in general, especially as it coincided with the delivery of sand arriving for the outdoor school. This meant that Chris and Andrew, two more long-suffering helpers, shovelled the sand out from the piles into a sort of flat surface. Gillian and I finished the job by moonlight while waiting for the vet to come and inject Sunshine, and I painted new fences until I was sick of paint – particularly white paint and post and rail fences. The charity stable was still a mess, so we managed to arrange for a group of community workers to come and renovate it. They did an excellent job, and open week could proceed.

By October I had time to take my first real look at the farm. The dogs trotted at my heels as we walked our land, played in the river or just watched the branches of the oak trees that swayed in the woods. I was at peace, and felt at home on our own farm. This didn't mean that life was easy, though! The winters were cold, and the central heating I'd enthused over was off more than it was on. We couldn't afford coal, any more than we could afford a full-time worker to help me with an ever-growing family of equines. New arrivals were Rhiannon and Melody, born in early spring to Morfydd and Sian, our rescued mares who now knew Beili was their home. Sunshine had settled in as well, and was a friendly youngster who walked towards people instead of running away from them. The dogs were settled and the ponies were relaxed and happy. Beili was becoming a true sanctuary, and a happy farm. No more sheep died in dark corners; it was an oasis of safety amongst an old community that accepted snaring and shooting as a way of life, where the local hunt no longer ventured onto our land and our neighbours respected our boundaries.

We were not always well-liked locally; attitudes varied from all-out hostility, carefully disguised by an insincere smile, to total disbelief. I sometimes wondered: how could they be expected to understand a 'veggie pacifist' who collected worn-out horses? There was predictable opposition to us riding on the roads that they deemed were too narrow (because drivers went too fast), despite the fact that, unlike their sheep who blocked the road completely, our riders kept to one side of the lane, allowing drivers to pass easily. I suspected that the real reason was my interest in their wild pony herds and fear that I would infect their children with my attitudes. I once commiserated with one near neighbour over the loss of a cow.

'Poor thing,' I said.

The reply was more to the point of her value and the loss of it, not the loss of life. It wasn't that the farmer was cruel; his stock was a credit to him, but there was no sentiment or perhaps none that he would admit to. He'd worked hard all of his life, and still did, and his farm was one of the tidiest in the area, but our ways of life were as opposite as they could be. However, I deemed that we co-existed amiably and frankly.

Pete still wanted to stick to our original plan and sell the farm, but agreed to postpone until after Christmas. I played for time, considering the options, but knowing in my heart that the place I once felt was alien was fast becoming 'home and sanctuary' to me as well as to the animals. Late one evening, I stood with Prince, my faithful gelding, in a moonlit field looking out across the yard. On one hand I was too blinded by worry to see a way forward, and on the other hand I was trying to think beyond the doubts and worry. I thought about the Trust, about a morning with a group of handicapped children who had come to meet the ponies, to ride, and who captured the hearts of everyone, while gaining the gentle acceptance of the ponies. I thought of all of the friends who helped out for nothing, their laughter, and the love that is now as much part of Beili Bedw as the old Lluest. The love that now radiated a welcome to new arrivals, both horsey and human.

Later that month, Pete and I went back to the old Lluest. We drove across the Mynydd Bach past Llyn Eiddwen, slate grey and mysterious as ever. A breeze chased waves across the surface of the lake: a surface sometimes reflecting the beauty of the mountains – mountains that were walked by Taliesin[43]. We drove past our favourite 'canter', and I could almost hear the war-whoops and the pounding hooves from not so very long ago, when Prince and I had thundered this way when he was fast and I was fit. Now he was lame and had been for six months, and I knew it would soon be time to turn my back on a life lived for gallops; we had enjoyed two years of borrowed time. I knew that we would never ride this way again or walk down the steep lane watching Cardigan Bay in all its beauty. We had trotted this way in snow, hail and rain, forgetting all the harsh days for one day of sunlight. This was hard. There were so many memories, and it still had the flavour of being home. I'd learnt to love at Lluest; to love the weak and the sick as well

---

[43] Taliesin was a famous sixth century Welsh bard who is thought to have sung at the courts of three Kings.

as the ponies like Prince whose fire would never fade. I was homesick again. I still missed this old place so much, for all its problems.

Pete drove into 'our' drive as he had so many times before. Our old sign lay on the floor, and weeds choked the gate that needed painting. The house stood as it always had, and I hoped always would. Our old Dutch barn, still upright by some miracle, creaked in the wind. The stables, that were the first home and an introduction to a new life for our family of wild foals, were empty and unpainted. The yard was full of grass, the gardens overgrown just as they were when fourteen ponies, a dog, Pete and I arrived all those years ago. The other dogs, Joker and Jemma, were born there, as were Tiggy and P Brain, the cats. Had its call lured Kitty or Tiggy back home? I called in vain, trying to ignore the feeling I had that both cats had died near Beili Bedw.

The house looked sad. New windows, that made it look like a church of some kind, had been installed and then deserted. Its new owners, who I'd hoped would love their home as I did, had left when they found it was less profitable than they hoped. Was Lluest's old magic lost now, as it stood empty and unloved? Yet the calm feeling of a true sanctuary and resting place was still there – the calm that created Lluest Horse and Pony Trust, and nurtured it to provide hope and love for the ponies who desperately needed it. Part of me wanted to sell Beili Bedw and come back to restore it, but Lluest had taught me many things, and one was that I had no duty to the sticks and stones of a house – my duty was to the animals and people who lived in our new home. Jester sat in the car; she remembered the road but perhaps she wisely realized that this was her 'old' home. I had one last look around, saying a final goodbye as a damp wind blew in with the tide – a damp wind that made me notice and realise how I was now used to the softer lands of Beili Bedw.

Pete drove down to the beach, where Jester ran around wagging her tail and sniffing at the remains of barbecues. Then we drove home, stopping for a drink and meal at our old local. I remembered nights when I'd worked for one of the landlords in our first year there, and the days when I worked for Trefor in return for grazing.

We arrived back at Beili Bedw at dusk, to a chorus of whinnies from Bluey, Jenna and Faith (a recent rescue by the charity). Faith was galloping now, as living proof that miracles do happen; perhaps Jenna and Prince would have a miracle too. There had been plenty of them amongst the tragedies. As for me, a new life was waiting for me. I had so much: a farm, the animals, friends and the charity. I didn't know what the future held, but I knew that Beili Bedw was our home and I would fight for it and all that Lluest Horse and Pony Trust stood for. It would be so easy to give up, and give in. Jester nuzzled my hand; Prince trotted up to the fence and blew on my face; Jemma, Joker and Gypsy hurtled towards me, tails wagging. Hooves thundered towards me – hooves and lives that depended on me. In turn, I depended on them and all my human friends too. They all played a part, giving their own special gift to the charity so that in turn it might give that love to others. The Lluest Horse and Pony Trust was too special to fail; it had to continue. Tomorrow would be another 'Lluest Morning and another new day dawning'. One day a new dawn would bring the financial salvation we needed and with it salvation for ponies – all the forgotten ponies, the weak, the ugly or the unloved. I was reminded of our song, especially written about the old Lluest[44], by friend Stella:

It's another Lluest morning,
And another new day dawning.
Hoof beats drum the ground,
Dogs bark at the sound,
And I know that life is good when they're around.

At Lluest we knew that within an ugly exterior hid a special pony, a pony who only needed love and good food to emerge from the chrysalis of its neglect into the butterfly world where love was not conditional on exterior beauty or ability to win prizes at local shows. But that love was our duty, the duty of the strong to the weak, of giving our riches to the poor and needy. Our riches were few and scarce, but who needed riches with a nose resting on your arm, or a chorus of whinnies that welcomed you home?

---

[44] The complete words are given at the end of Chapter 12.

Chapter 24

A nose on my arm

I t was already half past three in the afternoon. I knew that, because Prince and Sarah thundered up the field and leant over the post and rail fence, stamping their feet and demanding their dinner. I grabbed their buckets and raced off to the feed shed. Sarah, impatient as ever, kicked the fence, so I shouted at her as I ran down the yard clutching two full buckets. Prince waited politely, but he was hungry too. As they tucked in, the heavens opened again, so I rushed back to the boys' stable, grabbing a wheelbarrow and fork on the way. The boys were pleased to see me and crowded around the door eager for a pat. I pushed my way into the stable, dragging the wheelbarrow after me. Cariad skipped forward and nuzzled my arm. Phoenix blew in my ear and Ben almost fell over the wheelbarrow in his efforts to attract my attention. Jaws was displeased and pushed past Whisper who was waiting behind Phoenix and sank his teeth into Cariad's rump. She leapt out of his way, colliding with Trixie who lashed out at Copper in temper.

'Oi,' I yelled.

My delinquents sauntered back to the hay-rack and I set about cleaning up the newly processed 'hay'. Unfortunately, they soon got bored with eating, so I was trying to muck out with one hand and fend off a dozen noses with the other. Several fork-loads missed the wheelbarrow altogether as Sunshine chose a critical moment to grab my sleeve and pull. Irritated yells brought a minute respite but then a nose leant on my arm, another nosed my knee and I was once again surrounded by noses that blew a warm breeze on my neck.

'Oh, go away,' I yelled again, and marched forward pushing a variety of noses away from the wheelbarrow.

They seemed to have got the message at last, I thought, not realising that a conspiracy was brewing. I reached into my pockets for my mittens and realised that I had lost one. Whisper and Davy were playing together, and what they were playing tug of war with was blue, woolly and looked very much like the lost mitten. Leaving the full wheelbarrow unguarded was asking for trouble, but I didn't think that a thumbless mitten would be much use. Rescuing the mitten was easier than I had expected as Whisper and Davy turned their attention to annoying Rhiannon. Feeling rather pleased with myself I turned to retrieve the wheelbarrow in time to see Jaws grab the handle and turn it over.

'You pig,' I yelled.

Jaws wisely retreated to his friends, Cariad reared, Smokey trotted across the stable and I was surrounded by all twelve ponies celebrating a good joke. I was too tired to see the funny side and swore as I reloaded the barrow in record time. As I wheeled it away, leaving a clean stable, Ben lifted his tail and triumphantly produced a large deposit. Melody followed suit. I ignored them and refused to be lured back into the stable. Jaws looked disappointed.

The top stable was probably dirty again, so I plodded up the yard with the wheelbarrow. The stable was dirty, but it was late and I was tired and fed up, so I decided to call it a day after one more load. The rest could wait until morning. I wasn't concentrating as I mucked out Sian's stable, so I almost fended off a grey nose with a yell and a bad-tempered push. Luckily, I remembered whose nose it was in time to put the fork outside the stable. I stretched out my hand to touch her nose. Sian shied back in alarm.

'Alright, you silly cow,' I said, returning to the mucking out. I had so much to do and it would be dark soon. The grey nose demanded attention but retreated as soon as Sian realised that I had noticed her. I wheeled the barrow out of the stable and the rain gave way to hail. Somehow, I didn't fancy a trip to the muck heap in that. Sian watched me, ears pricked. There was no reason to think that today would be special; it was just another day of monotonous, exhausting grind, another day to struggle through, another day when I tried not to think of the money we owed, another day when I hoped that I wouldn't be too tired to notice if a pony was off colour. My head ached, my back ached and my skin itched, and now it was hailing too. What a day. Why did I do this job anyway?

Sian was still watching me. Wearily, I trudged to the feed shed, collar turned up but offering very little protection against the hail. I put some coarse mix in a bucket. Maybe today would be special. I hardly dared to hope that today would be the day Sian finally accepted me. It wasn't very likely; she had been with us nearly a year now, but, although she put up with being wormed and even groomed if she had to, she avoided human company as much as possible. I didn't blame her for distrusting the human race, as they had done nothing but abuse her and her foals. Sian had spent her early life on a mountain somewhere, breeding foals that were taken away from her to feed the horse-meat trade. Her friends, the other mares in the herd, disappeared too if they got too old to breed, so Sian learnt not to make friends. Foals came and went, but Sian hardly noticed as she struggled to grub enough food from a bare mountainside. She was a solitary, self-contained little mare, always ready to panic, ready to look after number one. Her attitude was unique; she wasn't a herd creature like most of her kind, and her friendship with our other pregnant mare, Morfydd, was just the acceptance of another companion as long as it lasted.

Her attitude wasn't surprising really, I thought. We had met at a local sale on that cold January day, when she was in foal again, and still had last year's foal at foot. Sian was just a grey mountain mare, nothing special unless you noticed a pretty head. The filly, not quite a yearling, was sold as 'quiet to ride' before we could do anything about it. The owner was a lout who broke a pony with the aid of a large stick, and if necessary he was prepared to reduce the pony to a pathetic cowering creature. I suspected that he tried to beat Sian into submission; she did stand quietly enough for him but her eyes rolled and I had the feeling she would have resisted if she had had the strength and energy to do so. The foal growing inside her had no chance of survival. If Sian was by some miracle not sold for meat then her owner would take her home and continue to break her in whether she was heavy in foal or not. So I bought Sian, then later in the sale I bought Sunshine the bay colt. At first, we allowed Sunshine to share a large stable with Sian because he was too weak to be a nuisance, but after two weeks he had his own stable leaving Sian to eat in peace. She couldn't believe her luck; she had never seen so much food and ate everything offered with gusto.

When our vet arrived to check the new arrivals and worm them, Sian had hysterics, but between us we managed to corner her and administer the doses. She hated the stable and yearned to be out, even if the weather was horrible. Dancer had been just the same and only accepted living in after a year with us. I could have kept her in and forced her to accept us, but I do not believe in forcing a pony like Sian to accept a human being. I knew that if I forced my presence on her she would accept that presence rather than risk a fight, but she would only do what she was forced to do, and as soon as she was faced with a weak person or child she would use her strength to win. She had made no attempt to injure any of us; the kicks we got from her were as much our fault as hers. If we gave her enough room then she had no need to panic, but if you tightened your hold on a leading rein then Sian was likely to land on you in her efforts to escape. So I decided it was best to let Sian have the foal as she'd had others in the past, with no intervention from the human race. Our woodland paddock had plenty of grass and was sheltered, so we moved Sian and Morfydd over. I had to carry them hay and stud nuts twice a day and was eagerly received by both mares, although, as usual, Sian refused to allow me anywhere near her.

We weren't sure when Sian would foal, so we moved them nearer the house in April, anticipating the happy event. The field was secluded and definitely off limits to all but a handful of special visitors who could be trusted to sit quietly. By the end of May, Sian had driven me to distraction. Her girth seemed to increase daily, but close examination of her udder was impossible. Of course, when she did finally decide to produce her foal she took us all by surprise. Sandra and Caz, two old school friends, had dropped in for a visit, so I took them over to see the mares. Morfydd came over to see us, but Sian, who refused to come near us, captivated my friends. We sat in the middle of the field, watery sunlight on our backs with the threat of rain peeping through the trees. It was the ideal day for a new life to dawn. At least this one life had a future; the other foals already born on the mountain this month did not.

'You know, I really think she'll foal in a few days,' I said. Caz gazed at Sian.

'How can anyone slaughter such a beautiful creature, especially when she is in foal?'

I sighed, thinking about all the other in-foal mares I watched sold for slaughter.

'It's a disgrace,' Sandra said. 'She's a nice mare, too.'

It was drizzling now, so we decided to go back to the house. I turned back for a last look at Sian and saw her turn to look at her belly. Was she going into labour? Sandra and Caz stayed for dinner chatting about Sian and all the others.

'Do you think she'll ever trust you?' Sandra asked.

'I hope so, but I just don't know,' I answered.

'What if she needs help with the birth?' Caz asked. 'Would she accept it?'

'Don't even think about it,' I warned. 'Anyway, she's probably had at least six foals so she should be OK.'

She was, too, and I missed the birth! I checked her again that afternoon and thought that she might be starting. I was on the point of panicking, but I decided to give her another hour. Of course, Pete had to come home at the wrong time demanding coffee. I decided to have a cuppa too, and Sian took advantage of a Ginny-free hour and produced little Melody. Sian owed her life to a dear friend who, together with riders and staff from her riding school, raised money by singing Christmas carols, so the little chestnut filly, who was saved by songs, had to be called Melody. I was entranced as I watched her for the first time. She was a beauty with a fine dished head and tiny ears, a rather damp chestnut who peeped out from behind her mother on a wet Welsh evening; a new life born into a true haven. Melody was safe and secure for life. She would have time to enjoy her growing up, unlike the mountain foals whose short harsh lives had to be devoted to the grim task of survival. At first, Sian guarded her jealously, teaching her to distrust all humans, but after a couple of weeks she went back to eating and eating. Sian never frisked or scampered and left love and devoted motherhood to Morfydd who, after a rather shaky start, became a devoted mum to Rhiannon and aunt to Melody. In fact, Sian never expressed joy, she just ate and existed like Dancer had. The fight for survival was the only important factor in her life. Dancer was the same when she came to Lluest, but she eventually relaxed and learnt to race the wind and play with her friend Mick.

Time is supposed to heal most wounds, but how can you heal a lifetime of losses, the fear of round-up and terror of a sale? Sian was a sad pony; most mares will defend their foals but Sian panicked for herself. If Melody kept up with her when she ran, fine. If not... I could not help Sian. I couldn't make her forget her miserable life any more than I could make her trust me and realise that not all humans are the same. I dreaded weaning the foals as it is an upsetting time for mares and foals alike. Predictably, Morfydd had hysterics; her grief upset us all and yet I grieved more for Sian who hadn't been able to love and enjoy her foal. Human beings have a lot to answer for. We condemned Sian to breed a foal every year, foals born of our greed or indifference, and we took them all away from her; somewhere we took all her love, hope, and trust too.

Melody grew up quickly into a clever, friendly, sensible little filly. Somehow, I was sure that she was just like her mother. Sian was clever and knew that Melody was still around and even called to her if they were within calling distance.

Sian knew exactly where her baby was that evening, too. Was that why she had sniffed my arm? Maybe Dancer had spoken to Sian. I wondered if putting Sian, who now accepted the stable, into that particular one with Mick and Dancer had been an accident dictated by lack of space, because some of the best things in my life had been a complete accident. Mick and Dancer had accepted Sian. Mick was still an old rogue, but he had accepted Dancer and taught her to be happy. Was Dancer repaying the favour by teaching Sian to love life too? I suppose that sounds pretty farfetched, but we had always known that Mick was telepathic, and all ponies are sensitive to the atmosphere of a place. Sian must have realised that both ponies were happy as she watched Dancer and Mick greet me with a whinny every morning. They were both old and their age saddened me – if only I could bring back their youth and make their lives as they should have been; if only all ponies had lives they deserved. At least Sian was young, probably only ten. Perhaps I could teach her.

Sian's ears pricked as she saw the bucket. She danced up to me but shied away again as I stretched towards her. So I put the bucket down and invaded her space. She backed away, eyes rolling, and tossed her head in threat.

'Stand,' I said, and inched forward. I could almost touch the headcollar. It was now or never, and I had to show her that I trusted her, so I knelt down in front of her and reached up to secure the leading rope. I felt her relax. This time she was relieved to be caught – it was her choice. She had chosen not to run me down, but we both knew she could have done so easily. She had wanted to be caught and be like the others, but old habits die hard and she hadn't been able to bring herself to have faith in anyone. She sniffed my face and then pushed her head into my arms. As I cuddled her the sun shone at last, and a pair of red kites wheeled over the back fields. I knew why I did my job as Sian opened my eyes again to the beauty of the world and to the animals that surrounded me. I stroked her neck and tried to slide my hand along her back. She flinched, although she didn't try to rear, so I just stood with her, touching her, hoping she understood she was home at last and that I would never let her down.

We stood together for a long time, watched approvingly by Dancer and Mick. Worries were a long way away for both of us, each healed by the love of the other. The radio blared out Radio 1 as the other ponies munched their hay, but Sian and I didn't notice it. It was dark now and way past short feed time, but even gutsy old Pepper hadn't complained. It was as if every pony in the stable had understood that Sian had come home at last. Finally, I remembered her bucket – it was there three feet away from us.

'Go on, have your dinner,' I said gently. Sian nuzzled me and watched me walk out of the stable before she ambled over to eat her dinner, pausing to savour every mouthful.

In two days, I had to face another sale. A year previously, two-and-a-bit ponies came home to a new life. This year there was no room. I fumed at the unfairness of life – if only I had... I could save another life. The endless procession that haunted my dreams haunted me in my working hours too.

Sian turned towards me, ears pricked, eyes gentle, one lost haunted soul recognising another. I'd seen so much misery and evil and I was tired and angry. Like Sian I kept up appearances, always laughing and joking – I did my crying in private, keeping my feelings bottled up tight. How could I forgive the men involved in the horse-meat trade where greed and cruelty were more important than an animal's life? Yet Sian had forgiven. She'd reached out to me and trusted me, and perhaps she was helping me, too. If she could forgive, then shouldn't I? I knew that I would face confrontation at the sales, but I would endeavour to face it without anger. I'd leave that to the men I dealt with. They could rave and threaten, but it didn't matter, because I'd spent a very special hour with a very special pony. Sian had finally come home – she was at peace at last.

Chapter 25

A happy herd

With a growing family of forty-plus horses and ponies, and not forgetting one very dynamic donkey, it isn't easy to make time to sit in a field watching the herd grazing around me.

The donkey was Dinah. She had been taken in by the Trust with her friend Champ, a very pretty pony. I had been called out to see them in a field nearby. Both were in a sorry state. Dinah was underweight, her feet badly needing attention, and her coat was matted. Champ wasn't much better. Now, here they were grazing happily, well-recovered and looking a picture.

Then there was Blackie, one of my trekkers, and one that actually preferred human company to that of his own kind. He had come with me from Gloucestershire, where he had suffered a kidney problem not so long after we bought him. Our then vet suggested we sell him through the sale ring, but I was determined to give him a chance. I nursed him, combining veterinary medicine (at £20 per bottle) with herbs picked from the hedgerows. Many children helped to collect dandelion leaves by the sackful, and I also gave him juniper berries. Blackie didn't seem to improve – in fact I noticed that his eyesight was failing. Just about that time 'Bright Eyes' was a number one record; the words usually reduced the whole stable to tears. Blackie was surrounded by love; in fact, he was even prayed for at the local chapel and school. I contacted a faith healer who told me that she felt Blackie was going to recover. A month later I phoned to tell her that she had been right. Blackie had lost part of his sight and was useless as a riding pony, but at least he was alive. We never found out what caused the attack. After a couple of weeks, I allowed his favourite rider to take him out around our fields, and after a few minutes he seemed to settle down. In time, his sixth sense became highly developed, and he avoided obstacles as if operating radar. He could be quite naughty, but incredibly he could jump two foot six over any obstacle, relying on my 'hup' to tell him where and when to take off. He became a happy pony, and sometimes I forgot his poor vision – like the time he decided to join the campers one summer, when he picked his way delicately in amongst the guy ropes. I don't know what saved him; perhaps it was the dandelions leaves or perhaps it was the strength of feeling that surrounded him.

Love had also surrounded Rice, who grazed nearby. His owners had been devoted and hard-working supporters of the charity. A change in their circumstances meant that Rice had to be found a new home. I agreed to take him into my trekking herd, and although he was getting on in years we were sure that he would enjoy the gentle ride out. Sadly, however, shortly after he came to me he became lame, and navicular disease[45] was suspected. His treatment could cost several hundred pounds with no guarantee of success. Rice was a friendly soul and he deserved a chance. I hoped that the coming trekking season would be a profitable one and that I could find the money for his treatment. I needn't have worried.

Winter postmen are usually viewed with suspicion, being the messengers of doom with assorted brown envelopes containing threats of varying degrees. I didn't recognise the writing on one envelope as I opened the letter. It was from Sian, the young lady who owned Rice, and contained a cheque for £100 to cover his treatment. Sian promised to pay for all his treatment, and over the next two months the family paid for X-rays and drugs. They visited Rice to check his progress, trying hard to be cheerful and sensible and ignore their sadness, and concentrating instead on doing only what was best for their pony.

I asked them why they wanted to treat him. Their reply almost restored my faith in the horse-owning public. 'When we bought him, we knew Sian would outgrow him but we felt we owed him a home for life. He is our responsibility.' They were so right.

I telephoned Sian's dad a few weeks later, to say that the medication wasn't working and that Rice would possibly need a nerve block and, if

---

[45] Navicular disease typically affects both front feet. It usually involves inflammation or degeneration of the small navicular bone at the back of a horse's foot, and causes lameness.

necessary, further courses of the treatment at £50 per pot. His reply was instant.

'Tell the vet to do whatever is best for Rice, as we'll back him one hundred percent.'

I gently explained that there might come a time when it was better put the pony to sleep, preferably at my farm. He repeated that whatever was best for Rice must be done and apologised for putting us to so much trouble. I couldn't help thinking that he had no idea how happy we were to look after Rice (now nicknamed Pud), free to do whatever was best, rather than what suited the owners' pockets. The family were not 'horsey' people, were uninterested in the number of rosettes their daughter and pony could win, and were unlikely to care if their pony had pigeon toes as long as he was well and happy. He was a loved member of the family, not a status symbol. Somehow, I preferred their company to that of the 'horsey' folk who bought and sold horses and ponies on a whim and pushed their offspring to win more rosettes than their neighbours. As for Rice, a tatty little pony of unknown breeding, no one expected him to respond to treatment. He proved us all wrong, became sound and happy and resumed light work taking care of a young girl who was paralysed from the chest down. Of course, his recovery was due to the drugs and veterinary care - or was it? At one point during his treatment, a friend tried to cheer me up by pointing out that miracles do happen. Time proved him right, as Rice had his own miracle: the miracle of caring owners.

∪

I usually combined checking the ponies with walking the dogs - a peaceful pastime and an excuse to be away from the phone for half an hour. At least, it was peaceful until a phone call from a neighbour that afternoon to ask if I had lost one of my dogs. I hadn't, but then I suspect the gentleman knew that anyway. There was a large black dog on his land. It had been around for a couple of weeks and was getting thin. The dog hadn't killed yet, but the farmer felt it was only a matter of time. I was about to give him the number of the RSPCA headquarters, but I was just up the road, and Julie and I were not very busy...!

'We'll be up in ten minutes,' I volunteered, grabbing dog biscuits, an improvised baler-twine collar and a lead rope.

We arrived at the farm to be told that the dog had gone but was usually in a large field nearby. Unfortunately, it was a very steep field, and just to make life interesting also contained a very large bull.

We walked around for several hours, not seeing any sign of the dog, and finally decided that our legs, as well as being tired, had been well and truly pulled. As we started our descent back to the farmhouse and Julie's car, I heard the farmer shout, and saw a black dog running away. Luckily the dog, which was in a blind panic, ran towards us.

'Sit down, Julie' I muttered.

As the dog tore towards us we could see the panic in his eyes. I just hoped that he would stop for food. I threw the first handful of biscuits, but he dodged and continued running. A second throw slowed him as he smelled food.

'Good dog,' I encouraged quietly. 'Come.'

His tail wagged as he gobbled up the biscuits, each one a little closer to me. Finally, despite his obvious hunger, he took one gently from my hand. He buried his face in the box of biscuits and hardly noticed the plaited baler twine that I had managed to slip around his neck. Julie removed the box and collected up all the biscuits I'd scattered as I didn't think they would do the sheep or cows a lot of good! The dog accepted our cuddles but his eyes were frantic. He was very thin and nervous.

'Poor dog,' I muttered. 'Come on, Julie, let's get him home.'

The farmer, who I'd forgotten was watching, was leaning on the gate. The dog trotted by my side, relieved to be caught at last, but as soon as we got near the farmer he tried to run away. I warned the family not to touch him and hoped the farm dogs wouldn't join us. Of course they did, but were soon sent back into the farmyard. Julie opened the back of her car and I lifted the dog in.

'What are you going to do with him?' the farmer asked.

'Contact the police and see if he's been reported missing,' I replied. 'If I can't trace his owner, he'll have to go to the pound, I suppose.'

'You did well to catch him,' the farmer said. 'Mind he doesn't bite you.'

I laughed. Somehow, I doubted the dog would bite anyone. Julie drove us back home while the dog tried to climb to the front and sit on my lap.

'What are you going to call him?' Julie asked.

'Hadn't planned to call him anything,' I answered. 'Look, we can't keep him. I hate lurcher types. He'd kill the cats, and the other dogs would hate him too.'

'How about Jet?' Julie interrupted.

'Well, yes, it suits him, but I'm not going to keep him,' I said finally...!

Of course, when we got back I had to introduce him to my pack! Fortunately for Jet, I decided to introduce him initially to Gypsy, who whined but accepted him. Joker ignored him after a few sniffs, and Gemma, without her mum to back her up, pulled a face and hid behind me. Jet was a perfect gentleman, accepting their superiority without question. Finally, Julie let Jester in; she sniffed, wagged her tail and lay down next to me, making sure Jet respected her position.

'Right, Julie, pussycats next,' I suggested.

Julie held Jet, by now wearing Jester's old collar, while I let P Brain and Perseverance in.

P Brain as usual didn't realise there was an extra dog and rubbed round him. Perseverance spat and ran away. Jet didn't move, even when P Brain finally realised much later that evening that Jet was not Joker and slapped him on the nose for daring to confuse her.

I rang our local police station at Llandeilo, where a lovely gentleman took Jet's details.

'Do you want us to take him to the pound?' he asked.

Jet's paw rested on my leg, his hopeful eyes fixed on mine, while all the other pets dozed and snored at my feet. My dogs, like all the charity's ponies, recognised another distressed soul and had already found a place for him. I thought of how my own dogs, especially Jester, always at my side through the worst weather and the unhappiest times, gave me so much. Just like my horses that had helped me, worked for me, and earned the reputation we had. Perhaps I did owe a stray dog a home.

'No, I'll keep him,' I said. The policeman explained the rules regarding the keeping of a stray dog.

If this was any other place, Jet would have been eternally quiet, grateful, and proved to be house-trained. Instead, although he was excessively and very loudly grateful, like all our recruits he caused his own eccentric brand of havoc.

The evening was fine; he ate his dinner and went out on his lead for his late-night walk without incident. A pity he spoiled it by cocking his leg as soon as I brought him back in. A roar from me abated the flow for a little while.

He watched and followed my every move, which was fine except that Jester slept in my room. It was her privilege, and not one she or I intended to let Jet share. He howled his protest until the dawn, stopping occasionally if my yells sounded very threatening. When he finally shut up, our resident jackdaws, who had probably had a sleepless night too, decided to give their brood of youngsters an early and noisy breakfast.

'Oh, crikey,' I moaned. Jester snored happily on.

I staggered out of bed late and very bad tempered, to be greeted by a very relieved Jet and plenty of evidence of his relief all over the front room. It was the first of many lapses.

When a police officer arrived at lunch time, I led Jet out to him and realised that I was shaking. Had he found Jet's owners? What sort of people were they to leave their dog unreported for two weeks? Did they love him or was he just another toy, and their interest as short-lived as it was for the latest video rented for a Saturday night? Jet wasn't happy, but the policeman tried to reassure him. The officer felt that Jet had been abandoned. He had taken several stray dogs to the pound already that week. Like all those involved in the messy end of animal welfare, he knew that a licence for all dogs was the answer. Only safely-insulated politicians who didn't have to look into a pair of appealing eyes transported to nearly certain death could think otherwise. Unfortunately, dogs, like most animals, are victims of human greed and apathy.

The policeman seemed pleased that here at least was one happy ending. As for me, I've avoided knowing how many dogs are destroyed daily in Britain, and about the puppy farms close by yet remote from my life, and the dealers offering good homes for all puppies in our local paper. I hadn't made time to think about anything but the misery I saw in the horse world. Jet's eyes in the first moment I saw him will always haunt me. Like all dogs he gave unquestioning loyalty even when his owners didn't deserve it. As Jet had bolted across that field, running away from raised voices towards something he probably barely remembered, his eyes accused every dog 'lover' in this country.

Over the next few weeks, when he chased rabbits, had countless 'accidents' in the house, bit our long-suffering vet, and chased the ponies, I tried to remember our human guilt. Jet tried too, learning to walk to heel, come, and leave and, mainly, not to chase ponies.

One evening we finally did manage to sit and watch my trekkers grazing peacefully. The other dogs lay around me, tails wagging. Jet, eager to please, copied, pawing at me just in case I relented and let him chase something. He was booked into the vet's to be neutered later in the week.

'Poor dog,' I said, cuddling him, knowing it was the sensible and right thing to do. Jet wagged his tail even harder. He would forgive me for his operation, but however much I loved and reassured him he could never bear to 'stay' as ordered when I walked away from him. Like our ponies, happy on a summer evening, he could forgive a bad start in life, but he could never quite forget it.

Dinah the donkey

Chapter 26
Mick's injury

I didn't like the look of Mick at all, as he stood there with his near fore leg just hanging. He was in a great deal of pain – a pony with less courage would not have made it back to the stable. It was his second injury in under a week. I settled him into his stable, making him as comfortable as I could, and rushed indoors to phone the local vet who arrived a couple of hours later.

He huffed and examined the leg while Mick trembled, in too much pain to do his usual trick of flattening vets. I was sure that I could hear the unmistakable sound of crepitus, the horrible sound of broken bone ends grinding on each other. The vet wasn't sure and injected Mick with cortisone. He promised to call again in two days – it seemed an awfully long time to leave a pony with a broken leg. My heart was breaking. Poor old Mick, always so quick to lead a mass breakout, but lately so kind and gentle, and always dependable with tiny children. I had a sinking feeling that his days of running were over. He didn't stop eating, but the weight fell off him as the pain and shock took effect. The vet arrived again as he'd promised and injected more cortisone. I asked about an X-ray, as the swelling had reduced enough to make that possible, but the vet didn't seem to think it was a good idea. I didn't know what to do – not wanting to condemn Mick to an early grave but not wanting him to suffer either. The vet was a nice gentleman doing his job to the best of his ability, but I wasn't impressed. Mick watched him go and I turned sadly towards the house. Perhaps it would be kinder to have him put to sleep. My stomach churned again. Some instinct told me to sleep on it and ask friends if they knew of a good horse vet. Luckily, they did, and that is how I met our 'new' vet.

He was out when I phoned, but his receptionist promised to send him over as soon as possible. I'd had a brainwave – a cunning plan! I didn't know how competent this vet would prove to be, so I made the appointment for him to see a mare with dodgy teeth, and the mare was Dancer who had a very uncertain temperament. Yes, Mr J would have some fun, I thought, and we'd soon see what kind of 'horse vet' we were dealing with. Dancer joined Mick in the stable while I waited for our visitor. When a car pulled in and a young man got out, I thought he must be a feed rep.

'Can I help you?' I asked suspiciously.

Jester and the other dogs were ready to send the stranger packing if I asked them to, but Jester was making her approval very clear.

'I'm the vet,' the stranger said.

I must have looked a bit mystified, as he didn't seem very old to me – probably not even my age. 'Oh, yes,' I muttered.

It was all Mick and I needed – a newly qualified vet.

'She's this way, and I've got another pony that I would like you to look at too. He's been seen by another vet but I would like a second opinion, would you mind?' I asked.

Dancer started to leap around as soon as she saw the vet, which was no surprise to me as she disliked all men. I waited for Mr J to back away or announce, as other vets had, that she was untreatable. But he had a few surprises up his sleeve, and instead of trying to rugby tackle and using his strength against her, he tried to win her confidence. He approached her slowly, talking all the time, and seemed in no hurry to start work on her.

'We'll have to dope her, I'm afraid, and the drug that's best is the most expensive one,' he said after a while.

'Whatever is best,' I replied. I then stood still, hoping he would manage to get it into Dancer rather than me.

'I'll have to clip her where I inject,' he continued. 'Do you mind?'

'No,' I answered with interest!

The rodeo that followed ended in a just slightly drugged Dancer, but who still had enough fight to try and box our ears. The only way I had the strength to hold her head was to balance it on my shoulder, which I wasn't going to try with her front feet whizzing past my legs. Another dose was given, and as this took affect she wobbled and then it took all my strength to support her head. Mr J worked away with his rasp.

'She's got an awful mouth,' he puffed. 'It's a "shear mouth" and there's lumps all over the place, like the Himalayas.' Finally, he said, 'Look, I can't do any more. We'll call it a day and I'll have another go in a couple of months.'

I lowered Dancer's head. Mr J patted her and stroked her.

'She's not such a bad old thing really, is she,' he said. 'Those teeth must hurt.'

It was then I realised that this young vet had definite possibilities. He was gentle and kind and took time to build a relationship with his patients.

Now it was Mick's turn. He stood to be caught, with only the toe of his injured leg resting on the ground. He looked a poor specimen, very old and tired. The leg was examined very gently.

Mr J paused and looked compassionately at me. 'It's an awful mess in there,' he began. 'I... think he's broken the ulna,' he continued.

I hardly dared to breathe. It was just as I had expected, but I couldn't bear to hear Mick's death sentence. I looked down at the ground so that the vet couldn't see that I was almost crying.

He cleared his throat. 'In this case, I really think it might be better to...'

He never got any further. Stella has always sworn that Mick is telepathic, and I had often been amazed by his reactions. He was a sensitive little chap, and that sensitivity had almost been the cause of his death several years before when owners failed to understand him. This time it saved his life, as he tore the lead rope out of my hands and barged into Mr J, knocking him into the wall.

'Oh, so he can move around,' was the chuckled and 'winded' response.

'Yes,' I replied, 'but he's always worse after the cortisone wears off.'

'Well, we could give him "Arquel", which is a non-steroid anti-inflammatory, but long term in a pony his size it isn't a good idea.'

'Is it fair to keep him? Would... would it be better to put him to sleep?' I forced myself to say.

I heard these words being spoken, but in my heart I was sure that Mick wanted to live, and I had an idea. First of all, I had to be sure this new vet was doing what was right for the pony and not what a new client wanted. What Mr J said next made so much sense to me that I wrote it down as soon as he'd left. All owners have wrestled with the horrible decision of when it is best to put a beloved pet to sleep.

'Well,' he said, ' I know that every horse is supposed to have four perfect legs, but we don't shoot humans with one bad leg. They have to endure some pain to get better. In this case I would give it a go. What do you want him for?'

'Retirement,' I answered, sure he would never work again.

'Oh, well then, just keep him quiet, and if he lies down...'

'Yes, he does,' I interrupted, 'and he can get up again.'

'Good. Well, if he starts lying down for long periods and doesn't eat, we'll have to think again.'

Mick glowered at the vet from the corner of the stable. It was the start of a long feud. Mick was checked regularly by Mr J, but never really appreciated the attention and continued to view him as the enemy. However, he was the ideal patient, clever, stubborn, but above all determined to live. I had to help him in any way I could. I had grown up knowing about the power of herbs and natural cures from my grandparents, so I knew that comfrey would help to knit his bones together. So I prepared comfrey tea, which Mick drank despite the vile taste. One of my herbal books suggested holly for broken bones, so I plodded off to pick some. Pete's Mum, who was staying with us, was puzzled by her daughter-in-law's interest, as she had never seen me show any interest in decorating the house before. When I explained that it was for Mick, she understood and helped me 'de-prickle' it.

Mick improved slowly, gradually putting a little more weight on his bad leg as March brought gales and rain. I was glad that the days hadn't become milder, as he was eager for excitement, sensing that spring was around the corner. For once I was thankful for the bad weather, as Mick had never liked the rain and usually preferred to stay in his stable if rain even threatened. He liked to walk, however, so I increased his stable size by removing one of the partitions, giving him first one, then two more stables to amble around. The addition of Bluey, as a companion to boss and herd around, did wonders for Mick's morale as he ordered Bluey from one hay net to another. At first he just walked towards me when I went in with his food, but after a while that got boring, so he added a few heart stopping steps of trot just for good measure, and then, to see if I really was going to have a heart attack, he added a buck or two!

It was time (I was told by the vet) to take Mick for his first walk on a leading rein. Stella and her fiancé Charles were expected that day, so I decided to let Stella do the honours, as Mick had always been her favourite pony. We chose the next morning to lead him out. It was a beautiful Easter morning, the sun was bright and warm, but for some reason everyone had a lump in their throat. Mick pottered up the drive to a paddock, stopping to sniff the air and gaze around at the beautiful land he'd nearly been forced to leave. He grazed, but much more important than the rebirth of the fresh spring grass was his own rebirth. Every step was a miracle, and I silently thanked the vet who had responded to an elderly pony with the will to live.

Half an hour later we returned Mick to his stable. Although he made it quite clear that he would have liked to stay out longer, he seemed to accept for once that we knew best. We were warned to accept muscle wastage on his injured side, but as his trips to graze increased his muscles strengthened. By the beginning of May it was hard to see any difference between his good and bad side when he was standing still. I still led Mick out to graze and kept a firm hold on him, but after he decided it was possible to gallop in his elongated stable, I decided to give in to the old fool and let him go in the hay field. The rest of his friends were in the holding pen, so he wouldn't go far as he would be lonely. I should have known better – Mick was always an 'escaper', and one day as I brought a ride back and we were walking sedately down the road, I spotted Mick three fields away from where I left him, cantering free, wind in his face and the sun on his back. He looked so happy... I wasn't! Impolite words were uttered. I leapt off Prince and threw his reins to a helper. The easiest way back to Mick was through a thorn hedge, so I was scratched, cross but most of all nearly hysterical by the time I reached Mick.

'Stand,' I pleaded.

He was about to leg it, but seeing the state I was in he took pity on me and stood to be caught with only the tiniest smirk.

'You bloody idiot,' I scolded.

His ears flicked mischievously and he burped.

It was the first of several scrapes that proved to us that Mick really was on the mend. The trouble was that everybody had forgotten about the old Mick, and had got so used to treating him as an invalid that they left gates open or forgot to do his door up, so I spent more than a few hours removing and retrieving my favourite equine delinquent. What he needed was a friend who was well behaved and who might encourage him to stay in his field or stable. His old friend Queenie was out of the question as she was a bit of a kicker. I knew that Mick would prefer a mare and eventually a thought occurred to me. I decided on Dancer, who was very timid and unlikely to copy any of his bad habits like breaking out. Dancer was at least twenty-five years old, possibly more, and because she had lived most of her life on a bleak mountain she appreciated good grass far too much to break out just for something to do. Perhaps she would also learn from Mick, who loved children. Well, his personality certainly made an impression on her as he herded her around the field. I hadn't had time to finish fencing the field so put up coloured string along the fence posts, hoping that the ponies would mistake it for electric fence and stay put. It would have worked too with any pony other than Mick. Two hours later I went out to feed my two favourite ponies and found them happily grazing on our drive, having broken out of good grass onto bad. But then the grass that you are not supposed to eat is always the greenest, I suppose! Mick skipped back under the string but couldn't resist poking a provocative nose back under it. Dancer, unable to remember how she had escaped in the first place, stood looking mortified.

'Pest,' I yelled at Mick as I went to catch her.

He was almost 'trotting sound' in June, and by July he could stand on his bad leg to have the hoof on his good leg trimmed. He lived in bored retirement for another eight months until a tiny tot, aged two and a bit, demanded a ride. Bluey had just been shod, and Blackie, although quiet, was too big. I can't remember who suggested Mick, who was looking over his stable door. When the saddle and bridle stopped by his door, he rushed towards Gillian, eager to be tacked up again. That first ride up and down the corridor cheered Mick up. Suddenly his ears were pricked and his step was light again. He had enjoyed the last few months, but after a while even escaping becomes boring. He then actually worked through the summer of 1988, giving pleasure to less able children and tiny tots. After a while, a plod around the school wasn't enough for the old rogue, so Sara rode him on an hour ride, dismounting to lead him up the hills. Mick loved it, and apart from pulling he was an angel.

One day, a lad called Timothy arrived. He had booked his first expedition on the two-hour ride. We led out Comet, but it was a windy day, and although Timothy could easily control Comet in the school, we were afraid that Comet would try and take off with him on the road. Eve suggested Mick. He was certainly fit enough, and Timothy was light, but

I had my doubts. It was the furthest that Mick had been ridden without a break. Mick stood and looked hopeful...

'Alright,' I agreed reluctantly.

Mick left the yard on his toes and returned an hour and a half later with ears pricked and a big horsey grin on his face. Timothy was impressed too. Apparently, Mick had pulled the whole way round, trotted, and at one point tried to retake his old place in the lead. He was an old pony – probably nearer thirty than twenty, and Mr J told me that his teeth were not good. I could have wrapped him up in cotton wool, which is what I most wanted to do, but Mick had made his choice. He enjoyed light work; but not total retirement. Perhaps even light work would shorten his life, although I thought that it probably wouldn't. I knew Mick well enough to realize that as long as he was happy, he would fight to live.

His spirit kept him alive for an extra two years. He lived those years to the full and spread love and laughter around himself. He taught yet another generation the joy of riding, stretching out a gentle nose that several children may well remember throughout their lives.

Chapter 27

Gwilym

My life has been a succession of love stories with horses and ponies of all sizes, some of them beautiful and some of them ugly and difficult. I believe that we are sent a very special horse or pony perhaps once in a lifetime if we are lucky. To have spent a life surrounded by special ponies is the greatest gift I could ever have had.

My work for the Lluest Horse and Pony Trust took me to many horse sales, so I should have been used to seeing ponies in varying stages of decay and neglect, but I had never seen anything like the stunted foal that tottered into the market, trying to keep up with the other 'normal' foals. I think I knew in the first seconds that I saw Gwilym that he would be coming home.

The foal's owner was warned to take him out of the market before the welfare people saw him. I chased after them as they grabbed Gwilym by the tail, steering him back through the crowds up to the filthy cattle box. The welfare people did catch up, and a vet was called. It was finally agreed that Lluest Horse and Pony Trust would buy Gwilym and take him home. A horsebox was kindly offered as transport and I travelled in it with him as he was too weak to stand and too stubborn and frightened to lie down. Gwilym was too small for any of our rugs so the saddler made and delivered him a beautiful stable rug in less than two hours.

Our vet arrived and confirmed what I had thought initially: that this was a foal with no chance. However, Gwilym had no intention of giving in easily, and he took to his special milk straight away. Unfortunately, he was passing blood, large amounts of worms, and was so desperately weak that he could only stand with help. Worming him helped, but we were trying to undo the damage inadvertently done by his poor mother who had probably never been wormed in her life. I wondered if she was still alive. It was a cold night, and as I lay in the stable holding Gwilym I felt that it was the end of his life. He was very tired and showing signs of colic. I held him and decided it was time to let him go. He would never recover and it was wrong to keep him alive. I phoned our long-suffering vet again at four in the morning, and later phoned our friend Ieuan who was intending to buy a special manger for Gwilym – a manger that we would no longer need. Ieuan arrived before the vet, and decided to try to lift Gwilym to his feet. I had my doubts, and Gwilym did not want to know, but by the time the vet arrived Gwilym was eating again, and demanding milk. I was too tired to remember who suggested bringing him into the house, but the vet picked him up and carried him in while Ieuan kept my dogs quiet. Gwilym looked around and settled down for a sleep while Ieuan rigged up a pulley so that I could lift him every two hours for a feed.

Over the next three weeks, Gwilym lurched from crisis to crisis and I shed many tears. I was so angry – if only his mother had been wormed and looked after, if only his owner had looked after his ponies and not just seen them as an easy way to raise some cash. When I was asked to allow his story to be used for a children's programme, I wanted to refuse as I was afraid that the lights would upset him. But I reconsidered, and the crew were wonderful. They made sure that they moved slowly and quietly, and as for Gwilym, well he enjoyed the attention. The picture of Gwilym, standing on his weak bent legs with his wizened 'old' pony's head, shocked so many people and left Ieuan and I in tears. It also made us realise that Gwilym was improving, even though he still had to be lifted to his feet for every feed.

The thing that I wanted most for Christmas was for him to get up and walk over to me while I was mixing his milk. One morning, I was about fifteen minutes late with his ten o'clock feed, as I had fallen asleep in my chair. He was cross because I was standing outside his pen and he really wanted his milk. I wanted him to stand so much, but all he did was try to stretch his head to reach it. I sat on my desk watching him, wondering, as I did so many times every day, if I was doing the right thing in trying to keep him alive. Then, miracle of miracles, Gwilym got up in a slightly bored fashion and walked over to me and drank his milk. Ieuan thought that I had won the pools because I was laughing and crying and completely incoherent.

Soon Gwilym was not only getting up unaided but lying in wait for the many visitors who came to wish him well, and biting those rash enough to come too close. For some reason he did not bite me, but Ieuan certainly had the bruise of a bite through a donkey jacket some weeks later. Gwilym was beginning to explore, and there was no danger of me oversleeping and missing a feed, as he would move his barricade and walk into the bedroom to get me. I got used to typing with his head on my lap, and Gwilym, who was never afraid of anything, stood watching while the printer, that sounded like a machine, rattled through the letters written to our supporters who rallied around to raise the money to pay for his treatment.

Christmas came, and the vet called in to see his patient, who responded to his attempts to see how steady he was on his legs by kicking him on the shins! It was going to be a special Christmas because out in the stable was an old grey mare, Holly, with her stunted foal Nest[46] who had also stood unaided for the first time. When Gwilym went for his first walk in January, wrapped up in his rug and hood, Ieuan had to lead him because he was so full of beans. All of the other ponies spooked at the strange little foal; that is, except for one old mountain mare who had barely recovered from being left to starve.

Gwilym was fascinated by Holly, and as she was the only pony not afraid of him, we put him in the next stable to her for a few minutes. It was meant to be. Very soon Holly had two foals to look after, and Gwilym finally learnt to eat the hard food which he had previously refused when offered.

Throughout the spring, major work had been going ahead to refurbish the stables, and in June we were ready for the grand opening. There was only one celebrity that we wanted to cut the ribbon, although I doubted that he would wear his garland of roses without protest. I led Gwilym out to be garlanded, and remembered that miracles can

---

[46] On the 19 December 1991, Ginny received a phone call from a person concerned for a mare in emaciated condition with a tiny foal at foot. After some difficulty in finding the pair, and then leaving instructions regarding their care – instructions which were ignored – the owner decided to sign them over to the Trust. After one day at the Trust, the mare collapsed and couldn't get up, so yet again a pulley was installed, this time in a stable, and used for three weeks to get the mare to her feet. The foal was suffering from respiratory problems, and was thin and weak as her mother had little milk.

On the 6 January 1992, after a confinement of eight weeks, Gwilym went for his first walk, and by early February Holly and Nest were well enough to spend an hour in the fields. Gwilym showed off, enjoying a good gallop with little Nest. Then on the 29 February he left the house for the last time to live day and night in the stables.

happen. Here we are, I thought, surrounded by the warmth and love of many of our supporters, and maybe all because a year and a half ago I had seen a tatty little foal out of the corner of my eye. Gwilym has given so much love to the human race; he loves children and curbs his enthusiasm when he meets older folk. He is old beyond his years, yet young and happy. He especially radiates healing to those that need it, and then in the twinkling of his eye causes havoc that only a two-year-old can, destroying his rugs with a malicious gleam in his eyes. His coat, crinkly and dull, never recovered from his early days of neglect, but his personality more than makes up for that. He shines like a beacon, reminding us all that, no matter what, life is worth striving for.

Gwylim and Ginny

Chapter 28

Jake

I was sitting at a respectful distance from the herd watching the newest foal explore the warm mountainside. The herd stallion was watching from a distance on the slope behind me, as I daydreamed in the sun. One of the older foals tiptoed nearer me, and as I watched him play I forgot about his father somewhere behind me.

I didn't hear the stallion approach me, and I wasn't aware of him until something breathed into my ear. I leapt up and turned to see the strawberry roan looking surprised and hurt to see I hadn't welcomed his polite advance.

'All right, boy,' I said, and knelt down again and let him sniff my hair.

I must have passed the inspection, as he settled down to graze close to me, pausing between mouthfuls to nuzzle my feet and hair. The stallion could have been a real beauty – a striking strawberry roan, around 13hh with a blaze and the most generous pair of eyes I'd ever seen. His eyes were full of warmth and gentleness, a gentleness that wanted human company and that loved his mares and their foals.

When I finally got up to go, the stallion marched up to me, nuzzled my face and determinedly demanded a cuddle. I wondered what in his wild life had given him such unconditional love for people. I had a feeling that I wasn't the first person to be honoured in this way. I later found out that 'the boys' would catch him and ride him to gather sheep, or even just for fun, until he got fed up and bucked the offender off. Yet in spite of possibly thirteen-stone men riding him, and no doubt hurting him, he always came quietly, gently eager for human company whatever the price.

The stallion needed a name but I couldn't think of anything suitable until 'My Brother Jake', an old song by Free, was playing on the radio just as the day ride was getting ready to leave. Jake. Yes, it did suit him, and he was just as happy to respond to that name as he was to any sound humans cared to make.

Over the next year I introduced the stallion to our customers when we rode out, hoping to educate people about what was really happening with these herds on the hills. Our ponies accepted the stallion as happily as he accepted them, although we kept the mares well away from him, just in case his natural instinct took over. He always greeted us with a whinny, standing quietly, while I explained how the foals playing in the sun were destined for the meat trade, which would one day claim his life too. The regular riders already knew what the casualties of this evil trade looked like, as they had watched our vet and me fight to save a wild mare almost starving to death with her tiny stunted foal.[47]

Ruth and Jane (two old friends) had come to visit, and as usual we headed for the mountains. Both had heard about Jake and were sort of keen to meet him, although years of experience of my casual disregard for their safety and mine made them wary. We found the mares first, all without their foals. I was heartbroken as we had planned to rescue two foals and I had wanted one of them to be Jake's. But then I heard a familiar whinny and trotted towards the sound. The girls followed, expressing doubts about my sanity. What we found humbled and saddened us all, spoiling what we had hoped would be a special day. Jake stood as all his foals played around him, and then quietly walked towards me. The foals followed, some of the braver ones stretching out to us as Jake stood aside. He seemed to be recommending them to us, asking us to choose, to help them; or perhaps he was just trying to pass on his own misplaced trust in humans.

Our ponies stood quietly behind us as we watched the foals. We were all feeling very emotional. I have watched thousands of these foals loaded into slaughter lorries over the years and had thought I was able to detach myself from their deaths, but how could anyone be detached from a father's love for his offspring, and for those responsible for their miserable existence. I just didn't know any more, but one thing I did know was that the foals could not rely on our laws to protect them. Their rights to proper food, parasite control and humane handling were a remote dream.

---

[47] Holly and Nest.

As we remounted I was afraid that Jake's time on the mountain was nearly over.

'I've got a feeling he's going to be at the market,' I muttered.

'Good,' said Ruth. 'Maybe someone will recognise his potential and buy him. He's wasted here when he could be with people.'

'Yes, but I'm sure there's something wrong with his teeth and mouth because his mouth smells, and he needs castrating and breaking,' I replied,

'You ought to buy him, then.'

'What with?' I snarled, and rode off in a temper.

The following morning we drove up to see Jake and his herd. Ruth's boyfriend took a photo of me kneeling with Jake. It was a cold misty day and I knew it was the last time I'd see Jake with his herd.

The next local pony sale was only a week or so later, and at home I was screaming and swearing at any long-suffering human rash enough to cross my path. Ruth and Becky (another old friend) left me muttering over my tea and toast, and no doubt plotted just a little.

When we got to the sale it was as chaotic as ever. However much improved lately, it was still a sickening reminder of human greed, stupidity and hypocrisy. One official and his friend enjoyed their macho images as they slapped sale labels on, whilst foals reared and slipped to avoid them. The first foal we decided on for the charity was a large iron-grey colt, with his father's gentle eyes and good bone. He stood with his friends, sweating and shaking, and endured all without retaliation and allowed us to touch him as soon as we had bought him, and he was sent into our pen. I'd seen our second foal early in the sale, as he tried to kick the owner that was trying to drive him through an entrance jammed with other 'caring' members of the human race. I later named one foal Jacko, and the other Albert after my grandfather. Both refused to be browbeaten, and were radiating defiance and hatred. Albert, his father a grey stallion, was quite prepared to attack any human silly enough to get close. As I was silly I soon had, in common with everyone else who had anything to do with him, an awful lot of bruises.

I don't know why I wandered off down a corridor, to come across a strawberry roan that was pacing around a pen.

'Jake,' I called, and ran over. He whinnied and greeted me before resuming pacing. His foal and three of his mares had already been sold for slaughter. They were calling to him and he wanted to go to them, but when a little girl leant into the pen he stopped pacing and let her play around him. Ruth and Becky found us.

'Buy him, Ginny,' Becky urged. 'Look, buy him for you, not the Trust. You really love him. You could break him.'

'How much cash have you got?' Ruth asked.

'About £60,' I said. 'It won't be enough and he may already be sold.'

'We'll give you some money,' they urged.

Jake was finally sent into the sale ring where the auctioneer said he was 'broken, quiet to ride.' The woman next to me laughed and the meat man was bidding. For all the people Jake loved, no one was prepared to buy him. I couldn't let go, and I bought him for £210 to whoops from the girls and other friends who had gathered.

Becky raced off with her flexible friend, and Ruth returned to the foals while I comforted Jake. He was sweating and restless, yet unfailingly gentle and careful not to tread on me or a steady procession of children who wanted to pat him.

Annette arrived with the box and I paid for the foals, asking if I could pay for Jake by cheque. I was surprised by the favourable answer and promptly forgot about Becky. I did, however, wonder if I was quite mad. The foals loaded easily, Albert being too tired to argue, and were duly deposited back at the farm where a less than enthusiastic husband watched in amazement as I returned for Jake. I don't think anyone had bothered to tell him or Brian who Jake was at that stage. Back at the sale Jake was surrounded by friends old and new, as his mares and foals were loaded into the slaughter lorry.

I put a headcollar and lead rope on him and warned everyone to keep clear and led him out to his new life. Although he whinnied and pulled a little every time yet another unwary human wandered across his path, he stopped politely. He loaded into the trailer, travelling quietly past the funfair with its lights and screaming children.

We unloaded Jake at the farm to gasps of approval, except from Pete who didn't seem too happy. Jake's first whinny was answered by Jacko and thirty plus equine residents of Beili Bedw. Jake spun around, pawed the ground and then, remembering his manners, followed me to the stable. As for me, I couldn't believe that Jake was mine, but the joy was not quite unreserved as I was sure that Jake had teeth trouble, and knowing my luck...

On Monday I telephoned our long suffering vet.

'Remember that stallion I'm always talking about?' I said.

'Yes,' was the reply. (I could imagine the look on his face.)

'Can you castrate him and anti-tetanus the two foals we bought with him?' I asked.

'Who owns the stallion? Is he quiet?' the vet asked.

'I own him, and yes, you know all mine are always quiet,' I replied.

'Have you any pennies?' he queried.

'Yes,' I lied.

'See you Tuesday, then. We'll do him standing.' He sighed.

I was about to try and negotiate the price but decided that Monday morning may not be the best time.

On the Tuesday a friend arrived and was persuaded to help with the castration. As usual I ignored the fact that she was a veggie with a sensitive stomach. The vet arrived late, in a bad mood, and insisted I take the front end. I did try to convince him that my friend was strong and better in front. I may have mentioned her squeamish stomach, but the problems were resolved by the use of string to tie up Jakes tail that she could hold without looking. After some head shaking, Jake accepted the injection to dope him, and the procedure went comparatively smoothly. Unfortunately, the weather turned wet, and as Jake had to be out he was soon swollen and uncomfortable. Luckily he responded to treatment, and as vigorous exercise was recommended he was introduced to the lunge. As ever he was the perfect gentleman, although when tired he would stop and refuse to move.

Jake's mouth and teeth were examined a little later during a rasping and vaccination session. My suspicions were confirmed. Jake had a bad tooth that was also split and possibly infected.

'Can you remove it?' I asked the vet.

'No.' was the reply. 'He'll have to go somewhere like Crickhowell.'

'Why?' I asked.

'You know why,' was the reply. 'With clients like you we can't afford the gear.'

I must have looked even more miserable than usual...

'You know,' said the vet, 'anyone else doing what you did for Jake would buy him and they'd live happily ever after, and that would be that, end of story, but you...' He shook his head and laughed.

The date for the operation was arranged, and our friends Chris and Linda offered a free lift with one of their horses who also needed dental treatment. Jake loaded easily, and Linda, who had admitted being nervous of transporting a wild pony, was soon under his spell.

He unloaded at the surgery and walked into the examination room, standing politely while the gag was put in his mouth. I had wondered how he would cope with walking into a green padded operating theatre, but although he hesitated as the 'ground' wobbled under him, he followed me, trusting me and all the strangers to do what was best for him. I had wanted to stay for the operation, but the smell and watching the vet (who I didn't know well) cutting into Jake's face proved too much. When I could take no more I left, thinking of a large number of helpers who would have a good and well-deserved laugh at my expense.

Linda and Chris fed me sandwiches and tea and pointed out that the operation was easy and safe. It seemed hours before I was called back to Jake who by then was coming round.

My beautiful pony had a large shaved area and two lots of stitches. Although still dopey, he still managed a greeting. The tooth had split and smelled pretty unbearable even after the vet had cleaned it up to show me. I wondered what made a pony living with toothache on a daily basis such a gentle and loving soul. Jake was soon on his feet, and the vet suggested I take him over to the grass verge for a walk. The verge, although separated from the busy A40 by a stone wall, still shook as large juggernauts thundered past. Jake settled, watching the lorries and trying a mouthful of grass, only shying a little when a Jack Russell escaped its owner's clutches and snapped at his heels.

Jake was reloaded for the trip back home after a check from the vet and most of his staff, who had all been won over by his gentleness. He travelled well and settled back into his stable routine until I tried to feed him his antibiotic, cleverly disguised in an apple, his favourite feed. He snorted it and ignored it. He was quite happy to let me push the feed into his mouth but then politely spat it back into his bowl. I rang the vet after an hour or so. Jake remained unimpressed until about four hours later, when I offered it to his friend who was eager to eat anything. Then, finally convinced I wasn't about to poison him, he scoffed the lot.

Our vet arrived three days later to remove the first lot of stitches. Jake threw his head around and stamped, pain finally making him lose his temper. By the time the last lot of stitches were due to be taken out Jake had finally had enough. He looked a mess, with pus dripping from his nostrils, and he stank. As soon as the vet tried to touch his face, he tried to rear and strike out. To make matters worse, the vet was late, tired and in a hurry.

'We'll have to twitch him[48],' he threatened as a hoof just missed his head yet again.

'Do we have to?' I whinged.

'Well, what else to do you suggest?' was the snapped reply.

Jake wasn't impressed by our attempt to twitch him and, to make matters even worse, for some stupid reason I let the twitch fall off. The car phone saved me from a much shortened life.

'Here, hold this,' said a bad-tempered vet, and stormed off to the answer the phone.

I patted Jake and gently removed the remaining stitches, expecting to have my head kicked in at any minute. He stood head down while I fumbled with the wound to check I'd got them all out. The vet reappeared and looked as if he was about to blow a fuse – who could blame him, with a 'helper' like me?

'I've got them out!'

'Are you sure?' he asked, as he knew that I had to be very close to the stitches to see them in the first place.

'Yes.' I said. 'He's a nice chap really. You can't blame him for messing about after all this. Will he ever get better?' I fretted.

'We could try more antibiotic, but as soon as you stop the infection will come back. I'll check him again next time I'm here.' Then he roared off, leaving me talking to Jake and later crying myself to sleep.

One of our regular customers suggested that I try a spiritual healer who lived locally. I laughed at the suggestion and laughed even more when the lady and her daughter arrived a few days later. Lyn looked like a normal housewife and arrived in a perfectly normal estate car rather than on the broomstick I'd half expected. She wasn't wearing flowing robes, but in spite of her normal appearance I was very wary of her. Lyn explained that she was going to lay her hands on Jake's face. I groaned, remembering his reaction to the vet, but Jake stood quietly and dozed off. Lyn also gave healing to two other ageing ponies, Dancer and Bluey, by then in their early thirties. I had started to accept the fact that it may be time to put them to sleep, as their condition was dropping in spite of all the good food I tempted them with. Dancer also accepted Lyn but I could still hardly suppress my giggles.

---

[48] A twitch is a device used to restrain a horse in a stressful situation such as veterinary treatment, as an alternative to a sedative. It typically involves a loop of rope tightened around the horse's upper lip.

Finally, Lyn turned to me, after seeing that I couldn't pick up a leading rein dropped on the floor. I had been working alone for about six months and my back was even worse than usual.

'It's you I should be giving healing to,' she said.

That did it. Scorn born out of fear of the unknown was replaced by pure terror. I was about to refuse, thinking that she would just waste more of my time, when I noticed the look of peace on her victims' faces.

'OK,' I agreed, 'but it won't do any good.'

Lyn laughed and went back in the house, where the dogs, including Jester, greeted her like an old friend. I got 'zapped' too. I felt absolutely nothing, as I'd expected, but for some reason I arranged for another visit the following week. Slowly I came to trust Lyn, and as her patients got better I was able to accept the healing coming through her, until finally I was able to ride and work reasonably normally. Lyn continued to treat any of my animals who either did not respond to conventional medicine or who needed a little extra help. Without her help, Bluey, Dancer, Jake and my beloved dog Jester wouldn't have continued to enjoy life for as long as they did. The sensible side of my nature does wonder about healing, while still recognising that it does help a sick animal. It does not promise a miracle cure and may in the end only help an animal to die peacefully and with dignity. It doesn't replace a vet, but perhaps in an ideal world healers would work alongside vets and doctors. Whatever healing is, and however it works, I know that every animal healed by Lyn has benefited, and in many cases an incurable pony has been cured.

Jake, helped also by a visiting homeopath, had recovered by the spring, so I saddled him up and led him down to the ménage. Becky then led him around, and I finally advanced on him carrying a chair, as at that stage I couldn't mount from the floor. Jake looked at the chair and me, and nuzzled Becky as I scrabbled aboard. He walked around the ménage as calmly as any of the riding ponies. Julie took over his schooling – or perhaps it was the other way around, as Jake let fly with a few bucks when he felt Julie was asking too much of a previously 'wild' pony. Jake never allowed himself to buck with me, even though my riding was clumsy. I'm sure Jake understood my need for a smooth ride, just as I understood his need to be ridden on a loose rein, guided Western style. It would be a long time before he was confident enough to allow a rider to collect him, though anyone, especially children, was welcome to sit on him. Jake progressed to giving rides in the school, and on his first ride outside Beili Bedw met and confidently passed a large lorry tipping some stone, road-men and their hut, some large drainage pipes and a moving JCB. Jake trusted Julie to guide him through the noise and men, while Prince was embarrassed into following Jake's lead past the 'monsters'.

Autumn meant another foal sale and more choices. Some of the foals were the last of Jake's efforts, and we managed to rescue two. Jake, who was by then working in my trekking centre, was once again surrounded by his foals. Although he was no longer free to roam, he seemed happy, enjoying his new life with a comfortable stable and abundant food. He would come cantering to my call with his foals playing hide and seek around him. The foals played and slept the summer away, sheltering in our wood and their fathers' love.

Checking Jake on the mountain

Part Four:

Memories and moving forward

Ginny on some time out with Jester near Cader Idris

Ginny at her happiest, as we hope she will always be remembered

Memories and personal tributes

To our knowledge, Jake's story was the last that Ginny wrote. Ginny's life was cruelly shortened on 13 September 1994 when she was just thirty-eight years of age. She died at home at the farm she loved so much, following a stroke. The extraordinary bravery and determination she brought to everything she did, particularly her efforts for the Lluest Horse and Pony Trust, shone through to the end. On the 22nd of September, Ginny's last wishes were carried out and she was buried in a beautifully sheltered spot on the farm, overlooking the mountains she loved. It was a simple, private occasion for family and friends, and her coffin was escorted by her two very special ponies, Prince and Gwilym. Her death was a great loss to the cause of equine welfare, and we are sure that she would have achieved so much more had she lived. After her death, Peter was deluged with letters of sympathy from people young and old, from occasional visitors, Ginny's friends, and some from her critics who actually really admired her.

Although Ginny often showed little patience towards people, deep down she appreciated very much everything that was done to help with her cause. During the early days of the Trust (when time permitted) she often wrote to supporters telling them personally of them her gratitude. Her infectious enthusiasm and willingness (or perhaps necessity!) to involve as many friends as possible in her quest for compassion in the equine world, was one of her main attributes.

Despite the less patient side of her nature, to many of us, she showed great compassion to those less able-bodied, in both mind and body. She welcomed adults and children to both Lluest and Beili Bedw. Several of her ponies had a hidden understanding of the varying needs of those special visitors: see, for example, encounters with Pepper (page 26), Rhona (page 138) and Ben (page 143). This work still continues at Lluest today, just as Ginny hoped it would, alongside her rescue and rehabilitation work for those horses, ponies and donkeys so much in need and deserving of care.

From Peter Hajdukiewicz

When you are young you never know how, or who, you are going to spend your life with. Had I known I was going to have the experience that I had with Ginny, I might have run in the opposite direction when I first met her! However, in many ways it was a wonderful time. We both shared a love of the countryside and outdoor life, and Ginny charmed me into her world with the enthusiasm and confidence that was so typical of her. I have some very happy memories, but also some sad ones. She was a remarkable person who had an amazing knack of influencing anyone who could help her achieve her ambitions, which led her through an extraordinary life with her animals. She is missed by many.

From Barbara Metcalfe

I met Ginny one September morning in 1977 in the hamlet of Coombe, near Wotton under Edge. Our youngest daughter had just turned five and she was booked in for her first riding lesson with Ginny. We accompanied the first few lessons, and that was really how we got to know Ginny, as she chattered away during the rides.

When Jerry joined Ginny's herd, she described how she bought him at Stow Fayre. Listening to her experience made us feel uncomfortable; to think that our daughter was having so much pleasure from riding whilst we learned that so many horses and ponies were suffering. We were completely oblivious to what was happening: inappropriate treatment at some markets; indiscriminate breeding, and the consequential horse-meat trade; not to mention neglect by some owners. We thought that horses were owned by the rich, therefore they must all be well looked after. How naive was that!

When the ponies were moved to nearby Kingswood, we and many other volunteers helped with the clearing of what were cow sheds, turning them into comfy stables, and also the building of the outdoor school.

Ginny was often heard shouting at the ponies – although she was a little person, she certainly had a voice! I remember Sarah, especially, being threatened with the 'knackers' yard' if she didn't behave. Although, understandably, some were horrified to hear this, I was

234

confident that Sarah would go nowhere except with Ginny. It was the tone of her voice, of course, that she and the others listened to (or not, in Sarah's case). They couldn't understand words! She took in and treated Bluey with laminitis; Blackie developed kidney problems, and rather than sell him as advised, she treated him. She also overcame and understood the behavioural problems that other ponies such as Prince, Jim and Jerry brought with them.

We were sad to see Ginny and Pete and the menagerie move to Wales. As well as our daughter losing her 'riding school teacher', we were also to miss the friendship that had developed between us. Luckily, we were already taking holidays in Wales, so were familiar with this beautiful country, and therefore kept in touch with Ginny and Pete. Then in May 1985 we became Trustees of the Lluest Horse and Pony Trust, and our lives changed!

I remember Ginny asking if Brian (my late husband) and I would become Trustees of the new charity, and asking 'What does it involve?' Ginny explained that the role of a Trustee is to see that the charity does what it set out to do, and makes sure that the money goes where it is supposed to go. I didn't think this sounded a particularly arduous task so agreed. Brian went along with me. He loved horses, and as a child had helped at a nearby farm in return for the odd ride. The only connection I had with horses was the occasional hack with a friend (no real lessons), and the fact that my grandfather once had at least one horse to transport his produce to market. I just remember the stables, and his unwillingness to talk with me about them. Maybe they were sent to war like over a million more and didn't come back. Also, of course, we now had a daughter, who was clearly going to gain a terrific amount of fun and life skills from caring for and riding horses.

Then there was a wait that seemed to go on for ever, to hear whether the Charity Commission would approve us. We couldn't really start fund-raising properly until then. Finally, we got the call from Ginny. 'Hello, this is Registered Charity number 516674.' We were both over the moon.

Soon afterwards we held the first formal meeting at Lluest. I became Secretary and Treasurer, and Stella became Chairman. Ginny of course was manager – unpaid. I admit to feeling a little daunted, as my typing was basic – very basic. I was given a typewriter and practised! I had little idea as to how to keep books, just common sense, surely: what came in from where, and what went out to where. I must, however, have had some persuasive skills, as I managed to persuade an accountant to check the books annually free of charge, for the time that I was Trustee. I was given a filing cabinet (which we kept in our bedroom) along with the sacks of used postage stamps that we collected as a means of raising funds. When we reached a total of about six sackfuls, I would take them to the nearby town of Dursley where a kind man would sort and pay for them. Then, after six years, along came a photocopier free of charge. Luckily there was room for that in the garage!

Quarterly newsletters were printed free of charge for many years. Competing with the bigger charities with funds to splash out on advertising, as well as professional folk to help and advise, made our work a huge struggle.

The distance between us in Gloucestershire and Ginny in Wales was overcome by Pete playing 'postman', as he travelled to and from work, bringing invoices, receipts and letters that needed attention.

The charity started with £100 (which Ginny and Pete donated) and four ponies: Smokey, Dancer, Phoenix and Jaws. Thinking back, I suppose it was a crazy, and some would say irresponsible thing to do, setting up a charity in this way, but we were all well-meaning and had strong feelings. (I certainly would not recommend that anyone should do this today.) We took no expenses from the charity for the first five years, then we claimed travelling. Ginny and Pete gave grazing free of charge.

Ginny worked as a volunteer manager, and it wasn't for several years that the charity was able to pay for someone to help her with the day to day running of the yard. Although it was the indiscriminate breeding and lack of care for the mountain ponies that tugged at Ginny's heart in the first place, the charity also took in welfare cases, such as Dinah the donkey with her friend Champ, little Faith, Daisy, Holly and her foal Nest, and many more. Once rehabilitated those suitable were (and still are) loaned to approved homes, and checked on a regular basis.

Ginny attended local markets monthly, as well as riding out regularly and getting to know herds on the nearby mountain. She worked with other organisations to secure a worming programme for the mountain herds. It would be wonderful to think that the issue of indiscriminate breeding had been resolved.

After seven years of being Trustees, Brian and I called a halt and handed over the reins to two others. After a break, I became Trustee again for four years, but ill health caused me again to call a halt.

However, I am glad that I did what I did, and I know that if Brian was still with me he would also be glad. To know that the charity is still working and striving to help the underdogs of the horse world makes it all worthwhile.

From Stella Gratrix

Captivated, enthralled and reeled in, that's what happened when you were exposed to the 'Lluest Magic'! I was first introduced to Ginny and the trekking centre in 1981 by the grandson of very old friends of my family who lived on the coast four miles away from the stables.

'Do you want to come pony trekking with my pals?' asked Iestyn.

'Love to,' I replied.

We drove up to the stables; I was introduced to Ginny, and after admitting I hadn't ridden for a few years, I was given a coloured mare called Katy to ride. Katy was a 'plodder'! I ended up at the back of the ride just in front of Ginny, who no doubt was assessing both my riding skills, practical and intellectual potential, and general ability to become a friend. All this was done in amicable conversation, while she honestly and earnestly displayed her zeal and enthusiasm for the equine world, all animals, and the beauty and wildness of the mountainous surroundings of Mid Wales. My last test was to see how Ginny's dog Jester reacted to me. Back at the stables, she leant against my leg and nuzzled my hand, and that was it, my fate was definitely sealed!

Actually, the pleasure was all mine. Working in special needs education, and being teacher trained, I was soon spending every school holiday at Lluest. My first job on arrival was always to muck out the house, which could have been *busy* with wandering hens, a crow, cats, dogs and the occasional pony. The stables, tack and ponies were much better tended, as when Ginny was on her own they were her priority. If we had parties of youngsters staying for riding holidays, there was food to shop for, prepare and serve, also sandwiches to make for day rides, and occasionally treats and goodies for an evening swim and beach barbecue.

Outside, Ginny was the boss. She taught horsemanship and stable management with enthusiasm, but woe betide the careless. Both pupils and staff soon learnt it was unwise to be lax; at five foot two she could pack a hell of a verbal punch. But then, when you're working with young people and larger powerful animals, the responsibility for the safety of all was hers, and she handled it well. Alongside this went her unending enthusiasm for riding and horse welfare, which was captivating. She chatted and encouraged both adults and children, many of whom had never ridden before, and she improved their ability and developed their love of riding. Later, she educated and evangelised about horse and pony welfare, which became her passion when she conceived the idea of starting a charitable trust for equine welfare in Wales. So many people were infected by that Lluest magic. I was one of them!

What joy it was to wake up, see the distant sparkling sea, walk up tracks and dew-spangled fields to attempt to catch a mixed bag of characterful ponies. Returning to the yard we then had grooming, tacking up, welcoming riders and getting them mounted. Depending on who the riders were and what horses suited them, I either rode Jadine, a 15hh hunter (officially belonging to Pete, but used in the trekking business), or Mick, a small pony – I weighed a puny six stone! Ginny always had me at the head of the ride while she observed and controlled the ride from the rear. Mick became very special to me; we developed an almost telepathic bond, in that he seemed to be able to read my mind and sometimes even knowingly make a decision when I hesitated. If we got caught in a sudden mist up on the mountain, I knew I could just drop my reins and trust that he wouldn't take us into a bog or too close to a steep edge. His wise nature later saved his life, and that story can be seen in Chapter 13.

Being a bit of a musician I wrote the song 'Another Lluest Morning' (included in Chapter 12), in which I tried to capture the enjoyment and beauty of life at Lluest.

As the years rolled by, the trekking became increasingly successful. As older ponies were retired from work, new ponies needed to be bought, and this took Ginny to local horse sales. Some were better than others, but she became more and more aware of the bad conditions that she found. Some of the ponies she bought were really her first rescues. On sight they were poor, but Ginny would get them right. She developed a drive to do something to improve conditions for horses, both old and young, at these sales, and this led on to her needing to educate the general public to these conditions, and also about the lack of care for the breeding of wild foals on the mountains which ultimately were sold for the overseas meat trade.

Ginny was a woman who made things happen. In retrospect it must have taken some time, but suddenly I found myself to have become

Chair of Trustees of the first Welsh horse and pony charity. Having another full-time career, I feel sure my working involvement was minimal in this process, and, as with the compilation of this book, a lot of the 'graft' was done by Barbara, who with her lovely husband Brian were also old friends of Ginny's. All of us at different times shadowed Ginny at different sales. Her first success was establishing the use of anti-slip rubber matting to prevent the falling and injuring of the wild foals scrabbling for a foothold on slippery concrete floors. I suppose in the eyes of the meat men and dealers she became known as a nuisance and at times suffered intimidation. Needless to say she was not one to be intimidated. Gradually, she saved, she educated, both locally and nationally through the media and just talking, talking, talking to all who would listen. I merely wrote songs, drove Ginny around, joined in the hard work and laughter when I could, and tried to persuade any horse-minded friends of mine to donate, visit and in turn become involved.

Later on, after the Trust and trekking relocated to Beili Bedw, a bigger farm near Llandeilo, I introduced my fiancé to the delights of the horse world. Ginny was at first distrustful of this city-born bank manager! On the first stay at the farm, she set him two tests. One was to demolish the inside of a stuffy, muck-ridden cow byre without the proper tools, the next was to carry a full hay bale into the middle of a muddy field that housed, amongst others, a pony called Jaws. Charles, with true northern grit, fought valiantly enough to earn a bit of respect from Ginny, and subsequently dealt with the paperwork of any donations made under Deed of Covenant to the Trust.

Like Barbara, there came a time when I had to withdraw from my role as a trustee. New blood, different thoughts and fresh drive are always a good idea and I left to start a family. During that time of course Ginny became ill and sadly passed away; such a loss to all who knew her and to horse welfare. I remember taking my daughter, Bethan, as a toddler to visit Beili Bedw on a Trust open day. She had her first ride on a pony that day, and sat on the bench in the peaceful field enclosure where Ginny is buried. Now, many years later, I hope Bethan's love of animals, and inclination to rescue any injured creature she might come across, was somehow passed on by the spirit of Ginny and her beloved Lluest Horse and Pony Trust.

When I first got to know her, Ginny showed me some of the stories she had written, recounting her unpredictable daily life, both amusing and heart-breaking. I often said to her that she should write a book. I

239

am so glad to have been asked by Barbara to assist her with getting this together in collaboration with Pete, Ginny's husband. Hopefully it will continue Ginny's work, not only to educate and raise funds for the Lluest Horse and Pony Trust now, but to give you a glimpse of Ginny's life and passion. I think at times it will be an emotional read, causing tears of both laughter and sorrow. But anyone who loves animals, the countryside and nature will enjoy just a taste of that Lluest magic!

Life at Lluest in 2023

Life at Lluest goes on, and just as Ginny taught Barbara's youngest daughter to ride in 1977 she also taught the current manager, Dionne Schuurman – although several years later! Dionne has been manager at Lluest since 2015 and is doing an amazing job. In August 2019 she became one of seventeen to complete the specialist level three diploma in Equine Legislation Welfare and Field Skills as a Field Officer. Dionne's current role is Operations Manager. The charity funds are still stretched, and just the equivalent of four full time members of staff are employed. Their work includes rescuing, rehabilitating equines (horses, ponies and donkeys), co-ordinating and supervising volunteers, fund-raising, running the farm, administration, book keeping and marketing. All of these tasks could not possibly be carried out by four people alone, therefore volunteers play a huge role in helping to keep the ponies fed and looked after; they also take part in fundraising activities and maintenance work around the farm, to mention just a few jobs. Needless to say, volunteers are always needed and appreciated. There are currently five Trustees (who are not paid) overseeing the running of the charity. As of autumn 2023 the Trust cares for an average of twenty five equines at the farm. Many more are cared for in approved foster homes.

The Trust still welcomes people with learning disabilities as well as offering placements and volunteering opportunities to adults with special needs. Lluest is also seeking funding to offer equine-facilitated learning sessions to a wide variety of young people and adults who would find benefit. Horses are at last receiving the recognition they deserve for the improved well-being and psychological benefits found in their company.

Visits to markets have fallen back since the Covid pandemic, when unfortunately the charity found it necessary to cut back on staff, but the hope and intention is to re-establish monthly visits to ensure that 'The

Welfare of Horses at Markets (and other places of Sale) Order 1990' is being upheld and that the conditions and treatment of animals is as it should be.

Lluest Horse and Pony Trust works alongside other organisations in Wales and beyond. Lluest has rescued two hundred and eleven equines since 2010, and given many more a helping hand. Struggling owners are given advice and, if appropriate, helped to find suitable homes for their horses, that are sometimes even taken into the ownership and care of Lluest.

The ongoing work of the Trust is illustrated by this relatively recent story about Connie:

During the first lockdown in March 2020 a walker came across and reported a tiny filly foal, that was desperately calling and trying to feed from her emaciated and deceased mother. A team from Lluest worked with the help of vets, police, and a welfare officer from another welfare charity to get the helpless foal to the safety of Lluest Horse and Pony Trust just as darkness fell.

Apart from being incredibly thirsty, the foal, now named Connie, was healthy and had not suffered any ill effects from her ordeal. Her owner never came forward, and although it was too late for her mother, Connie was given the best possible chance of a bright future. She was given around the clock care, and eventually another Lluest rescue cob, Abbie, adopted Connie as if her own. Staff and helpers had to continue to supplement the mares' milk as she could not produce enough. Connie is now living in a loving Guardian home with another Lluest rescue.

She owes her life to the walker who took the trouble to report her plight, to those who came together to get her to safety, to Abbie, and to all those people who had supported Lluest over the years leading up to her rescue.

∪

People and ponies have come and sadly gone over the thirty-eight years since the charity began, but Lluest still holds that magic, and we all hope that the Trust continues forever, as Ginny always wished. The charity depends entirely on donations and legacies for its very survival. Thank you for reading and making a purchase of this book, all proceeds from which will go directly to the charity.

Find out more

If you enjoyed this book and would like to find out more about the Lluest Horse and Pony Trust, please go to:

Website: www.lluesthorseandponytrust.co.uk
or
Facebook: https://www.facebook.com/lluest

or you can contact the Trust at:

Lluest Horse and Pony Trust
Beili Bedw Farm
Landovery
Carmarthenshire SA19 9TG
Tel: 01550 740661

Registered charity number 1150948.

Donations and volunteers are always welcome!

*Champ with Shelley, helping to promote the Trust's work
at a show in Gloucestershire*

Milton Keynes UK
Ingram Content Group UK Ltd.
UKHW011820111223
434184UK00003B/218